Back in Time for Dinner

www.transworldbooks.co.uk

Back in Time for Dinner

From Spam to Sushi:
How We've Changed the Way We Eat

Mary Gwynn

Foreword by Giles Coren

BANTAM PRESS

LONDON • TORONTO • SYDNEY • AUCKLAND • JOHANNESBURG

TRANSWORLD PUBLISHERS
61–63 Uxbridge Road, London W5 5SA
www.transworldbooks.co.uk

Penguin
Random House
UK

Transworld is part of the Penguin Random House group of companies
whose addresses can be found at global.penguinrandomhouse.com

First published in Great Britain in 2015 by Bantam Press,
an imprint of Transworld Publishers

Back in Time for Dinner accompanies the BBC series
of the same name, produced by Wall to Wall Media.

A CIP catalogue record for this book
is available from the British Library.

ISBN 9780593075241

Typeset in 11/16pt Fairfield Light by Falcon Oast Graphic Art Ltd.
Printed and bound by Clays Ltd, Bungay, Suffolk

Penguin Random House is committed to a sustainable
future for our business, our readers and our planet. This book
is made from Forest Stewardship Council® certified paper.

MIX
Paper from
responsible sources
FSC® C016897

1 3 5 7 9 10 8 6 4 2

To my mother, Jean, and my daughters, Lucy and Isobel

Contents

Foreword

Is there anything in the world more compelling than the idea of time travel? To go back through the decades and find out how things really were in the old days, to experience the daily highs and lows of life in another age, to remove our rose-tinted spectacles and see the past as it truly was, is a privilege granted, in real life, to nobody.

But television is different. Television can do anything. I myself was lucky enough to travel through time with Sue Perkins in our *Supersizers Go . . .* series for BBC2 a few years ago, and to live and dress and, most importantly, eat as people did in bygone days. But we never re-created those former worlds with the detail or intensity with which it was done for *Back in Time for Dinner*. And we were just a pair of boozy old TV presenters, the Robshaws are an entire family!

And what a family they are. So full of energy and intellectual curiosity. So down-to-earth, up for a challenge and game for a laugh. Frankly, I thought they were completely nuts to sign up for our crazy experiment. What family could possibly survive being thrown back into the 1950s then dragged through the 1960s, 1970s, 1980s and 1990s, always with new and unpleasantly scratchy outfits to wear, with none of the comforts of modern life, none of the foodstuffs we have come to take for granted, and every fortnight, just as they were getting used to it, having their beloved kitchen ripped out and replaced? Only, I suspect, the extraordinary Robshaws.

For me, who only had to come in and out of the experiment, in my own clothes, and could always go home to a tasty modern dinner, the whole experience was an unalloyed pleasure. In the 1970s and 1980s episodes I saw the kitchens of my childhood come alive again before my eyes in all their garish beauty, and it brought tears to my eyes (or was that just Rochelle chopping onions?). And in the 1950s episode I saw all the complaints of my parents about the grimness and the dirtiness and the rationing of those times – which I never truly believed – come alive again in a terraced house in twenty-first-century Walthamstow.

It was a real education to see how we have moved – very gradually over fifty or sixty years – from a world in which almost all our food was prepared from scratch by hand and most family meals were eaten together at a table, to one in which so much of it is factory processed and eaten alone, often on the run. I learned how much we have lost, in terms of nutritional health (we are fatter now than in the 1950s despite eating far fewer calories and only half as much fat), togetherness and romance. But also how much we have gained in terms of variety, social mobility and, crucially, female emancipation from the rigours of the stove and mangle.

Most excitingly of all, perhaps, I think the experiment offers a glimpse of how, after a half-century of technological marching towards convenience and cheapness, we might now, finally, be on the cusp of a move back towards a healthier relationship with our food, to a world in which some of the better things about the good old days – fresh, seasonal produce; local shopping; family mealtimes – can be resurrected, without the inconvenience of ration books, scratchy jumpers, depressing gender roles and endless worrying about 'the bomb'.

Giles Coren

CHAPTER 1

Enter the Time Tunnel:

from Austerity to Excess in Two Generations

' "A generation" – the average period, generally considered to be about thirty years, in which children grow up, become adults, and have children of their own.'

Oxford English Dictionary

THEY SAY YOU CAN tell someone's age by the songs that make them grow misty-eyed. But for me, like so many others, it's not just the songs, it's the food that transports me back to my earliest years. Born in the latter half of the 1950s, the early songs of the Beatles, Tommy Steele's 'Little White Bull' and the tender tones of my first junior crush, Adam Faith, all form part of my emotional DNA, but they still don't seem to evoke nearly as much feeling as the memories of the smells and tastes of my childhood.

I close my eyes and tune into my nose: little bottles of school milk warmed up on the radiator; 'egg in a cup' each and every day for breakfast while staying at my grandmother's; and the first time I ate duckling – rich, slightly greasy, served with green peas – while on a family holiday in Cornwall aged about six, and which if I close my eyes I can still taste today. Golden memories of a golden period . . . But were they really such idyllic years, or am I simply looking back with nostalgic yearning for a simpler time? Food has a way of instantly transporting us back into our pasts, but at the same time it says so much about our present.

The notion that our recollections of food take us further back in time than other types of memory is actually supported by scientific evidence. Rachel Herz of Brown University, Rhode Island, is a leading expert on the psychological science of smell and says: 'Smell is extremely linked to our memories, in particular to our emotional memories . . . If you want to bring a memory back, smell is the best thing.' Recollections of things that happened to us between the ages of eleven and twenty-five are most likely to be triggered via verbal associations, while memories induced by smell are most likely to take us back to the ages of six to ten. As smell and taste are inextricably linked, the foods of our childhoods hold a very special place in our hearts.

And for lots of us, once triggered, those memories carry us to the heart of our families and the times we spent together around the dinner table. But it seems today that family life as shared over a meal is under attack: fast food, fast lives, more choice – all these have an impact on how we eat together. What is happening to the modern family, and has the way we eat at home and outside it changed so fundamentally over the last half-century? Are we in danger of losing, or have we already thrown away, the emotional glue that binds us together – those food memories shared around a table?

One busy twenty-first-century family was given a unique opportunity to explore these issues and try to discover some of the answers. With the help of a little television magic, the Robshaw family of Walthamstow, east London, (and their kitchen) took a journey down a memory lane of dining to discover if what we perceive as a halcyon time of eating together was actually that, or whether in reality it was something quite different. By re-creating fifty years of eating in as many days, this remarkable journey helps us understand what the history of food and its preparation has to say about life in twenty-first-century Britain and how, in that half-century, family life has changed beyond recognition. What the Robshaws found is that our nostalgic visions of the foods of our pasts are not necessarily all that accurate.

For dad Brandon, a children's book writer and Open University lecturer, and mum and adult literacy tutor Rochelle, both born in the Swinging Sixties, would the television experience match their own personal memories of family dining in and outside the home? Rochelle says, 'Food is a way to share your past with your children', so what would Miranda (aged seventeen), Rosalind (fifteen) and Fred (ten) discover, not only about their parents' and grandparents' lives but also about how it felt to be a child in the previous century, especially in a time when children were expected to be seen and not heard? How would Fred, who likes to eat his breakfast on the sofa in front of the telly with his laptop on the go, take to 1950s-style formality? He worried about 'the hungry fifties' – no kiddie-friendly cereal, no juice, a smoothie unheard of – and about being sat at the table with Mum checking what he ate and ensuring nothing was left on his plate. For Rochelle, who, in common with most mums, worries about how and what her children eat when outside the home – especially Ros, who fills up on chips with her friends on the way back from school or dance classes – would it be a relief to have this control at home, and also to know that they had had a good, nutritionally sound, hot lunch at school? As the parent who works more outside the home in the present, she confesses, 'I miss the cooking and controlling what the family eat.' But would the restrictions on freedom that ensnared most women in a domestic net in the middle of the twentieth century be a worthwhile exchange for the ability to manage what her family consumed? 'The biggest challenge will be being in the kitchen on my own in the fifties,' she admitted as the experiment got under way.

Over half a century we have undergone a revolution in the way we eat. There have been fundamental shifts in attitudes to home and health, from a time when fat in the diet was seen as essential 'fuel food' to our current fears of a booming obesity crisis; ongoing debate about the role of the 'nanny state' (starting with the impact of rationing) in managing household diets; the changing role of women in the home and at work, and the huge impact this has had on family life; the effect of new technologies; the explosion of new food ingredients available; developments in kitchen equipment and labour-saving devices, such as the freezer and the microwave; the rapid rise of supermarkets and the way they dictate our shopping habits and diets; and the increasing impact of the media on everything from cooking advice and food scares to food fads and celebrities. Food sourcing, preparation and consumption have vividly reflected the important issues at the heart of family life, and they continue to do so. Writing for the Women's Institute magazine *Home & Country* in March 1935, renowned local food historian and cookery writer Florence White posited that the entire history of civilization might well be viewed from the point of view of food and cookery. She wrote 'the ramifications of the subject are widespread and endless.'

One vital source of information to help the Robshaws understand how families such as theirs shopped, cooked and ate together over the years was the National Food Survey (NFS), the longest-running continuous household food survey in the world, and one which provides us with a unique set of data on food consumption and expenditure, as well as on the changing patterns of household eating habits. It was originally set up in 1940 by the then Ministry of Food to monitor the diet of urban 'working-class' households in wartime, but was extended in 1950 to become representative of households throughout Great Britain. (In 1996 the survey was extended to cover Northern Ireland, allowing results for the entire United Kingdom to be presented for the first time.) The NFS ran until 2000, when it was replaced by a range of other surveys.

About 8,000 households took part in the NFS each year. The family member who did most of the food shopping was asked a set of questions about the household and its food purchasing. They were then asked to keep a diary for seven days, recording food coming into the household, including quantities and expenditure, and some detail of the household meals (including snacks and picnics prepared from household supplies). One thing that the NFS reveals very clearly about how the British public have approached and consumed their food over the decades is that, despite all the latest food fads and fashions that have come and gone, most people take a long time to change their eating habits. The NFS daily menus for 'meals at home' – breakfast, dinner, tea and supper (examples of which appear for each decade throughout this book) – completed in the main by Mum as the person who did the bulk of the food shopping and cooking, reveal an essentially conservative approach to meal times, even up until the final entries in the 1990s. Reading between the lines, it becomes clear that there is a time lag between the arrival of a new idea or development and the point at which it is widely adopted. Woks might have been on sale in Habitat as early as 1967, but we weren't cooking with them until Ken Hom got us stir-frying in the 1980s; the 1970s saw the arrival of wholefoods, with restaurants such as Cranks growing in popularity, but our total meat consumption remained stable from the 1950s through to 1990,

A NFS diary entry for a family in 1952 reveals the monotony of the post-war diet – stodgy and high in energy-giving fat and sugar, but with little in the way of fruit and veg.

decreasing only through the impact of the BSE crisis in that decade (although we had already begun to swap beef, lamb and mutton for chicken, and to move away from whole joints to more convenient cuts such as chops).

Interestingly, despite what appears to be evidence to the contrary, the National Food Survey supports the view that even in the twenty-first century cooking a meal for the family is still at the heart of what it is to be a parent, and more especially a mother. Recent research reveals that, despite all the changes in lifestyle and increase in convenience, preparing the daily meal continues to be seen as an important part of family life, just as it was back in the 1950s. Women still feel a strong sense of duty when it comes to feeding their families, and the need to cook meals for the household on a daily basis still underpins many of our attitudes towards meal preparation and cooking today. But this means that most of us also experience all kinds of negative emotions, especially guilt, when we resort to the use of what the experts term 'home meal replacements' instead of cooking from scratch. Indeed, for mum Rochelle the whole *Back in Time for Dinner* journey was a particularly intense one. For many women social pressure to be the homemaker and nurturer, and to embody the domestic ideal, has been a constant since our grandmothers swapped hard work outside the home in support of the war effort for the joys of domesticity. This vision of the woman as homemaker has been supported and encouraged through the medium of broadcasting, with both radio and television helping structure the domestic space with their depictions of women's roles in everything from documentaries to dramas and light entertainment. Today, when our image of domesticity and femininity is in turmoil, it remains a challenge to be addressed. And, as our family set out on their food pilgrimage through time, they would discover that this tension has been present down the decades, and has been and continues to be tapped into by advertisers, marketing companies and food retailers. As the Robshaws were to discover, guilt is not just a modern phenomenon!

Our twenty-first-century diet, ever more based around convenience and fast food, has progressively become a source of worry, and obesity is arguably one of the most pressing public-health issues facing the UK today. As far back as 1976 the problem was deemed 'to constitute one of the most important public health problems of our time'. Rates of obesity have increased dramatically over the last decade among all ages of the population, but the rapid rise in the prevalence of childhood obesity across the country is particularly alarming. 14.3 per cent of children (750,000) were obese in 2004 compared with 10 per cent in 1995, less than a decade earlier. Given the known relationship between obesity and other serious chronic conditions such as Type 2 diabetes and cardiovascular disease, preventing and treating obesity has become a major public-health goal. The question of how patterns of eating over the years have contributed to this dilemma is one with which the family will have to come to terms.

So, what did the five food-loving Robshaws find when, with food historian Dr Polly Russell as their guide, they started their television food journey back in 1950, just seven years before my own birth, and how did it contrast with the reality of their twenty-first-century lives? In 2015 their cheerful modern home, part of a street of late-Victorian terraced houses in east London, is bright and welcoming, with a spacious kitchen that forms the hub of family life. Food is plentiful, often organic, and comes from all over the world. The big fridge-freezer in the corner of the kitchen is stuffed full of easy-to-use, pre-prepared vegetables, bagged salads, straight-to-wok noodles, and yogurts – all short-cuts to eating that save time in this fast-living, frantic century. A bowl of fresh fruit sits on the kitchen table, while the biscuit tin with its cereal bars and snack packs is always to hand. And meals in and out of the home come from across the globe – a pizza delivery, Brandon's chicken and noodle stir-fry (Fred: 'Is stir-fry Chinese?'), a wrap filled with Turkish spiced shredded meat and hummus bought on a family trip to the local street market. Busy lives mean family members often eat at different times in different parts of the house and, like so many of us, find that three set meals a day have morphed into a series of snacks eaten on the hoof.

This modern family relies on convenience products to help cut corners, but they are always aware of rising food costs and their impact on both the family purse and, increasingly, on the environment. With the recession of the past decade we have become ever more concerned with the issues that our grandparents took for granted two generations ago, but which we are viewing now from the opposite end of the spectrum. Indeed, one of the most interesting factors that will become clear on this voyage through our food past will be the cyclical nature of the events and issues the family face – the merry-go-round of recession and economic boom is repeated unfailingly across the decades, while food waste, local ingredients and keeping to a budget all feature in a 2014 study on *Families and Food* run by Ipsos MORI to support the series. Evidence of resourcefulness on the part of families trying to use up food appear in its findings, and inspiration from TV cooks such as Mary Berry is mentioned alongside the use of recipes handed down by family and friends. Three of the fifty-six families in the study use eggs from their own chickens; several grow their own vegetables; while food shopping trips are still mainly done in person. Despite the arrival of online ordering, the findings show that most of us still do a big weekly shop at one of the large national supermarket chains, but 'top up' with several small trips for essentials, often on the way home from work. And, most reassuringly, although fast food and on-the-go products are popular with everyone during the week, the study reveals that Sundays are still special when it comes to families sitting down together. It might not be a meal in the middle of the day, or even a traditional roast (though for some that is still the case, with a home-made pud to round off the meal), but the day is still seen as a family time. Some things never change, it seems. But what our grandparents *would* struggle to recognize is the huge amount of choice that we now enjoy in our diets, and the global spread of our store cupboards. Mexican, Spanish, Middle Eastern, Greek – every day, without a second thought, we travel around the world via our plates. Meat and two veg is becoming a rarity.

This somewhat schizophrenic nature of eating patterns and flexible meal times, with the desire for speed and convenience set against the enjoyment of cooking for leisure and pleasure, might seem to us to be a thoroughly modern phenomenon, but where did it really start? Would the Robshaws find eating occasions, fifty years into the past, simpler and more straightforward (more enjoyable?), at a time when we imagine that the whole family sat down together at the table, Dad at its head, children not speaking until spoken to, as Mum, frilly apron to the ready, served up Spam and boiled potatoes? The theme of who ate what, where and when, both inside and outside the home, will be a constant as the series evolves.

Stepping back into a period of shortages and bland food, the Robshaws were in for a shock. Five years after the end of the Second World War the UK was still in the grip of rationing. The years immediately preceding the start of our experiment had been bleak ones for most of the country. Rationing of some foods was actually increased post-1945, and the diet for Britons became even more frugal than it had been during the war itself. Worldwide food shortages, a failed wheat harvest in 1946, and the Arctic winter of 1946–7 had all taken their toll. That staple of wartime meals, bread (even if it was the much despised National Loaf) was rationed for the first time ever between 1946 and 1948, and even potatoes were restricted in 1947, something that had not happened in the darkest days of war. Butter and meat rations were cut in 1947. The average adult's meagre weekly allowance in 1947 of 13oz meat (about 370g), 6oz butter (170g), 8oz (225g) sugar, 1½oz cheese (40g) and so on – compared to the slightly more generous allowance which included 8oz (225g) butter and 12oz (340g) sugar when rationing was first introduced in January 1940 – made the everyday process of shopping for, preparing and cooking food tortuous. Ingredients were basic and bland, producing negative reactions from husbands and families tired of austerity and ready to rebel, albeit in a very British fashion.

By 1950, when the *Back in Time for Dinner* experience commences, petrol had just become available again (though few people had cars), but otherwise food would continue to be restricted by rationing in some form for another four years. 'Austerity' Britain was still in full swing, but the decade would witness huge changes as the country shook off the impact of the war period, undergoing a transformation that continues to resonate in our kitchens to this day. In the 1950s we were eating almost twice as much fat and 900 more calories a day than in the year 2000; children were expected to eat what was put in front of them without complaint; and Dad was effectively banned from the kitchen. For a modern family, where Brandon, as the parent who works mainly from home, does the bulk of the cooking – 'I've got a feeling for food' – this aspect alone was going to be testing. And as the family progressed through the decades, living through the trends of the changing times, the challenges would continue.

As they set out on their journey, Rochelle summed up what they hoped to get from the experience: they were hoping to find out 'how the focus on food impacts on how we see the world . . . The Robshaw family are trying to come together on a plate.'

CHAPTER 2

This Is Your Life: the 1950s

Key Events

1950 Petrol rationing comes to an end

1951 Report showing the average British housewife works 75 hours a week

1952 All-party support in the House of Commons for equal pay for women

1953 Coronation of Queen Elizabeth II

1954 All rationing comes to an end when meat is finally taken off ration

1955 London becomes a smokeless zone

1956 Suez Crisis (leads to short return to petrol rationing)

1957 Creation of the Common Market

1958 M1 is opened – the first motorway in Britain

1959 Mini and the Barbie doll are launched

IN 1945, THE BRITISH people had looked to the future as a promised world of peace and prosperity. The reality had proved very different, for very quickly the country had entered a period of frustration and disappointment that would last well into the next decade. The dawn of the 1950s found Britain 'threadbare, bombed-out, financially and morally exhausted'. Continued rationing was not the only difficulty; large areas of cities and towns had been bombed beyond salvation, essential services were non-existent and, for many people, coping with the privations of their daily existence was immensely stressful.

Rebuilding the country and the lives of its people could not be done

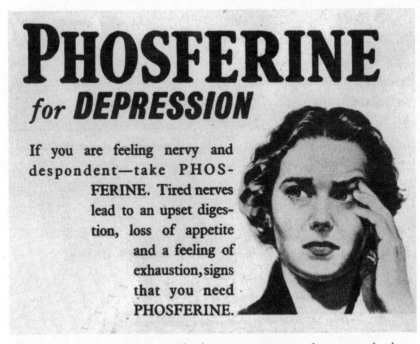

PHOSFERINE
for DEPRESSION

If you are feeling nervy and despondent—take PHOS-FERINE. Tired nerves lead to an upset digestion, loss of appetite and a feeling of exhaustion, signs that you need PHOSFERINE.

'Mother's little helper'. Anxiety and exhaustion were causes for concern for the 1950s housewife, worn out with her domestic duties.

overnight. The splendid world of opportunity and plenty, the vision of which an exhausted population glimpsed in the pages of magazines or on one of the new television sets, remained a mirage. As Rochelle comments at the beginning of the series, 'Older friends always say life was better in the fifties, but how can this possibly be true? I'm curious to find out . . .'

Home sweet home

The biggest challenge facing the country after the war was the shortage of housing, both in towns and in the countryside, and this would remain the case throughout the early 1950s. During the war German air raids had damaged or destroyed as many as a third of Britain's 12.5 million homes, with London suffering the worst of the devastation. The post-war boom in marriage – there were over 400,000 weddings in 1947 – and resulting rapid rise in the birth rate saw over a million children born in the five years following the war. And these fledgling families needed housing. More than 750,000 new homes were judged necessary and, for both the Labour government elected in 1945 and the Conservatives who succeeded them in 1951, large-scale house-building programmes were a priority. This was the age of the new towns, eleven of which had been established by 1950; and also of the prefabricated house, or 'prefab' – small, bungalow-type homes constructed from factory-made parts, which used fewer scarce resources than traditional housing, could be almost instantly assembled on site and offered mod cons such as mains electricity and modern plumbing. From 1945 to 1951, 89 per cent of the 1.01 million houses built were local authority dwellings (including tower blocks, which were first introduced in this period); over the next five years another 1.9 million went up, but these were mainly privately built. In 1951 over 50 per cent of the population lived in privately rented housing, while 30 per cent of housing was owner-occupied and the remainder local authority. (By 1999 owner occupation had increased to 68 per cent, with private rental at 10 per cent.)

Despite this intense building activity, the move into modern housing was by no means universal; even by 1958 only a fifth of the population lived in new homes that conformed to standards set out by the Housing Advisory Committee. As the 1950s dawned many households, like the Robshaws in their Victorian terrace, were still living in pre-war buildings – Georgian, Victorian and those built up to the 1930s. These were often relatively large, with high ceilings and entrance halls, and they tended to have rooms with distinct functions – a kitchen with a scullery at the back; a parlour for welcoming guests (or maybe two in better-off homes); a dining room; bedrooms; and, if funds permitted, a bathroom. Most included a walk-in larder, built facing north and with a cold slab made of marble or stone for keeping food cool. Many of these older houses had little plumbing, and the grimy terraces of the big industrial cities such as London, Newcastle, Liverpool and Glasgow often had no sanitation; in several areas they were also without gas or electricity. Coal fires provided heat in downstairs rooms, including the kitchen, which in many homes had a fireplace or grate. These houses needed modernization and the government introduced grants of up to 50 per cent for landlords to reno-vate, or to convert larger properties into bedsits.

People who moved into the rash of newly built homes found changes to the traditional room pattern, driven by the need for economy. Houses were smaller, with fewer rooms which had to per-form as flexible living space. Parlour and living room fused, while kitchen and dining room blended as the stigma of eating food in the same room as it was prepared began slowly to disappear. Although some complained of the 'cold new feeling' of many of these modern homes (especially the high-rise flats), people appreciated having heating, a bath, an indoor toilet, running hot water and a 'fitted' kitchen for the first time. The 'fitted kitchen', as we shall see, continues to be the dream for every decade, but each period has its own definition of 'fitted'. In the 1950s it was very basic: a fitted sink with drainer and cupboard underneath.

Many of the new builds also came with central heating, provided by electricity rather than gas. Electricity was more expensive than gas but was considered cleaner and more efficient, and by 1951 nearly 90 per cent of all households were connected to the National Grid. But even so, by 1960 only 5 per cent of homes had central heating and most owners of older homes turned to heaters run on electricity, paraffin or gas for warmth, or to coke or anthracite stoves, especially after the Clean Air Act of 1957 banned the use of coal in designated 'smokeless' areas. Hot water was provided by new immersion heaters, or came via a small economical system that instantly heated water by electricity or gas for the kitchen or bathroom.

Outside the towns and cities, the standard of housing in many rural areas in the early 1950s was considerably poorer, with pre-war conditions, such as no piped water, sewage systems, indoor toilets or electricity, still prevailing. Notes from a 1950 parish meeting in Galleywood, Essex, reveal the extent of the problems. A Mr Hull asks if managers are satisfied with the sanitation at the village school, where 'many children [are] afraid to use the lavatories . . .' A Mrs Cornell suggests that sanitation could be improved if the pails were emptied every night, and the Rev. F. A. Roughton admits that the Education Committee empties them only three times per week! Recognizing this disparity between standards in rural areas and urban, the Rural Water Supplies and Sewerage Act of 1944 had encouraged the extension of water and sewerage services to existing properties in rural communities. This led to government grants to support extensions of the networks and increased the number of rural households with access to piped water to 80 per cent by 1951. But when it came to everyday services, rural properties would continue to lag behind those in the cities well into the 1960s.

Women's work

Whether the house was old or new, inside it the task of rebuilding the home and the family in peacetime fell to women. In the later stages of the war, the government's minister of food, Lord Woolton, had told the female population – whom he termed 'domestic war workers' – that 'the government can and will build houses, but only women can build homes'. For many, it was a difficult role to accept. For the last six years, through necessity, women had become accustomed both to running the household and working in traditional male domains. In December 1941, the National Service Act (No. 2) had made the conscription of women legal. At first only single women aged between twenty and thirty were called up, but by mid-1943 almost 90 per cent of single women and 80 per cent of married women had been employed in essential work for the war effort; indeed Winston Churchill had said, 'This war effort could not have been achieved had women not marched forward in millions to undertake all kinds of work. Nothing has been grudged, and the bounds of the women's activities have been definitely, vastly and permanently enlarged.' But for the majority, these wide horizons were about to be drawn sharply inwards. Men, long absent, strangers to their children (and probably to their wives too), and many with their own wartime demons to contend with, reasserted their position at the head of the family and by the start of the fifties women had been firmly returned to their traditional place in the heart of the home.

Despite the increased opportunities in both education and employment for women in the 1950s, career choice was limited by the widely held view that a woman's place was in the home. The vast majority of girls left school at fifteen and, after basic on-the-job training, entered employment only to leave once they married. The 1951 census shows that, although only 30 per cent of all women were 'gainfully employed', the majority of those between sixteen and twenty-four were in work. However, most would be married by the age of twenty-five and, unlike today, becoming a dependent housewife was not regarded as a problem; rather it was those who didn't embrace this choice that were seen by society as going against the norm. In the early 1950s many employers operated a 'marriage bar', whereby married women were prevented from entering professions such as teaching and clerical work (although not lower-paid jobs), while those already in such jobs were sacked upon marriage. It was not just employers but the government itself that encouraged the idea that women should be at home. Motherhood (within marriage!) was seen as 'work' in itself – a view compounded by the explosion of child-rearing books, magazines and radio programmes bringing new ideas on the importance of mothers in the early development of their children. State-funded nurseries that had been set up during the war were closed by the post-war Labour government, and welfare payments to families were based on the assumption that wife and children were dependants of the man of the house, whose income was 'the family wage'.

The situation would begin to change by the end of the decade as manpower shortages started to shift prevailing attitudes towards accepting women in the workplace. Whereas in 1951 only 23.6 per cent of married women in the country were working, the figure had increased to one in three ten years later, while employment for unmarried women remained constant at around 72 per cent over the same period.

However, although some women undoubtedly felt their wings had been clipped, many were desperate for the home comforts and normal family life that had been denied them during the war. The new world of peacetime, with its order and security, created the perfect environment for a return to homemaking. As Nicola Humble wrote in *Culinary Pleasures*, 'Women of all classes joyfully and consciously embraced domesticity, almost as a holiday from the rigours of the past, freely entering into the fantasy that was the 1950s home. Domesticity, matrimony and maternity were not seen as a rejection of the old-style feminism of the suffragettes but as an intensely satisfying way of life.'

The role of homemaker was a big responsibility. A national nostalgia for supposed pre-war values – a looking back to a time of certainty and reliability in the world and at home – led to the idealized image of the 'perfect housewife', cheerfully and expertly combining the job of running the household with that of providing support and care for husband and children. A man returning from a hard day spent earning a living for his family should find a smoothly operating, comfortable home, a meal on the table and a smiling, well-groomed wife ready to help him forget his cares.

But behind the façade of the sweetly smiling housewife and mother lay a great deal of toil and menial labour. The slowly rising living standards at the start of the fifties might have led to a better quality of life for working-class women, but for the middle-class house-wife, who before the war would almost invariably have employed one or more servants, this was far from the case. Before 1940 residential domestic service had been the main employer of young women, but the war had meant emancipation for many, offering new jobs in factor-ies, workshops and offices that came with structured working hours, and now women were loath to return to work that placed them at the whim of domestic employers. For most housewives without help, then, the day-to-day reality of running a house was drudgery, and a survey of 1951 found that the average housewife worked a seventy-five-hour week (not including the weekend!). Although marvellous, labour-saving inventions were on show at the Festival of Britain in 1951 – where they were seen by 8.5 million people, or almost 20 per cent of the population of England – and were heavily promoted in magazines and advertise-ments, these were well beyond the reach of most women of the time. Lack of electricity in some homes meant that modern appliances such as fridges (which had actually become available as early as the 1920s) and the dishwasher that featured at the Ideal Home Exhibition of 1954 – 'Is it very much quicker than getting on with the job in the sink?' asked one doubtful visitor – remained a dream; for others, cost and space made such items equally unrealistic.

Making do

Chief among the hardships faced by Britain's housewives was the prolonged post-war rationing. As writer Susan Cooper commented,

National Food Survey Daily Menus 1950

Family of four, two sons

Breakfast
Bread & bacon
Toast & margarine
Tea with sugar and milk

Dinner/midday meal
Bread, butter & biscuits
Coffee with milk & saccharine

Tea/high tea
Rabbit pies, sprouts, boiled potatoes
Rice pudding (made with condensed milk)

Supper
Home-made chips
Bread & butter
Coffee with milk & saccharine

Family of three, young daughter

Breakfast
Bread, butter & eggs
Tea with fried sugar

Dinner/midday meal
Egg & chips
Fruit cake
Tea with fried sugar

Tea/high tea
Cow-heel cakes
Bread & butter
Tea with fried sugar

Supper
Fruit cake
Tea with milk & sugar *

'Wars end tidily in history books . . . But there was no single finishing line for the shortages of food, clothes and fuel . . . which gave
a dull grey tinge to post-war life. They slackened gradually.' Rationing
had made sense as part of the war effort, when people had warmed to
the idea of universal sacrifice for the good of the nation. Once peace
had returned it was harder to bear. In the early fifties, the diet for
Britons was even more frugal than it had been during the war, and it
was not until 1953 that rationing finally began to come to a very
welcome end. Bread and potatoes had been unrestricted since 1948
and jam came off ration in the latter part of the same year. Then came
a long four-year wait until 1952, when tea appeared once again as
a regular feature in the family shopping basket. The following
year sweets (much to young Fred's relief), then cream, eggs and
sugar were once more on sale, unrestricted by the government
though still in limited supply due to reduced post-war production
capacity. It would be another twelve months, in summer 1954,
before butter, cheese, cooking fat and finally meat would be released
from control.

It was the housewife who had the dismal task of implementing
the reality of the rationing policy, making the most of limited
ingredients to produce three meals a day. Women's magazines
responded with gusto to the need for ideas on how to manage. This
was the era of the mass magazine, as women sought out help and
advice; in 1951 the weekly *Woman* magazine sold 2.25 million copies,
up from a million five years earlier. Despite such encouragement,
National Food Survey records show just how challenging (and relent-
lessly tedious) it was to feed a family day in, day out and how little

* The pattern for these two families is for an early-evening meal rather than dinner at
midday, so it appears likely that both fathers had lunch outside the home and the kids
ate at school. Some of the ingredients are a complete mystery to modern eyes: fried
sugar is a strange idea, and none of us today are likely to tuck in to cow-heel pie. Cow
heel (literally the bone from the heel) was added in a piece to meat pies and pasties,
but only to add rich flavour to the rest of the meat, rather as we might add marrowbone
today. The first family is unusual in drinking coffee with saccharine.

scope there was for variety. Breakfast was typically toast and dripping or Weetabix and syrup. Dinner, served at midday as the main meal for the family, would be fried liver and onions, or maybe meat pie and peas followed by semolina pudding or rhubarb sponge – and remember, with a very limited sugar ration, the rhubarb was probably not sweetened enough for most palates. (My mother hated rhubarb and gooseberries for the rest of her life after enduring their sour taste during her wartime childhood.) Then there would be a high tea of leftovers from lunch for the children, increasing numbers of whom may have eaten their main meal at school, with corned beef or tinned pilchards, bread and margarine for Mum and Dad as an evening meal when he came back from work. Poor Rochelle found feeding her family in these early years of rationing-restricted cooking very hard. After serving up a meal of bread and pilchards, bread and dripping (National Loaf, of course) and quartered tomatoes to the family, she despaired: 'That's probably the grimmest meal I've ever cooked them!'

Dinner time

At the start of the decade, 70 per cent of men still came home at lunchtime for their main meal of the day; this had dropped to six out of ten by 1958. Though some commuted to and from the big cities (packed lunches were taken by those who worked too far from home to return for a meal), most worked within walking or cycling distance of where they lived and, unlike in the war years, few offices or factories of the time had canteens; nor were there many places to buy lunch. Even if women were working, they tended to eat lunch at home; in a countrywide survey of 4,557 adults in 1955/6, 82 per cent of women were shown to eat lunch at home, with only 7 per cent eating at work or in a canteen. But the whole family would gather for tea (more commonly known as 'high tea' in the north) at the end of the day. This meal, more likely to be lighter than at midday, was enjoyed by nine out of ten adults in one form or other, and the peak time to eat it was between 6 and 6.30pm. Offices mainly closed at 5pm, while work shifts were over between 4.30 and 5.00pm – plenty of time to come home for 'a look round the garden and a glass of sherry and a moment with the children on one hand, or for the manual worker, a change, shave and general clean up'. Ham, bacon, a piece of white fish, cheese or eggs, with bread, butter, cakes and biscuits were the dishes of choice for most rather than a heavy roast, pie or stew, which would more likely be served in the middle of the day. Vegetables make a poor showing on the NFS menus, with less than a fifth of respondents eating them regularly, though salad was more popular, with some 40 per cent of people choosing to eat it in summer – but it would have consisted of only lettuce, cucumber, tomato and vinegary beetroot with maybe a hard-boiled egg. As the decade progressed, people were swapping milk puddings and custard for tinned fruit to round off the meal, often served with evaporated milk. And as usual the meal was washed down with two or three cups of tea. Then 'a bite before bed' between 10 and 10.30pm, most likely in the form of another cup of tea or a 'health beverage' such as Ovaltine, along with biscuits or bread and butter.

The need to prepare separate meals for different members of the family put an additional burden on the housewife, not only because of shortages, which eased as plenty returned, but also because of the badly equipped kitchens in most homes – in particular, the lack of a fridge. Keeping food fresh was an ongoing challenge and leftovers could not easily be stored, while the high cost of food meant waste was anathema. Leftover milk was used up in puddings and batters, and when it soured it appeared in scones and breads; mashed potato turned up in all kinds of unexpected ways in recipes, bulking out breads, cakes and puddings. Inability to store food for long also meant that meals had to be shopped for on an almost daily basis, and this in itself involved a great deal of toil. Without a car – and unlikely to be able to drive even if she did have access to one – and with no network of supermarkets, the housewife of the early fifties would have to walk to her local high street almost every day, visiting several different shops to buy perishables such as fresh meat, fish and dairy products, then carry everything home in her basket. If she was lucky, local tradesmen such as the butcher, fishmonger, baker, greengrocer and, of course, the milkman would deliver to the door.

JUNKET makes milk a treat

The next time the children shy at taking milk, give it to them as Little Miss Muffet Junket. They'll eat it eagerly and ask for more. Tastes and looks so appetising. Four tempting fruit flavours. Easily digested, because the rennet enzyme it contains breaks up the heavy milk curd. Relished by infants during teething, as it is soothing and cooling to tender gums. Little Miss Muffet may also be used as a flavouring and colouring essence for other dishes. 7½d. bottle makes 3 one-pint junkets.

Little **Miss Muffet**
JUNKETS
RASPBERRY · ORANGE · LEMON · VANILLA

Before the war bakers had often delivered daily in vans (or sent a boy on a bike with a basket) but, though bread was not

'Waste not, want not' was the order of the day for the cost-conscious mum, who used up leftover milk in puds and batters.

rationed until 1947, the arrival of National Flour and the National Loaf made bread unpopular, and at the same time rationing of sugar and cooking fats meant finer bakery goods disappeared until the mid-1950s; as a result, bakers' deliveries fell away. National Flour was milled to specifications imposed by the government, leaving more of the wheat grain in the flour to ensure that precious wheat supplies went further. This more wholesome wholemeal flour made a heavier brown loaf that was viewed by the population, who saw white bread as a sign of affluence, with disfavour. But it was nutritionally better, with added calcium and vitamins – and to our modern palettes would have been tastier than white bread – and it was one of the foods that kept the nation well nourished during the years of rationing. Once restrictions were lifted and refined flours arrived back in the country, bakers once again expanded their range of products – cakes, crumpets and tarts – turning up on doorsteps with a basket of freshly baked goods to tempt their customers every day.

Today we still cook another wartime bread, the Grant loaf, by choice. This was a simple wholemeal loaf with only one rising stage and no kneading which had been invented by cookery writer Doris Grant back in 1944. It appeared that year in her book *Your Daily Bread* to encourage people to make their own. Doris was an early champion of fresh, natural ingredients and railed against food processing. She believed that 'healthy people are contented people' and in her 1955 book *Dear Housewives* wrote that 'the right kind of diet could even reduce juvenile delinquency'.

Despite the difficulties of producing meals, during the years of rationing many people in fact had a healthier diet in almost every way than they had had in the years of depression before the war. Average consumption of fat and calories fell, but intake of protein and vitamins showed a substantial increase. Even when shortages had been at their most severe back in 1947, the energy intake for Britons was around 2,750 calories a day (compared to around 2,000 recommended today); when 'the plenty of 1955' returned, this level increased by as little as 250 calories. The restricted diet did, however, cost more. The average British family of the time spent an astonishing third of its income on food (33 per cent in 1954 at the end of rationing), dropping to 25.7 per cent by 1970, compared to around 12 per cent today.

One of the reasons behind the nation's improved nutrition was school dinners. A hot midday meal had first been introduced in some British schools in the early years of the twentieth century and the 1944 Education Act finally made it compulsory for all local authorities to provide heavily subsidized school dinners and free school milk. The Act set out clear and strict guidelines: each meal should provide at least 1,000 calories and between 20g and 25g of first-class protein and 30g of fat.

The aim was to make it the main meal of the day for children and to compensate for any deficiencies in the diet at home – a neat continuation of the exertion of government control over what its citizens ate that went hand in hand with the reasoning behind rationing. The state was taking over responsibility for keeping the nation well nourished and it did have a beneficial effect: a Medical Research Council survey carried out in 1999 showed that the children of the 1950s were a whole lot healthier than their modern counterparts. The average cost of a meal was about 7d a day – around 73p in value in today's money – or free for children of means-tested parents (about 4 per cent in 1954) and by the early 1950s, though many children still chose to walk home for dinner or take a packed lunch, uptake had become widespread – and would continue to grow, reaching 70 per cent of all children by 1975.

This, however, had another social effect, in that it was part of a sea-change in the way families spent time together and ate in the home. The raising of the school leaving age to fifteen in 1947, and the increase in the number of children taking advantage of school dinners, meant that, as the years went by, more and more of the nation's young would eat their main meal of the day apart from their family.

Because of its scarcity and the problems associated with it, food became something of a national obsession. Books and films of the period demonstrate both this and the growing dissatisfaction with ongoing controls. Two popular and charming Ealing comedies, *Whisky Galore* and *Passport to Pimlico*, reflect the changing attitude of a public fed up with restrictions, queues and shortages. In the former (based on a true story), a close-knit community set on a fictional island off the coast of Scotland takes the law into its own hands when a cargo ship of whisky bound for America runs aground on its shores. The film culminates with a huge celebration as the islanders divide the spoils between themselves. In the latter a group of Londoners bowed down by the effects of rationing and wartime restrictions discover a hidden treaty that claims the area as part of Burgundy. The residents promptly declare independence and throw off restrictions.

Children's literature of the time also reveals this yearning for new beginnings and, above all, plentiful and good-quality food. C. S. Lewis's much-loved Narnia books, written between 1949 and 1954, contain vivid descriptions of everything from great feasts of celebration to simple meals such as the tea shared by Lucy with Mr Tumnus the faun, which included 'a nice brown egg, lightly boiled', buttered toast with honey and a sugar-topped cake, or Turkish delight and the steamed marmalade pudding cooked for the children by Mrs Beaver – mouth-watering portrayals of foods from the period before the war.

National Food Survey Menu 1952

Family with two daughters

Soft-boiled eggs
National Bread, butter & jam
Tea with milk & sugar

■

Liver & onion stew with mashed potato
Mashed turnip dumplings (made from National Flour & margarine)

■

Tinned spaghetti, National Bread & margarine
Biscuits & birthday cake
Tea with milk & sugar

Or

Jellied veal sandwiches (National Bread & margarine)

■

Bacon & biscuits
Fried egg, potato & turnips

Party time

By 1953, when the young Queen Elizabeth II had come to the throne, rationing was entering its final phase, and the Coronation on 2 June 1953 offered the nation the perfect excuse to throw a much-needed party. Described by the BBC as the 'most stupendous event in British broadcasting', this was the first big event to be broadcast live on television, allowing millions of ordinary people to join in the celebrations. Sales of television sets boomed and street parties were held across the nation, with neighbours combining their resources to provide a feast for everyone. To help them celebrate, households were given an extra pound of sugar and 4oz of margarine, and the Ministry of Food even granted eighty-two applications for people to roast oxen, provided they could prove that, by tradition, an ox had been roasted in their town or village at previous coronations. This was certainly dispensation to escape the ration books!

At last the housewife had an opportunity to show off her domestic skills, but what did she prepare for the occasion? Most guests at street parties dined on Spam and corned beef, paste sandwiches made with the dreaded National Loaf, cakes baked with dried egg but using the precious extra sugar ration and, as Rochelle and Miranda tried to make for their Coronation celebration, a special 'Jelly Crown Centrepiece', made using a recipe featured in an advert for Chivers Jelly. Decorated with piped cream, elaborate puff-pastry curlicues and studded with glacé cherries and angelica, the recipe promises it is 'easy to make'. But, as Rochelle wails when her pastry emerges from the oven like a volcanic disaster, 'that's obviously a lie!' Imagine preparing all this with no fridge in June. Luckily for the cook, the weather was typically British. A mere 11.7°C (53°F) was the peak in London on the day, with cloud and spots of rain on and off – perfect for keeping jellies set, but not such fun for those sleeping out on the Mall.

Although it was not enjoyed at the time by street-party revellers, one culinary legacy of the day was Coronation Chicken, a dish created specially for the Coronation luncheon served to some 350 foreign guests who could not be fitted into Buckingham Palace. Held in the Great Hall of Westminster, the meal was prepared and served by students and staff from the Cordon Bleu School in London and the Domestic Science School at Winkfield Place, Cranbourne in Berkshire, which had been founded by Constance Spry and Rosemary Hume. The recipe for *Poulet Reine Elizabeth*, as it appeared on the menu, was created by Rosemary Hume, although it is usually attributed to Constance Spry, who was herself responsible for the flowers at the Coronation. (She advised the minister of works on all floral arrangements for the day and did the Abbey flowers herself.) The challenges of planning a menu to serve at the occasion are summed up by the two ladies in the pages of *The Constance Spry Cookbook*, which came out in 1956: 'By two o'clock the guests would be very hungry and probably cold. There would be people of all nationalities some of whom would eat no meat. Kitchen accommodation was too small to serve hot food beyond soup and coffee. The serving of the food would have to be simple because all the waitresses would be amateurs.' Chicken was a rare luxury in the 1950s, which is why it was selected to be served at the banquet. The majority of chickens at this period were egg-layers, as fattening a hen for meat was an expensive process and the poultry-meat industry was still in its infancy.

The end of rationing, while universally welcomed, brought a different kind of challenge. Food shortages for more than a decade had forced housewives to use all their resourcefulness to create meals to feed their families. While this might have led to a bulldog spirit in the kitchen, the lack of ingredients had also denied women the opportunity to develop cooking skills that their mothers and grandmothers had taken for granted. War had stemmed the tradition of culinary instruction passed on from mother to daughter, and a whole generation of women existed who had learned to cook from Ministry of Food leaflets and demonstrations, if at all. Shortage of basic ingredients such as butter and sugar meant that many women were unable to make the most everyday dishes, such as a simple sponge cake, batter or crumble – recipes that their mothers would have held in their heads. Concern about this loss of ability is reflected in books and magazines of the time. Organizations such as the Women's Institute (the largest women's organization in the country, with 446,475 members in 1950) and the Women's Gas Council saw the need to address not only this loss of essential cookery skills but also the local knowledge of regional dishes that was in danger of disappearing. The WI created special books and leaflets, including detailed pamphlets on breadmaking and pastry, and a fifty-page booklet entitled *County Fare*, which was handed out from their stand at the Ideal Home Exhibition and contained recipes aimed at preserving culinary heritage, such as Melton Mowbray Pork Pies, Potted Severn Salmon and Kentish Pickled Cherries.

A day out

One of the underlying causes of the prolonged period of rationing had been the high levels of food that was imported into the country at the outset of the war, at a time when agricultural production had been falling due to the inter-war depression. British farmers, with the much lauded 'land girls' to help, had increased their output during the war years, contributing to the war effort by doubling the tonnage of potatoes grown and upping output of vital grain. After the war politicians recognized the need for the nation to be more self-sufficient and a second agricultural revolution was heralded. The aim of the 1947 Agriculture Act was to create 'a stable and efficient agricultural industry capable of producing . . . part of the nation's food . . . and at minimum prices'. This was to be achieved through price guarantees for farmers, as well as a system of grants and subsidies to support the adoption of new techniques and to increase efficiency. The aim was to raise output between 1952 and 1956 to around 60 per cent above pre-war levels, and this was achieved. But it came at a price to the British countryside. In his paper on post-war agriculture, J. K. Bowers writes: 'The lasting achievement of post-war policy has been the changes it has wrought in the landscape and the natural environment.' The emphasis on high yields saw the loss of hedgerows as small fields disappeared, merged into industrial-sized areas that could be managed with modern tractors and combine harvesters, and the effect of large-scale use of pesticides on water quality and habitats would have a profound effect on wildlife.

Simultaneously, the middle years of the decade saw the general public begin to turn in increasing numbers to the countryside for leisure. With the end of rationing and petrol back in the pumps, the nation could finally start to consider how it might let its hair down a bit after years of living in grey times. And one way was to go for a drive. Car ownership began to rise from 1951, and by the mid-fifties more and more families were able to escape into the countryside at the weekend. It was also government policy to encourage people to spend time outdoors: the 1950s saw the establishment of the National Parks to ensure that everyone had access to our most beautiful countryside, and there was a growing appreciation of the benefits of physical exercise 'and the feeling of freedom and of spiritual renewal gained from open-air recreation'. Encouraged by women's magazines, the picnic became a regular feature of family life each summer. Our mid-fifties family would have driven off in their new car with a picnic hamper carefully packed with hard-boiled eggs, sandwiches, home-made cake and a flask of tea all prepared by Mum. For most people sandwiches were the basis of a picnic, carefully wrapped in waxed paper to keep them fresh. The fillings would invariably be old favourites such as egg and cress, canned pink salmon, bloater paste, corned beef or Spam (the name comes from 'spiced ham' and it was a 'luncheon meat' made from chopped processed meat, usually pork, compressed into a loaf and sliced). At least by the mid-fifties the sandwich had escaped the confines of the National Loaf. If the housewife wanted to be daring, however, maybe she would have tried something more elaborate, such as one of the recipes from 'The Winning Picnic Pack' – six picnic recipes that appeared in *Woman* magazine sent in by Wooden Spoon Club readers entering a competition. One, a Layer Loaf, is made up of a scooped-out small sandwich loaf, filled with layers of sliced meat, hard-boiled egg and chutney, with each layer coated in aspic jelly (a savoury jelly made from meat or fish stock and much used at the time to keep elaborate cold dishes from drying out), pressed down, then wrapped in greaseproof paper and sliced 'when wanted'. Mmmm.

National Food Survey Daily Menus 1955

Family with three children

Bacon & eggs
Rolls with butter
Tea

■

Stew & potatoes
Rice & prunes
Tea & cake

■

Chips
Morning rolls & butter
Tea & cake

■

Tea & biscuits

Friday
Family with three children

Cornflakes with milk
Bread, margarine & jam
Tea with milk & sugar
∎

Boiled fish in milk, boiled potatoes & beans
Gingerbread
Tea with milk & sugar
∎

Scrambled eggs with toast & margarine
Biscuits
Tea with milk & sugar
∎

Bananas
Bread & margarine
Tea with milk & sugar

Eye appeal is buy appeal

In the mid-fifties the austerity years were left behind as Britain rode the crest of a new economic boom. In 1953, Chancellor Rab Butler's 'New Look' budget cut both income tax and purchase tax; in 1955, in the run-up to the general election, he exempted 2.5 million people from paying income tax (although several of the qualifications for exemption were revoked shortly afterwards). The Welfare State was up and running; more powerful unions were demanding better pay and working conditions; and, with the country suffering a labour shortage as the decade progressed, more part-time work became available to women, gradually freeing them from their stay-at-home role. Taken all together, these things meant that Britons were starting to feel more affluent. And, as the shackles of the grey years slipped away, they started to spend. Consumerism had arrived, based around the idea that happiness was there to be purchased – every medium from advertising, television and radio to magazines and newspapers supported this notion to some degree.

Here in the UK a second television channel was launched, with ITV beaming into homes for the first time. The evening's viewing on 22 September 1955 featured a variety show, a boxing match and a series of drama excerpts with well-regarded actors such as Alec Guinness and John Gielgud. An hour into viewing, at 8.22pm, in a break from the variety show, Britain's first television advertisement was broadcast to the nation. It was for Gibbs SR toothpaste, and over the evening a total of twenty-three adverts appeared for products such as Cadbury's chocolate, Guinness, Brown and Polson custard powder, Batchelors canned peas and Esso petrol. As the decade progressed, TV advertisements would become as famous and as talked about as the programmes they supported. Tony Hancock would 'go to work on an egg'; in 1956 the first Brooke Bond chimps made an appearance, drinking tea from china cups in an elegant country house, with a voice-over from Peter Sellers; while cosy married couple Philip and Katie first embraced life with Oxo in 1958.

And there was one particularly notable beneficiary of the power of advertising. A new icon was set to enter the national consciousness, as up in Great Yarmouth, on the coast of the North Sea, a Birds Eye factory produced the very first frozen fish finger. Yet it was so nearly not to be!

Clarence Birdseye was an American scientist who, with his invention of the blast freezer in the 1920s, had transformed the commercial quick-freezing process, which in its turn would revolutionize the way we store and cook food at home – although it would be several decades before anyone other than the wealthy owned a domestic freezer.

Ad slogans of the decade:

* Tide's got what women want (no wonder you women buy more Tide than any other washing product)

* There's always time for Nescafé

* Katie says: Oxo gives a meal man appeal

* Don't say brown say Hovis

* Heinz 57, Heinz 57. You've a family to feed (jingle on new ITV channel, 1955)

In 1955, when Britain had a glut of herring, Birds Eye prototyped two different versions of a new product, developed at the Great Yarmouth factory by a Mr H. A. J. Scott: 'herring savouries' and the blander alternative 'cod sticks' were tested on consumers in Wales and Southampton. To the surprise of their makers, cod sticks came out the winner with the tasters, and such was their success that within a year over 600 tonnes of the renamed fish fingers had been eaten by British consumers. What a difference there might have been if the trials had gone for herring – maybe no cod wars, and, as herring is both more sustainable and healthier, perhaps a different view of this humble foodstuff.

At the time of their invention, few homes had fridges, let alone freezers, so initially most housewives would have had to cook the fingers on the day of purchase, but such was their popularity that within a decade they would account for 10 per cent of British fish consumption.

In 2011, when the fish finger gained a place in the History Association's *A History of the UK in 1000 Objects*, it was estimated that 114 packets of fish fingers are sold every minute in UK supermarkets. In the 1950s they must have been a particular boon on a Friday, as the Catholic practice of avoiding meat and serving fish on a Friday was still followed in many homes and institutions such as schools and work canteens. (In the 1960s Pope Paul VI loosened this restriction except during the forty days of Lent.)

In other areas besides food, the kitchen was the engine of the technological and economic boom, with the housewife as the eager driver. Buying things for the home became the means of expressing personal style and taste, and the 1950s dream was centred around the kitchen, where women longed to be able to create the perfect home without suffering the sheer drudgery of housework they had known in recent years. With little domestic help available, middle-class women increasingly turned to modern labour-saving devices to assist them in their pursuit of perfection.

Improvements in kitchen design appeared as architects and designers began to plan with the housewife in mind. The idea was that technology would enable consumers to 'buy leisure'. Fitted kitchens, designed by time-and-motion experts to help the user save time and energy, emphasized a professional approach to domestic management. Stainless-steel sinks, new electric cookers and refrigerators – although the fridge would not become universal for another decade – all came with simple lines for easy cleaning. Colour entered a formerly grey area, and up-to-the-minute fashions in the design of kitchen appliances were promoted to create as much desire for the latest model as for a new hat. Formica (gold-sequined was introduced in 1955) covered every worktop, while a serving hatch to the dining area enabled the housewife to communicate with her guests as she prepared food in her new domain.

Where durability and economy had once held sway, designers now worked with planned obsolescence in mind. Equipment and appliances would need to be replaced more regularly and acquiring the latest model became a goal. The housewife's spending power was recognized as an important factor in driving the economy, whether it was her own earnings – usually seen as a supplement to the main wage-earner of the house and therefore an ideal target for these new essentials – or as something for her husband to buy her. Men were just as keen on the value of a settled home life, expecting to return to a wife and a proper dinner at the end of the working day.

The loosening of restrictions on hire purchase by the Board of Trade in 1954 also contributed to the boom in Britons purchasing all kinds of new-fangled electrical goods. A BBC *Eye to Eye* documentary of the period shows an upper-middle-class housewife listing all the purchases she has made through HP: 'the mixer, the fridge, the washing machine, the dishwasher and polisher, the bedroom suite, the carpet, the lounge three-piece and the TV set and my car'. The interviewer asks her: 'What do you get with HP?' and she replies: 'I have more free time, the children have more variety in their diet, I can help my husband entertain.'

With HP available from virtually every retailer, luxury goods like

the Kenwood mixer became a real possibility for the house-wife. Kenwood's original mixer, a simple two-beater affair, had been invented in 1947 by British electrical engineer Ken Wood, whose motto was 'eye appeal is buy appeal'. The redesigned mixer, with its multitude of functions and christened the Kenwood Chef, proved a great hit

'Welcome home, dear!' The housewife welcomes her husband home with a smile, a hot meal and no worries.

when it was launched at the Ideal Home Exhibition in the fifties. It also won the hearts of housewives in the USA, where an advertising campaign in women's magazines went as far as to reveal the secret of why the American housewife looked younger: it was because she used a Kenwood mixer!

And with the new goods came plenty of support to enable the user to get the most out of her purchases. Magazine articles introduced the consumer to the latest appliances, and manufacturers provided advice and support for the user. Mary Berry's first job was at the Bath Electricity Board showroom, conducting demonstrations to teach customers how to use their electric oven and visiting them in their homes to help them get the best out of their appliance, while a 1953 article in *Good Housekeeping* gave pointers on using equipment to ensure 'you get the most out of each piece . . . and save time and energy throughout the year'.

Down-to-earth advice came from Marguerite Patten, a former Ministry of Food adviser whose wartime recipes had demonstrated ways of cooking home-grown food and preparing interesting meals with rations. In 1943 she had taken charge of the Ministry of Food Advice Bureau in Harrods (of all places!), giving demonstrations of four or five recipes a day in the famous Food Hall. By the 1950s the growing popularity of liquidizers and electric mixers brought reports of people being showered with hot soup and other liquids because they had failed to hold the lid on their blender, and their pleas for help saw Marguerite and her team at Harrods demonstrating how to use these machines properly. Her recipes for dishes such as Rabbit Pâté, Speedy Tomato Soup, and Mock Cream (made from milk thickened with cornflour and enriched with butter) helped people make the most of their equipment.

Marguerite had also been one of the very first cooks to appear on national television. In 1947 she took part in a new programme, *Mainly for Women*, making yeastless doughnuts with dried egg, which came out rather flat but were very popular with viewers. By the mid-1950s she had a regular television programme, BBC's *Cookery Club*, which began broadcasting from a specially built kitchen in the Lime Grove Studios in west London. The programmes all went out live and included a monthly competition for viewers to send in recipes; winners were invited to appear on the programme itself. With cooking fats, meat and sweets newly off ration, many of the recipes Marguerite cooked were for pastries, breads and cakes, and she was 'deluged' with requests for real chocolate icings to put on cakes and desserts. Frying was a frequently used method of cooking in her recipes, as fats were viewed as an important source of energy at the time. Her recipes for deep-fried chips, puff pastry, sausage rolls using home-made flaky pastry, lemon meringue pie and chocolate biscuits were all snapped up by eager home cooks.

Another legendary television cook of the day was Fanny Cradock, who burst into the nation's consciousness with dinner-jacketed husband Johnnie in attendance in 1954. Her intricate food and complex presentation turned food preparation into a form of theatre and we still feel her influence in the twenty-first century. Maraschino cherries and tomatoes sculpted into roses garnished every dish and aspirational cooking became the order of the day.

Eating out, dining in

By the end of the decade new trends in everything from food and drink to appliances and furnishings were slowly starting to transform life for the average Briton, many of them popularized by the medium of television. ITV, the infant commercial channel, was busy advertising foods such as the recently available ready-sliced loaf, as well as the latest kitchen equipment, while articles in magazines and newspapers introduced readers to modern ideas of sophistication, from eating out to foreign travel. Food, whether at home or in the world outside, was taking its place in the fantasy of a more affluent, dream existence.

In the wake of this, writing about food was the up-and-coming career choice for some and, as John Burnett writes in his book *England Eats Out*, reading about it was a popular recreation. Magazines, books, newspapers and even television all rhapsodized about the glamour of entertaining in the home and the excitement of eating abroad. Elizabeth David (whose first book, *Mediterranean Food*, had been published in 1951 into a world controlled by rationing) was writing articles for *Vogue* from 1956 onwards on the joys of eating in France, and that same year an issue of *Good Housekeeping* found Barbara Wace and Anne Deveson, 'two travelling journalists', cooking up 'a ragout of gastronomic souvenirs' in an article on 'Travels in Tasting'; it opened with the statement: 'Part of the joy of a holiday is collecting exciting new tastes . . . crushed rosemary . . . a jar of olive oil'. This was at a time when the only herb regularly found in a British kitchen was curly-leaf parsley and – as Elizabeth David had found necessary to advise readers of her cookbooks earlier in the decade – olive oil was bought in small bottles from the chemist, where it was stocked for medicinal purposes.

However, there was still a considerable mismatch between what the housewife was reading about in magazines, cookery books and newspapers, or watching on television, and what she was cooking in her own home – or even what she actually ate outside it. Most people of the period regarded ingredients such as garlic with a great deal of suspicion. In 1946 Peter Pirbright, in his wonderfully colourful and entertaining cookery book *Off the Beeton Track*, had written: 'You know the contempt for garlic in this country is somehow connected with the vague notion of wicked dagoes, loose living and general frivolity. Garlic is almost considered a moral issue . . .' Pirbright had taken issue with the English way with vegetables, turning his ire on Mrs Beeton herself and accusing her of perpetuating 'crimes against food'. But he saved his loudest complaints for canned and pre-prepared foods, and looked ahead to emerging trends in home cookery in the 1950s with advice on cooking and eating spaghetti properly (with a description of cooking *al dente*) and a recipe for good hamburgers. Other food writers would follow his banner, such as Rachel and Margaret Ryan (both of whom wrote regularly for the WI's own magazine, *Home & Country*), and recipes appeared for American and Italian standards such as risotto, macaroni cheese and meatballs, all of which would emerge as firm favourites with the British public in the years ahead. But despite Pirbright's championing of garlic, the general view was slow to change during much of the fifties, even with a booming economy and a huge increase in the types of food available to a public theoretically keen to embrace a new world of flavour. Despite appearances and the mass of information, the reality was that things changed very slowly.

Top cookery books

■ *Good Housekeeping Cookery Book*, 1948

■ Rachel and Margaret Ryan, *Quick Dinners for Beginners*, 1950

■ Elizabeth David, *French Country Cooking*, 1951

■ Elizabeth David, *Italian Food*, 1954

■ Dorothy Hartley, *Food in England*, 1954

■ *Be-Ro Home Recipes*, 19th–21st editions, 1956–8

■ Constance Spry and Rosemary Hume, *The Constance Spry Cookery Book*, 1956

■ Marguerite Patten, *Cooking for Bachelors and Bachelor Girls*, 1958

Nevertheless, for a small but slowly increasing number of people, as the end of the decade approached, eating in public began to be seen as a desirable recreation, and eating out for pleasure became part of the wider social trends among British people. Geoffrey Warren's *The Foods We Eat*, a book based on a survey by W. S. Crawford Ltd of national eating habits undertaken in 1955–6, illustrated this move, revealing that 8 per cent of adults lunched in a café or restaurant on a Saturday, which by this time was either a half day or a whole day off work, probably as part of an outing. The following day, however, saw this number drop to 2 per cent, as the family gathered together for their traditional Sunday meal at home. 'Sunday dinner' was still sacrosanct and 'a symbol of security' – in 1958, 90 per cent of all adults surveyed ate their meal at home, for when 'mother has the brood gathered – she is sure for at least one day in the moving busy week they are having enough good nourishing food under her eye'. Sunday dinner (just one in four people called it 'lunch' in 1958) was usually a roast: beef, lamb or pork. Eating out in the evening was rarer – only 2 per cent of adults would do so during winter, rising to 5 per cent once summer arrived. Tea was still the drink of choice for most people with their midday meal, whether at home or eating out. Nearly two thirds of adults drank a cuppa with their dinner, with coffee coming a poor second. Even fewer drank water or soft drinks, while beer, wines and spirits were drunk only occasionally by 1–2 per cent of the population, and more likely in the summer months.

The late 1950s was also the age of the drinks party and the dinner party. Hosting a successful one was an admirable way for a wife to impress her husband's work colleagues or, even more importantly, his boss – or should that be his boss's wife? Magazines and newspapers of the time were filled with advice on every aspect of throwing the perfect party. And this was competitive – the house, the table, the food and, of course, the wife, all had to look the part. A feature on 'Giving a Party' in a 1950s issue of *Woman's Own* magazine offers plenty of tips to ensure the success of your evening. And as the writer promises: 'Main thing to remember about party giving is it's a super chance of showing off your home to your friends.' The menu for a drinks party with 10–14 guests, budgeted at £2.15. 6d, includes the classic and inevitable canapés, chicken-and-ham vol-au-vents, with cheese straws, coffee nut layer cake, 'meringue surprise' and almond petits fours piped into shapes and iced, all washed down with glasses of cider cup. If you are a working girl, you are advised to prepare a 'great deal the night before', while it is essential to make sure you manage to have a rest 'with your feet up' beforehand, as the party is 'unlikely to succeed' if the hostess is 'tired or anxious'. Clothes, of course, were an important part of the display. A smart and sleek 'hostess dress', hair done at the hairdresser and elaborate make-up were all part of the show, and a little frilly 'hostess apron' would be donned to protect the finery as the meal was wheeled in to the waiting guests via that ultimate alternative to the much-missed servant, the hostess trolley.

This pressure on the housewife to perform is revealed in a small A5 recipe notebook of my mother's that dates back to 1958. The little book, with recipes in her handwriting for Goulash, Beef Stroganoff and Cheese Soufflé next to a note to call the chimneysweep, also holds a browning newspaper cutting taken from the *Sunday Express* of 9 March: 'How to put on a banquet for 30/- and still have time to be the serene hostess when your guests arrive'. The menu is elaborate – and in French and Italian with the English translations alongside:

Crème aux Epinards (cream of spinach soup)

Salmis de Pigeonneau (casserole of pigeons)

Crêpes Parmentier (potato pancakes)

Croques-M'sieur (fried bread and cheese)

*Spumoni Zabaglioni (Italian ice cream in
chocolate meringue baskets)*

But don't worry, because everything can be prepared in advance: 'YOU DON'T have to get hot and flushed over the kitchen stove while gay chatter drifts from the living room.' All the hostess has to do on the night is answer serenely 'when an infuriating guest invades your kitchen and asks, "Can I lend a hand or am I in the way?"' At the time my mum was snipping out this piece of advice, she was living with my father in a little two (and a half)-bedroomed house set among farm-land on the edge of a Surrey village, recently bought with a loan from her father-in-law, with no central heating, half a mile from the nearest shops and unable to drive. She had two four-month-old babies. And, like many women of the time, although she enjoyed food and cooking, my mother's skills were limited. How must she have viewed this menu with its complex recipes?

Like all the women's magazines of the time, the WI's monthly publication, *Home & Country*, rose to the challenge of helping the housewife entertain, but was maybe a little more down to earth in its approach than some of its Fleet Street cousins. A feature from 1957 offers ideas for entertaining with offal recipes, including Brains and

Annoying guests are of no concern to the well-organized hostess, calmly cooking up a storm in her new 'fitted' kitchen.

Pineapple (tinned pineapple was viewed as the height of sophistication at the time), Baked Stuffed Sheep's Heart, and Veal Kidneys Baked with Crumbs, the latter to be served up behind 'a wall of mashed potato'.

Brave new world

What a very different world it was that the average family woke up to at the end of the 1950s from that of just ten years previously. The country had moved from austerity to affluence, and the new Elizabethan age was settling into its stride. New hopes and aspirations for everything from the kind of home you lived in to the sorts of food you served your guests to the car you drove – all took on a special significance as the country looked towards the next decade. More women were working (by 1959 one in three married women was in employment), television was introducing people to innovative ideas about what to eat and where to holiday, and a group of consumers was emerging who would have a huge effect on the way we viewed ourselves as a nation. The teenager was about to enter the stage, and the world was ready for the next 'revolution'.

The war babies and those baby boomers born just after the end of the war were better educated than ever before and, at the end of the fifties when levels of employment were high, they were now entering the workplace with greater freedom and more disposable income than their parents before them. They had also benefited from the better nutrition imposed by rationing and the introduction of school dinners, which saw them enter puberty earlier. Youth culture emerged as a distinctive entity for the first time, as young people started to spend on clothes, cosmetics, motorcycles, records and other entertainment. Although they made up just 10 per cent of the population, their spending accounted for over 25 per cent, and as they lived at home with their parents with none of the responsibilities of marriage or families, they could afford to splash out on the latest consumer desirables.

The generation gap widened as the young embraced rock and roll, the coffee shop and all things American. And food was part of that all-American experience – everything from milkshakes, sodas, Coca-Cola, the ever-present chewing gum and, above all, the hamburger. The Wimpy fast-food restaurant, which had launched at the Ideal Home Exhibition in 1953, had been growing in popularity year by year, attracting those who had never really eaten out before.

By the end of the decade the growing sense that things were finally changing, and that the new was something worth embracing, had taken hold. The path was clearly set for the Swinging Sixties.

Spending an average of seventy-five hours a week on housework, most women worked hard to provide a comfortable, well-run home.

CHAPTER 3

Lost in Space:
the 1960s

Key Events

1960   End of National Service

1961   Contraceptive pill goes on sale in the UK

1962   Cuban missile crisis

1963   Assassination of John F. Kennedy; Beatlemania grips the country

1964   New town of Milton Keynes conceived

1966   Mao launches China's 'Cultural Revolution'

1967   BBC starts broadcasting in colour

1968   Assassination of Martin Luther King

1969   First moon landing

THE 1960s WAS NOT so much the Age of Aquarius as that of the baby boomers – in the early 1960s 40 per cent of the population was under the age of twenty-five – and this new generation enthusiastically embraced everything from free love to the space age. This was the decade when mass consumer culture would arrive, setting patterns and trends that we still follow today. Music, fashion, celebrity-obsessed media, personal fulfilment through shopping and car dependency all made their presence felt in these years. Alongside them came great leaps in science, and nowhere was what the prime minister, Harold Wilson, called the 'white heat of technology' more in evidence than in food production and the domestic kitchen. Developments in freezing and packaging technology, intensive farming methods and food production techniques all changed what we put in our shopping baskets; advances in design and materials changed the way we prepared and served our food; and a burgeoning advertising industry promoted items previously regarded as luxuries as everyday necessities while 'make-do and mend' was banished to the history books.

But although Bob Dylan sang 'the times they are a changin'' in 1964, for many Brits in the early years of the decade it probably seemed that things stayed pretty much the same. The 1960s may have been swinging for some, but most of this activity took place within a relatively small area of central London, with Carnaby Street and the King's Road as its epicentre, a world away from the lives of the majority of the population at the time. The media picked up on the goings-on of art students, models, musicians – the new pop stars – and hairdressers, but the saying 'if you can remember the sixties you probably weren't there' really doesn't hold true under inspection. For most of the country the permissive society seemed another world. And for Mum there was still a great deal of hard work involved in caring for the family, despite the raft of labour-saving appliances coming on to the market.

National Food Survey Menus 1960

Family with two children

Bacon, bread, butter & marmalade
Tea with milk & sugar

■

Minced beef dumplings with carrots
Biscuits
Coffee with milk & sugar

■

Eggs, baked beans, bread & butter
Biscuits
Tea with milk & sugar

■

Bread & cheese
Biscuits
Tea, coffee, Horlicks & milk

Saturday
Family with four children

Bread & treacle
Tea

■

Corned beef hash & Yorkshire pudding
Dry bread
Fruit malt
Tea

■

Pork sandwiches with stuffing
Pineapple slices
Iced cakes & biscuits
Tea

■

Fried mushrooms
Bread & butter
Biscuits
Tea

Below the surface, however, change was starting to creep in – as Brandon exclaims when Rochelle serves up a sixties meal, 'Is this spaghetti bolognese? Things are looking up!' – and by the end of the decade it would be making its presence felt in all areas of family life.

The birth of lifestyle

The 1950s had seen a flood of innovations enter the marketplace and gradually trickle into the home, making life easier for the housewife and cook. By the 1960s, however, consumption was no longer based on practical need but focused more on status and desirability. The longing for style and novelty overtook the requirement for durability, and the influence of the US, Italy and Scandinavia on design found its way into our homes, especially the kitchen. The space age was at its peak, and the impact of all the new technology developed as a result was filtering through into the domestic arena in fabrics, furniture and appliances. The era of the 'lifestyle' had begun. With it came an explosion of colour and pattern, as Britons finally shook off the drabness of the war years with wholehearted enthusiasm.

The fitted kitchen was the epitome of the application of science to design and technology. As Polly Russell told Rochelle as she entered her 1960s kitchen, 'The dream of the fifties kitchen has become a reality!' The houses of the new towns and the flats in the modern high-rise blocks boasted up-to-date kitchens that were seen as very desirable. The Parker Morris report of 1961 laid down minimum standards for space and heating for social housing, and architects took inspiration from Le Corbusier and Bauhaus to create high-density modern living, to build 'streets in the sky'. But the term they coined for their designs, 'Brutalism', was all too apt in notorious building schemes such as Sheffield's Park Hill Estate, which opened in 1961 with nearly 1,000 flats built in blocks of four to thirteen storeys on land cleared from old slums. Victorian and other older properties, viewed as old fashioned by their occupants, also began to feel the benefits of modernization, often undertaken by home owners themselves as they embraced the new trend for 'do it yourself'. 'Time and motion' was the order of the day: engineers measured patterns of use to identify maximum efficiency and applied these ideas to the creation of the 'perfect' fitted kitchen. Lines were sleek, with units, work surfaces and flooring constructed from new, easy-to-clean, man-made materials such as Formica, Arborite and linoleum, which had been the darlings of designers, manufacturers and magazine feature editors throughout the 1950s and which now started to appear in kitchens across the country. Sinks came with integral draining boards in enamelled colours; up-to-the-minute eye-level ovens and hobs set into worktops appeared in the smartest kitchens. Metal finishes such as stainless steel and aluminium were used for door handles, all fitting with the universal theme of modern, clean, hygienic living. Free-standing fridges, cookers and washing machines were, for those fortunate enough to own such a thing, universally white enamel. For the first time kitchens featured a range of wall-hung cupboards, with a raised eye-level oven in the trendiest versions, making the most of precious storage space. And there was a good reason for this – there were plenty of new con-sumer goods, both food and equipment, needing room in the 1960s kitchen, and in the economically built modern housing space was at a premium.

Another significant innovation was the introduction of an eating area into the kitchen – increasingly the norm as people moved into the new-build homes or upgraded their older kitchens – as the modern fitted kitchen worktops freed up space for a small table and chairs. Now the kids could eat in the kitchen while Mum got on with her housewifely duties, although there was rarely enough room to seat the whole family for the main meal at the weekend or in the evening. The formal dining room still served that purpose.

Top cookery books

- Marguerite Patten, *Cookery in Colour*, 1960

- Elizabeth David, *French Provincial Cooking*, 1960

- Peg Bracken, *The I Hate to Cook Book*, 1960

- Katharine Whitehorn, *Cooking in a Bedsitter*, 1963

- Robert Carrier, *Great Dishes of the World*, 1963

- Len Deighton, *Len Deighton's Action Cook Book*, 1965

- Arabella Boxer, *First Slice Your Cookbook*

- *The Cordon Bleu Cookery Course*, weekly part work, 1968–70 (72 parts at 4/6 each)

- The Galloping Gourmet, *The Graham Kerr Cookbook*, 1969

Revolution in the kitchen

The new decade also continued the deluge of labour-saving devices that began in the 1950s, powered by electricity and targeted at the time-conscious housewife. Electric kettles that could switch themselves off when they came to the boil replaced a whistling kettle on the hob, while toasters, although invented decades earlier, finally became commonplace – no more toasting forks or burnt toast under a grill. However, although this was the decade when we all went electricity crazy, house fitters had still to catch up. Most kitchens came with a distinct lack of electrical sockets for all these appliances.

But the innovation that brought about one of the biggest changes in national eating habits was without doubt the arrival in many more homes of that now-essential piece of kitchen equipment, the re-frigerator. In 1956 only 8 per cent of households in the UK had owned a fridge. In the 1950s, the UK domestic-appliances industry had still focused on a largely prosperous middle-class market, but in the 1960s this began to change. Imports from Italy made by companies such as Zanussi, Ignis and Indesit concentrated on the cheap end of the market, meaning ownership of such goods was opened up to the working class. In 1956 Hotpoint had carried out market research with 'housewives' to find out what they felt was important in domestic appliances, and as a result began to create products with a real user in mind as opposed to those imagined and developed by male designers for some mythical woman. By 1960 a quarter of British households had a fridge, by 1962 a third of all families possessed one, and by 1970 they were to be found in 50 per cent of homes.

This was a trend born of necessity. The post-war housing boom had seen many new homes constructed either with tiny larders or none at all and, as more women went out to work, fridges were becoming a vital part of everyday life. Food writer Margaret Ryan opened a feature on 'You and Your Refrigerator', which appeared in the Women's Institute magazine, *Home & Country*, in the 1960s, with a paragraph that must have resonated in homes throughout the land: 'On that exciting and delightful day when we first see our very own refrigerator in our very own kitchen, our minds almost certainly turn . . . to the joy of keeping milk, meat, stock and so on without the dread that the cautious sniff will meet the unmistakable smell of "going off"!' For the sixties housewife, freedom from the difficulties of keeping food fresh in a warm kitchen, from the need to use up spoiling food and from the tyranny of the daily shop must have been liberating indeed. These new appliances, such as fridges, washing machines and televisions were not viewed as status symbols, but were identified instead as 'material goods now thought necessary for a relatively comfortable life' – and advertisers recognized this as they targeted 'the affluent working class' with such labour-saving products.

A report by the Ministry of Agriculture, Fisheries and Food (MAFF) on the National Food Surveys for the years 1956–65 reveals that fridge ownership had a significant effect on how people shopped and ate. It encouraged families to splash out and spend on the ever-expanding range of convenience foods that depended on the fridge, such as fish fingers, fruit juice and ice cream, all being heavily promoted through the rapidly growing medium of television advertising. Interestingly, weekly household food expenditure per head was higher for fridge owners. They bought more of the new quick-frozen food and also showed healthier buying habits with the purchase of more fruit and veg, which could be kept fresher in the fridge; and they purchased more brown bread and less sugar than those without fridges. This different attitude to food amongst fridge owners spread across all social classes – the report refers to it as being 'food conscious'. Rather than looking on food as fuel, these families enjoyed food for its own sake.

Snap, crackle and pop

It wasn't all good news, however, as the changes in eating habits were not necessarily all associated with improved nutrition.

With the fridge installed in pride of place in the heart of the kitchen, the next step was to fill it. And manufacturers were coming up with all kinds of ways to tempt every member of the family to try different food experiences. Mum might still be responsible for all the food shopping and preparation, but advertisers were starting to recognize the power of the rest of the family – children and husbands – to influence what she put in her shopping basket. And no meal would reflect the changes wrought as sharply as the 'most important meal of the day' – breakfast.

As a meal, breakfast had changed little since before the war. The National Food Survey shows that the average family in 1960 was starting the day with an early-morning cup of tea (in 1958 most people drank six cups a day). Porridge or cereal was eaten by one in five, followed for over half the population by a cooked course made up of eggs and bacon with maybe a sausage and tomatoes. But with a fridge in place alongside that other new gadget, the electric toaster, households were suddenly ready for change. Sliced white bread, sugary breakfast cereals and spreads such as Nutella (launched in 1964) would all make this meal easier to prepare and eat, but also less nutritionally balanced. Working mums in a hurry to get out of the house could now leave families to get their own breakfast – cereal, bread and jam on the table, milk, butter or margarine in the fridge.

Thus the 1960s marked the moment when sugary cereal started to become a regular part of our breakfast table. In 1959 only around a quarter of adults ate cereal or porridge at breakfast, rising to a third in the winter. Cereal consumption rose by 42 per cent over the next ten years, to 75g per week (about two to three bowlfuls, depending

Sugar consumption rocketed in the 1960s to the highest levels in our history as snacks and convenience foods fed our increasingly sweet tooth.

on the cereal). Cornflakes had arrived in Britain in 1924 and by 1936 UK sales topped £1 million, and other cereals such as Rice Krispies, Shredded Wheat and Force (wheat flakes) had also been popular in the inter-war years, but wartime milk rationing had had a big impact on eating cereal. Now, with a fridge in place and new products such as Coco Pops (launched in 1961) and Froot Loops (in 1963), all with plenty of added sugar and supported by advertising focused for the first time on children, the decade saw the nation's sugar consumption swell to an average of 50kg per person per year – greater during the 1960s than in any other decade in British history. Many cereals came with cartoon characters associated with them, such as Tony the Tiger with his distinctive roar for Frosties, and Snap, Crackle and Pop, the Rice Krispies elves. Promotional packs came with a little plastic gift hidden in among the cereal. How many families argued as mine did about who would get the precious toy, be it Noddy figure (in Ricicles), badge or plastic spaceman? My sisters and I fought desperately to be allowed to tip all the new pack's contents into a bowl to find the frankly disappointing item. Then there was the challenge of getting all the cereal back into the packet! Other brands advertised a free gift but – unbelievably – the shopper had to collect as many as fifteen tokens from separate packs to send off for the toy.

Cereal is an interesting example of the time lag that occurs between the introduction of many foods and their progression into daily use. Many of the sugar-coated varieties, such as Frosties, had arrived in the 1950s but it was the new television advertising and promotion aimed at children in the 1960s that saw their popularity increase. They were still an occasional treat in the 1960s, however; but when the post-baby boomers (those born between 1964 and 1978, often dubbed Generation X by journalists) grew up and had children of their own in the 1980s and 1990s, these sugary treats were remembered as special, as something we wanted to give our children, and so they became everyday foods – with disastrous impact on obesity levels.

Toast was another staple that made its presence felt more strongly on breakfast tables in the decade, its popularity boosted by the arrival of the electric toaster. Cereal, toast, tea with milk and sugar, with bacon and egg on a Sunday, are regular entries from many of the families in the National Food Survey of the period. Bread, named by baker and author Andrew Whitley of The Village Bakery as the first 'convenience food', changed fundamentally in the 1960s. Mass-produced bread, made using the new mechanized Chorleywood process – which reduced the time from mixing to readiness for the oven to less than an hour – was now available in all kinds of outlets, from supermarkets to dairies, and proprietary brands from the big milling companies became household names: Mother's Pride, Sunblest and Wonderloaf. As Elizabeth David was later to write in *English Bread and Yeast Cookery*, it was the total antithesis of homely basic bread. The Chorleywood process uses lower-protein wheats to produce a softer, finer loaf that keeps fresh for longer, and vitamins and nutrients removed during the milling process were now put back into the flour in the form of additives alongside bleaches, emulsifiers and preservatives. Refined, white and cheap, 80 per cent of modern white bread is now made by this method.

On the road

The other important technological advance of the 1960s lay outside the kitchen, but it too would change our eating habits, along with the rest of our lives, for ever. By 1961, 31 per cent of British households owned a car, and by the end of the decade the number of cars and vans on Britain's roads had doubled to 12 million. But even with this increase in ownership many of us continued to walk to the shops – even well into the next decade in 1973 between 55 and 65 per cent of all shopping trips were still made on foot. The growing demand for cheap, economical vehicles inspired designer Alec Issigonis to come up with the Mini, launched by the British Motor Company in 1959 and still the symbol of 1960s Britain for many people. Princess Margaret drove one, Twiggy, the Beatles and Steve McQueen were all seen with a Mini. Car ownership was glamorous, showing how modern and sophisticated we were, and it changed British lifestyles hugely – to the point where, today, people walk very little in comparison to previous generations. It also altered the way that British people shopped for their food and ate out. It could well be argued that the car was partly responsible for raising the standard of British cooking. Prior to the 1960s, most commentators agreed that, outside London, the standard of food to be found in restaurants was low; as the car took more travellers out for meals, the situation began to improve, albeit rather slowly!

And these proud car owners needed better roads on which to drive their new purchases. The first stretch of motorway in Britain, the M1 8¼-mile-long Preston by-pass, had been officially opened on 5 December 1958 by the prime minister, Harold Macmillan. Within a year 72 more miles of the M1, from Watford to Rugby (now junctions 5–18), were opened, having been completed from start to finish in a mere nineteen months. Travelling on the motorway cut journey times by almost an hour, and the surprisingly few (to modern eyes) drivers using it would have found no crash barriers, lighting or speed limit.

As they sped across the country, travellers using the motorways needed refreshment. The 1960s were the glory years of the now often maligned motorway services. These were part of the cutting-edge vision for the new roads and were planned to embrace the latest in contemporary design. In the early sixties the motorway service restaurants became fashionable destinations to dine at in their own right, while the open-all-hours venues offered a congenial alternative to the coffee bar for young Britons and attracted celebrities such as the Rolling Stones and Dusty Springfield through their doors. The Beatles, according to one waitress at Newport Pagnell, were *very unruly*, throwing bread rolls at each other, while Jimi Hendrix heard the place mentioned so often that he apparently mistook the Blue Boar Services at Watford Gap for a London nightclub.

Newport Pagnell service area began operations under the aegis of caterer and hotelier Charles Forte in August 1960; it was the second to begin service in Britain, after Watford Gap, but as the latter catered only for lorries and had opened behind schedule with just a wooden shed selling sandwiches, Newport Pagnell was the first to be used properly by the general public. Such was the interest that the doors had to be opened two hours early to let in the waiting crowds. According to *The Times* of the day, this included 'lorry drivers in oily overalls, families returning from their holidays, mothers and babies, girls and dogs, salesmen and business men'. Decor was bright and modern, and food and service were carefully planned, all adding to the ambience. Meals were eaten with a view of the motorway, as restaurants occupied

The Blue Boar: a fashionable destination for everyone from pop stars to lorry drivers.

the glass-paned covered bridges below which the traffic sped. Menus in the snack-bar areas included new fast foods such as hamburgers and hot dogs, alongside soups and desserts called 'sweets', and for the truckers and long-distance lorry drivers (and many others) there was that great British essential, the fry-up of eggs, sausage, beans and chips. In the more formal restaurants, white-hatted chefs worked in the kitchens, smartly dressed serving staff waited at table, while customers were greeted by welcoming hostesses, like those on airlines, specially trained in the arts of hospitality and even midwifery. Food was elaborate and up to date for the trendsetting customers:

Appetizers
Iced Melon
Prawn Cocktail

Grills
Lamb Cutlets
Chicken Maryland, Corn, Banana Slice, Pineapple
Fried Potatoes
French Beans
Grilled Tomatoes

Rolls and Butter

Sweets
Crème Caramel
Continental Gateaux

Cheese and biscuits
Camembert
Caerphilly
Danish Blue

But for modern 1960s diners there was one big drawback. Newport Pagnell had applied to the local council for a licence to serve alcohol, but it was promptly turned down. At a time when drink-driving was not regarded as such an issue as it is today, this was viewed as an example of British puritanism.

The rise and rise of convenience

Until well into the 1960s, town and even village high streets still had a range of independent small and specialist local shops, offering personal service and expert knowledge – grocer, greengrocer, baker and butcher. During the war and the long, slow recovery of the fifties most people had lacked transport and needed to shop locally, visiting several shops several times a week and interacting personally with the shopkeeper; the produce they bought was often local too. But once restrictions on both food and petrol were lifted, Britons became increasingly keen to explore new ways of shopping. The expansion of co-operative societies, multiple shops (retail chains) and department stores selling more and more pre-packed produce, supported by advertising on radio and television, saw a shift away from local produce to branded goods which were viewed as more desirable. People began to shop for pleasure and demand more choice, and by the 1960s a growing number of housewives were willing to pay for prepared foods that might save them time and money. As more women went out to work and, with longer journeys to work and more widespread provision of works canteens (which reached 35,000 by 1976), men no longer came home for lunch, home baking and cooking declined at the same time as the range of processed foods rocketed.

The Co-operative Society had introduced the first self-service store in 1942, with other multiples such as Tesco and Sainsbury following suit in the 1940s and 1950s. The greater shelf space introduced by the abandonment of counters meant they could offer more choice, and customers enjoyed the freedom to browse and select their own products. By 1956 there were more than 3,000 self-service shops in Britain, many converted from existing grocers, and this number had grown to 28,000 by 1969. At the same time we started to visit the new 'supermarket' stores built on a larger scale and more likely to sell fresh meat and greengrocery products. In 1950 there were around fifty, but this number had risen to 3,400 by 1969. These new stores offered choice, convenience and, for a wartime generation fed up with queuing, much faster service.

Another nail in the coffin of the local store was the abolition in 1964 of the Retail Price Mechanism (RPM). Pushed through by Ted Heath, then president of the Board of Trade, it was one of those apparently dull but actually controversial pieces of legislation that would fundamentally reshape the country. Price maintenance measures introduced in the 1890s had until then allowed manufacturers to set the price at which shops could sell their products; any shop selling for less would be breaking the law, and this practice favoured the smaller, more expensive independent shops over the multiples. Now, as the law was swept aside, supermarkets – which could take advantage of the economies of scale that came with new food-processing technologies – were free to undercut and drive down prices on all their products. Manufacturers, initially delighted to be gaining large bulk orders, eagerly formed relationships with the supermarkets and the smaller shopkeepers found themselves unable to compete. Between 1957 and 1966, nearly a fifth of independent retail establishments closed, at a loss of around 160,000 jobs. The reduction in numbers of local shops also saw the disappearance of deliveries to the home, which led to further isolation for many elderly people unable to get out, and mothers staying at home with young families. The whole nature of food shopping changed from a socially interactive experience to an essentially solitary activity.

Consumers, whose growing affluence was finally allowing them to access the lifestyle they glimpsed on television and in advertisements, flocked to the supermarkets in their newly purchased cars to stock up on refrigerated and convenience foods. The daily shop was suddenly a weekly shop, freeing up much of Mum's time, and the whole shopping experience now came with an element of impulse as women added extras to their trolley as they spotted tempting items on shelves. As the range of goods extended down the aisles, all in seductively bright, bold packaging, with the newly introduced trolleys allowing you to buy more than you could carry, family meals and life changed. Convenience became king, at last giving the overworked housewife with a dependent family a vision of some kind of life of her own. Vesta curries and chow mein (launched in 1961 and the first taste for many Britons of 'foreign food'), Green's sponge-sandwich mixes, chocolate Swiss rolls, and Heinz tinned ravioli and spaghetti hoops (launched in 1965) all found a place in the weekly shopping basket. During the decade, Sainsbury

Self-service grocers and supermarkets offered the busy housewife a wealth of choice and convenience, all at tempting prices.

saw the number of lines it stocked double from 2,000 to 4,000 (in 2014 there are around 30,000 food products in Sainsbury's aisles).

Another newcomer – surprising to modern eyes – started to appear on everyday family menus in the mid-1960s as, thanks to modern farming practices, a former luxury became a staple. Up until this period chicken had always been regarded as a special-occasion dish. An article on entertaining for a tennis party in a WI magazine of July 1930 includes a recipe for Wall Street Chicken (named after the Wall Street crash of 1929) that demonstrates its luxury status (and has a topical dig at bankers at the same time):

Wall Street Chicken

If somebody gives you some money, follow the recipe given for meat [beef, far more affordable than chicken at the time] below but with chicken and green peas ever so slowly stewed and moistened with their own water. Leave the peas whole and mask the turned out mould with the rest of the water boiled to half its bulk, thickened with ground rice, and, if Wall Street has been really good, richened with cream.

Up until the 1960s, most chickens were reared for egg-laying, as feeding them up for the table was very expensive. Pre-war, the average chicken flock was made up of only around 400 birds, and in the1950s a mere one million chickens were being eaten in this country annually. A bird was viewed as such a treat that for many families it was the choice for Christmas dinner rather than turkey. In the early sixties, however, the supermarkets encouraged UK producers to embrace American production techniques in order to reduce prices and create a demand. Companies such as Lloyd Maunder, who supplied Sainsbury into this century, invested in freezing and packaging technology that revolutionized the production of chicken, turning it from an un-affordable luxury to the dinner-time staple that we know today. This period witnessed the birth of the battery chicken – high stocking dens-ities, close control of the availability of food, water and light, selective breeding and medication. As a result of these methods, by 1965 the price of chicken had fallen by 30 per cent from its level a decade earl-ier, while the cost of pork and lamb rose by 30 per cent and beef by 40 per cent in the same period. We turned into a nation of chicken eaters: between 1960 and 1970 alone individual consumption rose by some 96 per cent, and by 1967 Britons were consuming a massive 200 million chickens a year. Today in Britain we eat 2.2 million chickens a day!

All kinds of other ingredients, especially 'exotic' vegetables which we now regard as commonplace, began to find their way into our shopping baskets as the decade advanced, many of which had been tried for the first time by the increasingly adventurous travelling public on a package holiday to the Costas or Greece. Aubergines, courgettes, green peppers (and occasionally red) and fennel all feature in recipes in Marguerite Patten's encyclopaedic 1960 *Cookery in Colour*, such as Ratatouille, Spanish Omelette and Peppers au Gratin. Avocado was another newcomer, becoming not only a bathroom-suite colour but a staple of dinner-party menus, served with a spoonful of vinaigrette dressing, stuffed with prawns – or even, as suggested in the 1962 book *Woman & Home Cordon Bleu Cookery*, 'they are also delicious as a sweet', mashed, sieved and mixed with double cream, sugar and lemon juice.

TV dinners

If the 1960s was the decade of convenience, then its apogee was the TV dinner. Like so many trends in eating from the period, the original TV dinner had arrived on the scene in America back in 1953, when food company C. A. Swanson produced the first pre-packed complete frozen meal in a single serving. (Swanson trademarked the name TV

Brand Frozen Dinner with their original launch of a Thanksgiving dinner made up of turkey, cornbread, frozen peas and sweet potatoes.) Taking inspiration from the airline meal – then seen as the epitome of glamour – and served on the aluminium-foil tray in which it was heated up, the idea soon caught on for the home.

The ready meal made a virtue out of the fact that it would save the busy housewife precious time, but many advertisements were at pains to stress that by putting the meal in the oven or adding boiling water, cooking for the family still retained that 'home-made' touch. And to the modern reader used to the speed of chilled meals heated in the microwave, the time-saving element still seems nominal. A quick meal from the period, such as the Vesta Beef Curry prepared by the Robshaws, was still unlikely to take less than 25 minutes to prepare and often required several pans, but the relative speed and exotic nature of these meals made them a hit with the British public. In 1966 alone Sainsbury sold nearly half a million Vesta ready meals. (The supermarket chain had also introduced its first range of Chinese ingredients in its Bristol store in 1961 in response to requests from the local community.) But as Rochelle and Miranda comment when preparing the Vesta curry for the family to eat on their knees in front of the 1966 World Cup Final, 'It's not cooking, it's just opening the packets and stirring.'

By the sixties the term 'TV dinner' had become synonymous with any meal on a tray eaten in front of the telly, whether it consisted of a pre-packed ready meal, a time-saving dish made using one of the new convenience products, such as tinned spaghetti or freeze-dried packs like Vesta curries or chow mein, or a dish cooked from scratch by Mum. Marguerite Patten's classic *Cookery in Colour*, promoted as the 'perfect companion in the practical kitchen of the modern home', offered an illustrated recipe for every occasion – and one of those occasions was 'Television Snacks and Sandwiches'. Turning to the relevant page, we find that Marguerite recognizes that the advent of television has changed catering habits at home, as instead of an evening meal 'the family enjoy a substantial snack while watching their favourite programme'. The much-loved author suggests dishes that are 'easy to serve and eat on a tray' – an autumn 'risotto' made with long-grain rice, pork luncheon meat, sultanas and apple; or macaroni cheese, sausage burger, Pilchards Mornay; or a Television Grill made up of fried rashers of bacon served with pineapple rings and halved bananas cooked in the leftover bacon fat. To round off the meal, a special treat might be a dessert such as Angel Delight, a chemical-laden powder in banana, caramel or chocolate whisked up into a synthetic mousse with added cold milk, then left to set and more than likely finished off with a sprinkling of multicoloured hundreds and thousands. Alternatively, the family might indulge in the ultimate luxury, a slice of Arctic Roll, made possible only because the new fridge came with a tiny, boxy freezer section that might just squeeze in a tray for ice cubes, a Neapolitan ice-cream block in pink, white and brown, fish fingers and a bag of frozen peas. In his autobiography, *Toast*, Nigel Slater remembers how, for his family, Arctic Roll was seen 'as something of a status symbol . . . served with as much pomp as if it were a swan at a Tudor banquet'.

This was the beginning of a more informal eating style for many people as family life became centred around the television. And the desire to try something different, to treat the family as they watched *Dixon of Dock Green*, *The Avengers* and *Doctor Who*, was satisfied by these marvels of technology, as we sat down to enjoy new foods eaten in front of visions of the future. We all believed we would be living on space food designed for astronauts by the end of the century. For me in the late sixties, Monday night's Latin homework was normally completed in front of *Star Trek*, followed by a switch to *The High Chaparral* on recently launched channel BBC2, as at the same time I finished off a meal of lamb's liver with its revolting tubes and pipes, or maybe chops with mash and peas, served on a tray and rounded off with tinned fruit salad (known as fruit cocktail) and my favourite Dream Topping, a sugary-sweet cream substitute that left a coating on the teeth for hours afterwards.

In 1966 the World Cup would offer the perfect television-viewing event for the men of the family to bond in front of the box with a tray on their knees. These meals were invariably washed down with a cup of sugary tea rather than the lager of today. And before the final, Geoff Hurst, a member of the England team, recalls, 'We had begun to get the hang of nutrition, so steaks were out and I had Welsh rarebit, tea and rice pudding.' All except two national teams followed a controlled diet. Smoking was forbidden, or tolerated under controlled circumstances; players who did smoke were expected to cut down. Alcohol was forbidden by thirteen countries but West Germany allowed two bottles of beer per evening. Half a century later, in 2014, the England team had its own dietician and each player had an individual diet plan of carb-rich meals; the Italian team even enjoyed specially tailored fruit shakes every day. In the twenty-first century food is seen as part of the foundation of the athlete; in the 1960s it was just fuel. But we don't seem to have seen the benefits!

As well as meals, watching the football on television was the perfect time to indulge in another new craze: snack food. And it is the snack foods and sweets that appeared in this decade and went on to become everyday treats that are now recognized as the culprits in our modern high-sugar, high-fat diets. Families in the early sixties already ate more biscuits than fruit and veg, and between 1959 and 1969 sugar consumption rocketed by 42 per cent. New sweets such as Toffee Crisp, Opal Fruits, Spangles and the precursor to the much loved Cadbury's Creme Egg, the Fry's Creme Egg (1963) all helped to push our sugar consumption skywards. And other culprits in this boom appeared – flavoured crisps and snacks proliferated in what became known as the 'flavour wars'. In 1962 Golden Wonder launched the first flavoured crisp, Cheese and Onion, and went head to head with competitor Smith's, who were much loved for their packs of crisps with little blue paper bags of salt, by introducing ready-salted crisps. Smith's countered with Salt and Vinegar. By the time England beat Germany in the

World Cup final, Golden Wonder was the UK's leading crisps manu-facturer and the country's fifth biggest grocery brand, and by the end of the decade the crisp market had doubled in size.

Gender in the kitchen

Supermarkets, modern kitchen appliances and gadgets, as well as other labour-saving equipment such as Hoovers and washing machines, meant the 1960s housewife spent fifty-five hours a week on domestic chores and cooking – down a quarter on their mothers ten years previously. But this welcome liberation didn't necessarily lead to actual free time for her-self, for any time that was saved would be spent on home, family and her own appearance, for what husband wanted to return home from a day at work to a tired, listless companion? In most households the husband was still the main wage earner: he was the provider, with the house-wife as accessory rather than partner. Countless ads of the period show a wife dressed like a sex kitten but ready at the kitchen stove with a frilly apron to protect her clothes, while cookery books and magazine articles depict the hostess fully made up in cocktail dress, stockings and high heels, again with a tiny apron. Looking good for your husband and being a good host for your guests was very important. In an article for *Woman* magazine, journalist Godfrey Winn declared: 'Even in 1964 the average wife does not want to dominate but be dominated . . . she likes her menfolk to be master in the house, to make all the big decisions.' To post-feminism eyes, it is a shocking view of women's role in the home.

At the same time, however, more men were challenging the notion of the kitchen as a woman's domain, driven by the fact that, with ever

---

* NFS menus from the mid-1960s illustrate changing family patterns of eating. Here, the first shows a substantial evening meal shared by the whole family, while Mum, with husband working outside the home, snacked on a banana with bread and butter for lunch. The second shows how families began to eat separately – Mum finishing off the Sunday-dinner leftovers for lunch, the children having a high tea once home from school, then a meal for Mum and Dad at the end of the day.

National Food Survey Menus 1965

Thursday
Family with one teenager & one child

Bacon & eggs
Bread with butter & marmalade
Cocoa & tea with milk & sugar

■

Bananas with bread & butter
Tea with milk & sugar

■

Meat pie, potatoes, cauliflower & peas (frozen)
Apple pie with custard
Cocoa & tea with milk & sugar

■

Biscuits
Cocoa & tea with milk & sugar

Monday
Family with four children

Porridge
Tea with milk & sugar

■

Yorkshire pudding, potatoes, cabbage, dried peas & gravy
Tea with milk & sugar

■

Salmon with bread & butter
Buns
Tea with milk & sugar

■

Luncheon meat, chips, eggs & beans
Bread & butter
Tea with milk & sugar *

greater numbers of women entering the workplace, more women and men lived alone than ever before. Up until that time it had been considered rather unnatural for a man to cook for himself at home, but it soon acquired a certain cachet and an essentially female task was reworked so that culinary skill was linked to sexual success. Male cooks and chefs, such as Graham Kerr, who became famous as the Galloping Gourmet (and whose recipes Brandon has a go at cooking for the first time in the 1960s episode of the series, finding the experience hard work within the limitations of the sixties kitchen), and thriller writer Len Deighton, appeared on television and brought out books that addressed themselves specifically to men. A defining image of the time must be that of the bespectacled Michael Caine, playing Harry Palmer in the film version of Deighton's *The Ipcress File*, slicing peppers and breaking eggs, one-handed, while he promises, 'I am going to cook you

Michael Caine was the epitome of 1960s masculinity and cool as he cooked up a meal for his date in The Ipcress File.

the best meal you have ever tasted in your life . . .' Deighton had trained as a pastry chef, and his famous 'cookstrips', which used a combination of words and graphics to explain how to make dishes such as Chicken à la Kiev or Baked Alaska, appeared in the *Observer* for two years. His book, *Len Deighton's Action Cook Book*, published in 1965, promised a move from 'guns to gastronomy' on its cover and came with clear, step-by-step instructions that concentrated on the masculine attributes of science and speed. The book is full of wit and good recipes, with advice about the importance of buying a fridge and the assumption (probably correct!) that readers would have no experience of such exotic fruit and veg as asparagus, chillis, salsify or pomegranate. Reading the *Action Cook Book* one is aware of a strong gender division: Deighton's keenness on garlic and coffee beans, his insistence on using only the best kitchen utensils and the liberal doses of alcohol in his recipes are at refreshing variance with the patronizing 'little woman' tone of books aimed at the female population in the 1960s.

Bedsit blues

If the 1950s had witnessed the birth of the teenager, the 1960s saw her grow up fast. The newly affluent young, working and with money in their pockets, were all ready to fly the family nest. As the Swinging Sixties moved on, many young people were choosing to spread their wings before they got married, leaving home and settling into lodgings. Harold Wilson's government oversaw the expansion of the universities, with the result that student numbers doubled during the 1960s, leading to more young people living and studying in towns like Bath, Keele, Newcastle and Warwick, while expanding work opportunities meant more young people lived away from home. Fifties boarding houses, celebrated by travelling salesmen and northern comedians, came with a landlady in situ offering communal dining and services such as laundry and cleaning. Cheaper bedsits, many in large, older houses that were suitable for multiple occupancy, catered for young singles and students unable to afford a place of their own. The arrival of compact fridges, electric rings and smaller cookers, tinned and packaged foods meant that young people, like both the Robshaw girls, could live an independent, if rather unglamorous, life away from home. Many of the kitchen-sink dramas of the period evoked the squalor of the bedsit – *Georgy Girl*, *A Taste of Honey* and *Up the Junction* – while writers such as Lynne Reid Banks, whose book *The L-Shaped Room* was filmed with Leslie Caron as the unmarried pregnant French girl who moves into a London bedsit, found them a rich ground for inspiration.

Bedsit living involved cooking for yourself, for young men as well as women, usually for the first time, without a kitchen and in very restricted conditions. After experiencing the joys of feeding herself in two such rooms as a young journalist working in London in the late fifties, Katharine Whitehorn was inspired to write her book *Kitchen in the Corner* (reissued as *Cooking in a Bedsitter* in paperback in 1963) to help this new generation of people moving away from home. Unlike their mothers, who, if they were lucky, had left home to start married life in their own establishment, these girls (and boys) were less well off, their living conditions more cramped. As Katharine wrote in her introduction: 'Cooking a decent meal in a bedsit is not just a matter of finding something that can be cooked over a single gas ring. It's finding somewhere to put the fork down.' One had to be inventive in order to chop, cook and eat when there was only one pot and no table, so out went the traditional meat and two veg meal with its multiplicity of pans and utensils. Her recipes for Poor Man's Goulash, Egg Casserole ('more elaborate but worth it') and Tripe Catalan (with instructions to buy tenpence worth of tripe – about 4p today) all serve one and take around 30 minutes to prepare and cook – though this last dish was an exception with its cooking time of 2¼ hours, which must have put quite a strain on the single gas ring and created an interesting atmosphere to sleep in, probably dispersed by the cigarette smoke in the room. The newly liberated singleton was also expected to entertain in his or her little nook, so the book also comes with a trifle recipe made with frozen raspberries, half a pack of lemon jelly and a wine glass of sherry and rum, serving six. Goodness only knows where they all sat or what they ate from! Imagine cooking this as part of a meal sitting on the bed to stir your jelly as it melts. As Katharine points out: 'No one who cooks in a real kitchen can imagine the unbelievable inconvenience of having no tap near the cooking. Nothing can be washed, swabbed, diluted, strained, or extinguished without first making that trip to the water-hole down the corridor.'

And catering for yourself, based around easy-to-store-and-heat-up pre-prepared products and fast food that could be eaten in a bedsit, created another source of stress that was also being echoed in households as busy families looked more and more for convenience and time-saving when preparing and eating their food. If curves were all the rage in the early 1960s, by the end of the decade society had declared there was an ideal body shape for women: they needed to be slender and androgynous, and no one better exemplified this than the British model Twiggy. The problem was that the diet of the decade was piling on the pounds rather than reducing them, as with increasing affluence Britain moved towards a 'richer' diet containing more protein, fats and sugar, sowing the seeds of the obesity crisis of the twenty-first century. A growing number of people were also starting to skip breakfast, especially young adults, either because of deliberate slimming or through being in too much of a rush to get to work.

La dolce vita

As the much-promised benefits from the spread of suburban housing, labour-saving gadgets, convenience foods, high levels of employment and better earnings began to be felt, the nation started to enjoy its leisure time and become more adventurous in how it spent it. For true modernity and freedom from inhibition, the public was becoming more likely to look abroad. The 1960s was a golden era for Italian film, and directors such as Michelangelo Antonioni, Pier Paolo Pasolini and Federico Fellini produced some of their most famous movies in this period. In 1960 Fellini's classic *La Dolce Vita* (*The Sweet Life*), with its iconic scene of Anita Ekberg cavorting in the Trevi Fountain in Rome, revealed to the world a vision of an exotic, luxurious destination, where lust for life and enjoyment of food and wine went hand in hand. Hollywood stars and American filmmakers were lured to Rome and the bars and restaurants of the exclusive Via Veneto buzzed with famous faces such as Audrey Hepburn, Brigitte Bardot, Elizabeth Taylor and Kirk Douglas. This was the birth of celebrity culture, as paparazzi photographed the stars embracing the glamour and decadence of the period.

The average Briton, grown weary of the greyness of life during the previous decade, lapped up this vision of Italian sophistication and pleasure. And if they couldn't actually go to Rome to experience it for themselves, by the 1960s they wanted a slice of it in their homes and on their dinner tables. Italian design, fashion and ideas were eminently desirable, and popular dishes of the day, promoted on television, in books and newspaper columns by food writers like Marguerite Patten, Philip Harben and Clement Freud, reflected this trend. Many people were tempted to try unfamiliar dishes in restaurants recommended to them by writers in one of the new Sunday-newspaper colour supplements, and then to experiment with cooking the dishes for themselves. Recipes appeared for spaghetti bolognese, minestrone (Marguerite Patten's recipe for Quick Minestrone from her 1960 *Cookery in Colour* is based around a packet of chicken noodle soup), pizza and lasagne, all aimed at helping the cook re-create the sophistication of eating foreign food back in their own home. A 1960s survey entitled *The British Eating Out* undertaken by the National Catering Enquiry reported as a fallacy the view that 'Britons are sometimes said to be rather conservative in our food choice'.

Meanwhile, for the newly affluent young with this week's wages burning a hole in their pocket, the coffee bar was the place to hang out, whether it be the the Mocambo in Knightsbridge, El Toro in Muswell Hill, the Moka Bar in Frith Street (opened to much fanfare by Gina Lollobrigida back in 1953), Liverpool's famous Kardomah or any one of a thousand copies. Replacing the milk bars of the pre-war years, the coffee bars took their tone from the stylish espresso machines made by Gaggia of Milan. Italian coffee ruled, the atmosphere was trendy and contemporary, with music provided by a juke box, and the booths were overwhelmingly filled with teenagers (dubbed 'Spendagers' by the *Daily Mirror*), happy to while away an hour or two in a convivial place for the price of a cup of coffee. In 1960 there were an estimated 2,000 coffee bars in Britain, 200 of them in London alone.

The coffee-shop boom was shortlived, however, as proprietors realized there was not a lot of profit to be made from serving coffee alone. Two thirds of them had closed their doors within five years of opening and many turned their premises into trattorias and cafés, initially serving light meals, pastries and desserts with simple service and informal surroundings. But as their popularity grew the menus expanded to serve more substantial dishes, such as spaghetti bolognese (of course!) or, for the more adventurous, melon and Parma ham, or minestrone soup to start, followed by linguine with clams or veal milanese. More familiar might be liver and bacon, or a classic steak – bistecca fiorentina. Gelati, zabaglione and tiramisu rounded off the meal, followed by good coffee served with paper-wrapped almond biscotti and maybe a liqueur such as a flaming sambuca or a sticky crème de menthe frappé. The Italian theme was all part of the ambience of this 'trattoria revolution', with raffia-wrapped Chianti bottles hanging from the ceiling, 'O Sole Mio' playing on the music system, and Venetian gondoliers poling their craft across the walls in lurid paintings.

The trendsetters of the day frequented the better versions, such as La Terrazza in Romilly Street, Soho, opened in 1959 by Mario Cassandro and Franco Lagattolla (known simply as Mario and Franco, and dubbed 'the godfathers' of the capital's trattoria boom) and patronized by the new 'royalty' of film stars, pop stars, actors and hairdressers, and even the occasional authentic royal, such as Princess Margaret with photographer husband Tony Armstrong-Jones. Another Italian, Alvaro Maccioni, described in his 2013 obituary as 'one of the small group of Italians who transformed Britain's restaurant landscape', had arrived in London in 1958 and worked at La Terrazza. He went on to open his own place, Alvaro's, in the King's Road in 1966. Brigitte Bardot, David Bailey and Jean Shrimpton were soon regulars, and within a few months of opening the restaurant was so popular with the elite of the day that the story spread that its telephone number had been made ex-directory. These restaurants helped launch a transformation in the British way of eating as clones opened in cities and towns across the country.

Chop suey and chicken tikka

One of the biggest factors in our changing eating habits in the 1960s was the wider cultural diversity of the British population. Since 1945 immigration had begun to have – and would continue to have – an impact on everything from what we ate to the way we spoke and, alongside the growth of car ownership, increased longevity and the introduction of the contraceptive pill, it was one of the biggest post-war social developments in Britain. The way we eat out now, with its great ethnic range, is down to the impact of those who have arrived in these islands since the start of the twentieth century. Since 1900 one in ten Britons has emigrated, and from 1946 even more new citizens have arrived here.

Despite two Commonwealth Immigrants Acts (in 1962 and 1968) that placed restrictions on the numbers of Commonwealth citizens who could settle in the United Kingdom, the 1960s saw an unprecedented surge of immigration to the country. Despite hostility in some quarters, people flocked here from the Caribbean, India, Pakistan and South

Ad slogans of the decade:

* Go to work on an egg

* All because the lady loves Milk Tray

* Bird's Instant Whip – Just add milk

* Wonderloaf – As fresh as the news every day

* Christmas morning she'll be happier with a Hoover

* A Mars a day helps you work, rest and play

* The Milky Bars are on me

* I'd love a Babycham

Asia, as well as thousands of Hong Kong Chinese, a lot of them attracted by the huge expansion of opportunities in the catering industry. Eager to introduce their ways of eating to their adopted country, many of them opened their own restaurants – as well as shops selling their traditional foods – and in the British they found a nation ready to embrace these exciting dining opportunities. As ever, food and eating became a way of establishing and strengthening social bonds. Eating in the local Chinese or Indian restaurant acted as a bridge between cultures, a kind of 'internal tourism' that worked for both sides of the system.

By the end of the 1960s there were 4,000 Chinese catering establishments in Britain – compared to 2,000 Indian and 500 French restaurants – and there were well-established Chinatowns in London's Soho and in Manchester. The cuisine these immigrants brought with them was mainly Hong Kong Cantonese, with dishes adapted to suit

Western palates and to make the most of limited ingredients. In the early days chips were served with almost every dish, Chinese or Indian, and, to keep prices low, meals were often high in fat, salt and sugar. Beansprouts and onions were mixed with tomato paste and added to chicken or mushrooms to make sweet and sour. Chop suey, meanwhile, was actually invented in San Francisco and isn't to be found anywhere in China. Even the classic banquet dish Peking Duck is thought to have been invented in Britain. Christopher Driver, who in 1970 became editor of *The Good Food Guide*, called it 'a collision of food cultures'. Chinese food was seen as tasty and exotic but without the strong flavours of Indian cuisine, so it was more popular with women and children. Service was polite and speedy, while the clearly laid-out menus with their set choices of differently priced banquets made ordering simple and offered a range that suited both students escaping hall catering and businessmen entertaining clients. However, Chinese cooking was still far too exotic to try at home. When Habitat introduced the wok into its cooking range in 1967 it came with an instruction manual because the concept of stir-frying was completely alien to the majority of the British public.

A survey in 1966 on 'The British Eating Out' showed that at the time 34 per cent of people ate out for pleasure once every few weeks, and 3 per cent did so more than once a week. From these small beginnings this number had risen to nearly three meals a week outside the home for the average person ten years later. As the nation grew accustomed to eating out in exotic Indian and Chinese establishments, other new kinds of restaurants emerged to satisfy the demand for food that appealed to all ages and classes, and there was soon something for everyone. Inspired by the likes of Doris Grant and concerns about what kind of food we were eating, Cranks opened its doors in Carnaby Street in 1961; for the more affluent meat lover the first of the London Steak Houses opened in Baker Street in 1962; while following on from the Wimpy in the 1950s, our love affair with all things American continued as the first Kentucky Fried

Chicken opened in Preston in 1965. For most Britons, apart from the old stalwart fish and chips, this was their first foray into takeaway food – an emerging trend that would explode in the next decade. And the Italian influence of the trattorias moved into fast food too in the form of the first Pizza Express, which opened in London's Wardour Street in 1969.

Out in the world

While sixties Britons enjoyed eating exotic food on their own high streets, growing numbers were also able to experience foreign food in its place of origin. The rapid expansion in opportunities for foreign travel, newly available to all social classes in this decade, had a huge influence on the way the nation ate. In the fifties and early sixties *glamorous* food was by definition foreign, and for most Britons, still influenced by memories of years of culinary restrictions, queuing for the dubious pleasures of Spam, snoek (whale meat) and the National Loaf, *good* food was also foreign.

Foreign holidays had always been the preserve of the wealthy. A visit to one of the holiday camps set up after the war by Billy Butlin and Pontins, or a trip by train to a Victorian seaside resort was the norm for the average Briton until well into the 1960s. But by 1969 expectations had changed. Greater affluence and job security started to pay dividends for more of the population. People were working forty-hour weeks and enjoying a fortnight's holiday every year, and increasing numbers wanted to spend these in the sun, travelling to the warmth of the Mediterranean on a 'package' holiday to resorts such as Benidorm and Majorca in new jetliners with cut-price 'tourist class' fares. In 1965 Clarkson Tours offered fifteen days 'all inclusive' on the Costa Brava for £30! A suntan became fashionable for the first time and was seen as evidence of sophistication rather than the mark of someone who laboured outside on the land. The modern tourists wanted reliable weather, a change of scene and, just as important, different food and drink from their everyday meals. By the end of the decade more than 2.7 million Britons were heading for the sun.

And on their return they wanted to eat more of the flavours and foods they had tried (often with great trepidation) while they were away. The meals they ate while abroad were on the whole casual, peasant-style cooking which could be reproduced at home, even if they might still serve them with chips – pizza, lasagne, scampi Provençal. Although they had first been published in the 1950s, it was really the 1960s, when they all appeared in their distinctive Penguin paperback editions, that saw Elizabeth David's books have a real influence on how mid-dle-class people cooked and ate for special occasions. Dishes such as slow-simmered Boeuf à la Bourguignonne or Daube à l'Avignonnaise required the cook to shop for specific ingredients and then have the time to prepare and cook the dish, so they fitted the bill for weekend entertaining (and with a little ingenuity could be prepared in a bedsit).

And enjoying a glass of wine with your food was all part of the experience. As David wrote in her article *An Omelette and a Glass of Wine*: 'I do regard a glass or two of wine as . . . an enormous enhancement of the enjoyment of a well-cooked omelette.' She continues: 'One of the main points about the enjoyment of food and wine seems to me to lie in having what you want when you want it.'

Elizabeth David's invitation to sample the joys of foreign dishes reached a wider audience as her classic cookery books appeared in Penguin paperback editions.

Drinking, which had been at low levels since the early twentieth century – due in part to the huge loss of life among young men in two world wars, as well as to higher taxes and reduced pub opening hours – began to increase rapidly in the 1960s and on into the 1970s. Rising affluence meant changing lifestyles and tastes, and those changing tastes of the sixties set the pattern for the current day. We moved from being a nation of beer drinkers (we drank 3.5 litres a head in 1950, rising only slightly to 4 litres in 2005) to being consumers of wine and spirits. Various factors lay behind the increase in sales that began in these years. New drinks such as lager appeared; foreign travel accustomed us to the idea of wine with a meal; wine producers began to target the affluent baby boomers; from 1964 supermarkets could sell wine without the restrictions of the Retail Price Mechanism; and taboos on women drinking started to wither, expanding the whole drinks market. One of the biggest changes was that far more women and young people now began to drink alcohol. The new teenagers of the 1950s and early 1960s had preferred the coffee shop and milk bar to the pub, but as affluence took hold and TV advertising showed alternatives such as Babycham, which were promoted as both fashionable and feminine, drinking alcohol became the norm. Licensing policy, which had historically been based on the principle of reducing harm where possible, shifted after the 1961 Licensing Act towards the more liberal idea that legislation should support responsible drinking and manufacturers started actively promoting drinks to women and young people.

Two faces of the future

By the end of the decade the nation's attitude to food preparation had split itself into two distinct camps, which seem totally at odds with one another but actually related to most people's experience of cooking and eating at the time, and reflected the needs of different cooking occasions. Everyday food for the family was quick, convenient and increasingly pre-prepared and processed, while at the weekend exotic meals from foreign locations were cooked completely from scratch, especially when there was a need to impress guests. We still approach food in the same way today. Katharine Whitehorn herself summed up this divergence, the contrast between convenience and authenticity: 'There's proper food which is more French than anything else, which is what I basically love to do if I've got time . . . Then one tends to go with a terrific bump to "short order stuff". The important thing is to keep in one's own mind the distinction, when it's hamburger night and when it's a proper food night.'

A flood of cookery books appeared to satisfy demand for both styles of food preparation. On the one hand there was the quick and easy: simple ideas for novice cooks and busy working women (and men). Colourful and quirky, they came with cartoons (Len Deighton's *Action Cook Book*), as cards (Robert Carrier's wipe-clean cookery cards), or in the form of menu-planners such as Arabella Boxer's *First Slice Your Cookbook*, and *Cook Now, Dine Later* from Catherine Althaus and Peter ffrench-Hodges. In complete contrast, there was the elaborate 'authentic' approach to cooking, designed to impress guests and enable the cook to display a knowledge of dishes from far-flung destinations.

By the end of the decade we find all the members of our family at home in the new consumer society. Mum Rochelle is serving up 'exotic' party treats from the fridge – cocktail sausages, devilled eggs, celery sticks stuffed with Primula cheese – to celebrate a win for Lulu in the Eurovision Song Contest and handing round the After Eight mints, while the kids feast on crisps and ice lollies such as Zoom, Fab and Orange Maid. It's all a far cry from the 'making do' of the 1950s – their first car has given them a taste of the freedoms to come, Brandon's been in the kitchen and on the booze and, with feminism about to burst on the scene, Mum can see change on the horizon. But will the 1970s deliver on the promise of an escape from the kitchen with more free time to spend with the family?

CHAPTER 4

Happy Days:
the 1970s

Key Events

1970 Germaine Greer's *The Female Eunuch* published

1971 Decimal currency introduced

1973 UK joins Common Market; miners' strike leads to the three-day working week; international oil crisis as OPEC raises prices fourfold

1974 First indication of problems with the ozone layer

1976 Summer heatwave – standpipes in the street; UK inflation rate hits 16.5 per cent

1977 Queen's Silver Jubilee

1978 First test-tube baby born

1979 Margaret Thatcher becomes Britain's first woman prime minister

BY THE TIME THE 1970s arrived, much of the optimism and hope of the previous decade had started to unravel, making way for a period of contradictions and extremes. Economic decline, inflation, stagnation, bitter disputes between unions and management, the three-day week, power cuts and speed restrictions in the early seventies, the IRA bombing campaign on the mainland and the winter of discontent – all were set against the blisteringly hot summer of 1976, glam rock, disco, punk, gay liberation, environmentalism and feminism. For children and teenagers it was the age of the Space Hopper, the Chopper bike, the Slinky, the skateboard and the troll. We watched *Dr Who* and *Top of the Pops* religiously, laughed at Monty Python and Morecambe and Wise, danced to the Bay City Rollers and Donny Osmond (well, I did!) at the start of the decade and were listening to Bruce Springsteen, Madness and the Sex Pistols by the end.

While the 1970s witnessed a general rise in affluence, this was set against a backdrop of deep recession. Many household budgets were under pressure as wages failed to keep up with prices – something noted by several housewives in the National Food Survey records of the time. But despite record inflation levels, the mid-1970s saw income inequality reach its lowest levels, as did the number of people living below the poverty line, while social mobility peaked. There's no doubt that many people felt the pinch, but at the same time families with parents in work were enjoying higher living standards – foreign holidays, consumer goods, weekends at the garden centre and affordable new homes in the suburbs. A steady shortening of the working day and an increase in leisure hours meant families spent more time together than in any previous decade, and many view these years as a golden age for the family. People started to look further afield for entertainment, and the trend towards foreign holidays and eating out at ethnic restaurants, which had emerged in the sixties, increasingly became the norm.

Within the home, easy consumerism led to greater comfort than ever before and convenience was king. The kitchen underwent a radical makeover during this decade. Gradually transformed from the wife's domain into a place where the whole family could congregate, it became warmer, more cheerful and somewhere in which to relax. Decorated in warm colours – golds, reds, browns and greens – and hung with pot plants in macramé holders, with natural materials and tiles that echoed nature, the 1970s version of the fitted kitchen had arrived on the scene, with a fridge that slid neatly under the counter and all kinds of gadgets. Appliances seen as luxuries at the start of the previous decade now became common: by 1976 eight out of ten households had a fridge, two thirds owned a washing machine and three out of ten a freezer. And nine out of ten homes had a television. The big retail chains opened stores in new shopping centres like Brent Cross,

As the 1970s progressed, a new pine country-style kitchen was the perfect place for the family to congregate and enjoy a meal together.

and a weekend trip to buy electrical goods or furniture from an out-of-town site became a family outing.

The 1970s also saw other trends emerging. A combination of frozen foods, the birth of artificial flavours and the latest processing technologies meant that the food we ate became further removed from its natural form, while industrialized, intensive farming wreaked havoc with wildlife and the countryside, and the destructive effects of pollution became recognized. Concern over these issues led to the beginnings of a counter-culture, and this was the period that witnessed the birth of the environmental movement, with a shift towards concern for the planet and, in domestic terms, an enthusiasm for wholefoods, vegetarianism and healthier methods of cooking.

While some social historians see it as a decade of struggle, most of those who lived through the seventies seem to have different recollections. A survey conducted in 2004 by the New Economics Foundation concluded that Britain was a happier country in the 1970s than at any time in the thirty years that followed . . .

Down the pub

The decade might have witnessed the blossoming of the feminist movement but, at its outset, for most women the idea of Women's Lib was focused more on how to reduce the amount of work they did in the home – whether by taking short-cuts with convenience foods, using labour-saving devices or cutting down on some of the regular chores like the weekly defrosting of the fridge – than on burning their bras and sharing childcare. Even though more women were working than ever before, the majority continued to take full responsibility for housework and cooking, and many were still spending between two and four hours a day in the kitchen, cooking and cleaning. The thought that men might enter the kitchen to relieve their wives of the drudgery of cooking two or three meals a day seven days a week was not part of the equation (although a survey by Birds Eye in 1976 revealed that by then 74 per cent of husbands did help with the washing-up – but it doesn't say how often!). In fact, while his wife was attempting to embrace feminism via the convenience culture, the 1970s husband was more likely to be found down the pub enjoying a pint of warm beer with his mates over a game of darts.

Although the decade would see an increase in social drinking at home, a visit to the local pub was still a regular feature of life for the seventies male. At the time 90 per cent of beer was drunk in the pub, with only 10 per cent bought from off-licences or supermarkets (as opposed to a 50/50 split in 2014). The public house was still a very male-dominated environment. In some parts of the country women would still not venture into a pub alone, and it was actually legal to refuse to serve a woman. Primarily drinking establishments, in the 1970s public houses had strictly enforced opening hours – weekdays and Saturdays from 11am to 3pm and 6pm to 10.30pm, and on Sunday from midday until 2pm, then again from 7pm until 10.30pm. (This remained the case until the Licensing Act of 2003 introduced more flexible opening times.) Many pubs were still traditional-style buildings with a specially designated 'posher' lounge or saloon bar for middle-class drinkers or those with wives or girlfriends in tow, and a public bar with bare boards, hard seats and cheaper beer for labourers, who didn't need to worry about entering in their work clothes. In the modern pubs built in the new towns and post-war housing estates of the 1950s and 1960s, this distinction had gradually disappeared. As we all became increasingly middle class and traditional manual work began to evaporate, everyone congregated together in the same bars.

If women were frowned on in many establishments, family-friendly pubs were non-existent at the start of the decade: children were most definitely not welcome through their doors. But busy mothers still wanted the kids out of the way while they got on with the housework (or visited the hairdresser) at the weekend and, like many children of the 1960s and 1970s, I remember hours spent sitting with my sisters in the family car (in the sixties a Triumph Herald, then a Vauxhall Viva in the seventies) in the car park outside my father's local. Handed bottles of Coke and bags of crisps through the window, we were expected to wait patiently, or maybe play in the pub garden, until such time as my father was ready to take us home. However, as the larger breweries realized there was profit to be made from selling food as well as drink, the decade brought a gradual change towards more family-friendly establishments. Chains such as Berni Inns, Harvester and Beefeater had 'carveries' offering an all-in, moderately priced Sunday roast, chicken in a basket and ploughman's lunches, and many pubs started to become indistinguishable from restaurants. Social eating, once the prerogative of men in their clubs, started to morph into a shared experience for all the family.

The sweet taste of convenience

Early in the 1970s Dad would head back home from the pub still expecting to find a meal on the table. And what might have been waiting for him in 1970, as convenience took hold in the kitchen? Continuing the pattern emerging in the 1960s that saw more men working further away from home, and the increase in employment among married women, lunch was no longer the principal meal of the day as it had been twenty years before. Afternoon tea for the children, with cakes, bread and jam, had also vanished. Now an evening family meal was the norm, with convenience foods coming into their own. The NFS report in 1975 shows a family of five in Thurrock enjoying a more traditional family supper of bangers, mash and baked beans, followed by tinned rice pudding; Mum and Dad also finish each day with a cup of cocoa. But in the same year a Perthshire mother of three small children doing her Saturday shop was buying convenience items such as sliced white bread, McVitie's chocolate wholewheat biscuits, Heinz tomato soup, tinned peas, baked beans, a ready-made beef pie and sausages to feed her family. Teabags and instant coffee also start to appear regularly on shopping lists.

For many families, dessert at the time was likely to be that speedy and much-loved treat Angel Delight, which had been launched by Bird's at the end of the 1960s and by the start of the 1970s had doubled the size of the instant-dessert market. It turns up in NFS diaries from Motherwell to Plymouth. With its long list of ingredients, it was truly artificial in all aspects, including taste, but in 2014 it remains the UK's bestselling instant pud:

Angel Delight ingredients: Sugar, Vegetable Oil, Modified Starch, Emulsifiers (Propane-1, 2-Diol Esters of Fatty Acids, Sunflower Lecithin), Gelling Agents (Tetrasodium Diphosphate, Disodium Phosphate), Milk Lactose, Milk Proteins, Flavourings, Colours (Beetroot Red, Annatto, Mixed Carotenes), Whey Powder from Milk, Anti-Caking Agent (Silicon Dioxide)

When it came to the first meal of the day, our family's 1970s breakfast was very similar to what many families still eat more than forty years later. Cereals, toast, tea, with maybe an egg at the weekend, were the basics of the meal.

Alpen, that stalwart of the seventies breakfast table, was launched in 1971 as the result of a Weetabix executive's holiday to Switzerland that year. As the first muesli on sale in the UK, its emphasis on natur-alness chimed with the start of the health-food movement that was beginning to take root. The irony was that Alpen, though sold as full of natural ingredients, was high in sugar. Alpen Original Muesli has 23.1 per cent sugar (although this did include some natural sugars from the dried fruit). Nowadays the traffic-light labelling system for

National Food Survey Breakfast 1970

Family from Scarborough
with four children: 16, 13, 12 and 11
housewife: 46; husband: 53

Fried egg
Bread
Cheese
Alpen
Marmalade
Butter
Tea
Milk
Sugar

foods uses red for those that contain more than 12.5 per cent sugar (12.5g per 100g), so today Alpen is defined as a high-sugar food. In the 1970s it would also have been served with whole milk, all that was on offer at the time. Tea was still the drink of choice for most people, five times more popular than coffee. And tea leaves brewed in a pot were still the preferred choice over teabags to make the daily brew. Despite having been around since 1953, the teabag would not achieve dominance in the tea market until the 1980s. A teapot, tea strainer and tea cosy were still essentials in the 1970s kitchen.

As well as appearing in many breakfast cereals, sugar consumption on the whole was still on the rise, continuing the trend begun in the 1960s. But the nation was busy looking the other way, ignoring sugar as a problem and obsessed instead with low-fat eating. In the 1960s an American scientist, nutritionist Ancel Keys, had linked high cholesterol levels to heart disease and stroke in a huge piece of research known as the Seven Countries Study, which followed 12,763 men aged between forty and fifty-nine and initially ran from 1958 to 1964. This led to the first recognition of the health benefits of 'the Mediterranean diet' and, as a result of the findings, Keys declared fat to be public enemy number one. Food manufacturers recognized this as an ideal opportunity to encourage us to spend on so-called 'healthy' products, and supermarket shelves filled up with everything from low-fat yogurts, spreads, juices, cereals such as Alpen and Special K, and Nimble bread with its ad campaign of a girl floating under a balloon – 'She flies through the sky like a bird'.

But one man was voicing the opposite view. In 1972 a prophetic book was published, although it was derided at the time by the food industry and some scientists, including Ancel Keys himself. Instead of laying the blame for the West's escalating rate of coronary heart disease on our consumption of fat, Professor John Yudkin identified another culprit – sugar, which he found not only contributed to heart disease but also raised levels of insulin, directly linked to Type 2 diabetes. His book *Pure, White and Deadly* posited that fat, on meat or in the form of butter and lard, had been eaten for centuries, but in the past sugar was a very rare treat, mainly for the well-off; only in the mid-nineteenth century, with the development of refining processes for cane and later beet to produce table sugar, did it become a regular part of our diets. Yudkin wrote: 'If only a small fraction of what we know about the effects of sugar were to be revealed in relation to any other material used as a food additive that material would promptly be banned.' It was not a message that the food industry, increasingly adding huge amounts of sugar to its new 'healthy' low-fat foods to make them palatable, was willing to hear. But Yudkin, reviled at the time, has since been proved all too prescient.

In 2012, with obesity levels ten times higher than when Yudkin's findings first came out and seventeen years after his death, his book was republished, and its legacy has since been re-evaluated and recognized.

Ad slogans of the decade:

* Golden Wonder Peanuts – Jungle fresh!

* Just One Cornetto, Give It to Me (sung to tune of 'O Sole Mio')

* Angel Delight – It's delightful, it's delectable, it's de-smoothest . . .

* Cadbury's Fudge Bar – A finger of fudge is just enough to give your kids a treat

* Cadbury's – Everyone's a Fruit and Nut case

* Milky Way – The sweet you can eat between meals without ruining your appetite

* Birds Eye Chicken Pie – It can make a dishonest woman of you!

* Campari – 'Were you truly wafted here from paradise?' 'Nah, Luton airport!'

* Alpen – Every body should feel as good as it looks

* Findus – Success on a plate

* Hands off my Curly Wurly (Terry Scott in schoolboy character 'My Brother')

* For mash get Smash

The amount of sugar we now eat has rocketed by 31.5 per cent since 1990 alone, mainly thanks to the 'invisible' sugar added to the kinds of foods for which we really acquired the taste in the 1970s, including orange juice, everyday processed foods such as baked beans, and even that greatest of staples, bread. And sugar is a worldwide problem today – in 2014 the WHO decided to recommend that sugar consumption be cut from the shocking levels of 22 teaspoons a day for the average person to almost half that.

Burning up the fat

As the seventies progressed, the average diet became less heavy than it had been in the previous two decades. Less beef and lamb, fewer heavy pies and offal-based dishes, and more pork, poultry, cheese, pasta and breakfast cereals were being consumed, with a rise in processed foods like cooked and canned meats, quick-frozen foods such as peas and fish fingers, puddings, pastries, biscuits and ice cream – all labour-saving products to help the busy housewife get a meal on the table as quickly as possible.

Even though people began throughout the decade to move on from the classic meat and two veg as a standard meal, we were still primarily a nation of meat eaters. On average people ate double the amount of meat that we do now, and for most of the decade potatoes still made up as much as a third of all fruit and vegetable intake. The average Briton's consumption of fats, including butter, margarine, lard and oil peaked in the late 1960s and early 1970s at around 320g per person per week (that's more than a block and a third of butter each per week!). By the twenty-first century it had dropped to 198g. The National Food Survey tells us that lard was by far the most popular cooking fat at the time – three times as popular as vegetable fats, and almost eight times as popular as olive oil, which was being promoted heavily in advertisements that ran in women's magazines as an alternative cooking fat, though it was still a fairly high-priced luxury. Chips featured in many family meals (a poll in 2008 showed that 58 per cent remembered a chip pan in the kitchen in this period), cooked in lard, and chip pans were responsible for so many kitchen fires in the early 1970s that the government started a safety campaign that launched on television in 1976 and continued to run until 1988. It was viewed as very successful in improving public awareness of the dangers and in the first twelve months a decline of up to 25 per cent in incidences of chip-pan blazes was reported. But five years later in 1981, chip pans were still the biggest cause of domestic fires – they were responsible for 31 per cent of all such incidents, and 15,000 of them that year alone caused twenty-one deaths and 13,672 injuries. Even in 1990 a television ad campaign led by Keith Floyd was necessary to publicize the dangers, and it is only since the introduction of the electric deep-fat fryer and the arrival of the oven chip that such accidents have reduced. By 2012 chip/fat-pan fires had fallen by over three quarters in ten years to 2,600, with fatalities down to just twelve that year.

Women's lib enters the kitchen

In the early 1970s there was little evidence of any fundamental change in the role of women in society, despite the improvements that had taken place in the post-war years. Thanks to new technology, domestic chores were at long last becoming less time-consuming; families were smaller; more women were staying on in higher education; and over half of those aged between twenty and forty-six were working. But although women might now reasonably begin to expect the same opportunities as men, in reality this was not happening. Cheap accessible contraception, liberal laws on divorce and abortion, and a sexual freedom celebrated in the media had all changed the landscape, but it was men who were the main beneficiaries. Society still saw the role of women as essentially domestic – as that of the carer. Even in work, most women were taking gender-specific roles such as secretaries, carers, cleaners and teachers.

Germaine Greer's *The Female Eunuch*, published in 1970, called for a revolution in female consciousness, but even she recognized that the struggle would be a long one and 'for a long time there may be no perceptible reward'. The language and behaviour of what we today call sexism was the norm, and the so-called permissive society was still dominated by men and their paternalistic view of the world. The first British feminist magazine, *Spare Rib*, was launched in 1972, at a time when, as co-editor Marsha Rowe (another young Australian journalist) has since said, 'Feminism in the seventies was about all the things that now everyone takes for granted.' But change was in the air. The Equal Pay Act (passed in 1970) came into effect in 1975 and established that women should be paid the same as men for the same work. That year also saw the passing of more anti-discrimination legislation that covered everything from housing to pensions, introduced paid maternity leave and outlawed dismissal on the grounds of pregnancy.

However, although this was all definitely a move in the right direction, in reality the effects were minimal. Many employers worked around the terms of the new legislation to escape having to treat women the same as men. And although wages for women did rise from 65 per cent to 76 per cent of men's by 1977, the following year saw the gap start to widen again, while in its first eight years of existence the Equal Opportunities Commission would launch only nine anti-discrimination investigations. Another factor holding

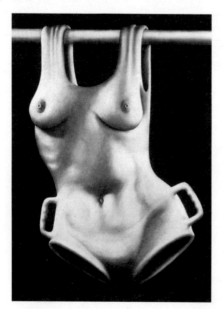

The shocking cover image set the tone for Germaine Greer's ground-breaking The Female Eunuch, *which challenged women's perceptions of their traditional role as homemaker.*

women back can be laid at Margaret Thatcher's door. Despite becoming the first woman prime minister at the end of the decade, at its outset she successfully torpedoed proposed legislation from the recently elected Heath government aiming to ban discrimination against women. As education secretary she insisted on so many exemptions that the proposed Act lacked any credibility and never came to pass. (In 1970 she also oversaw the withdrawal of free school milk for under-sevens and as a result was dubbed 'Margaret Thatcher Milk Snatcher', while the *Sun* named her 'The Most Unpopular Woman in Britain'.)

Yet change *was* in the air. The practical effects of the political situation had begun to change expectations. Job losses and restrictions due to the three-day week and deep recession of the mid-seventies meant that for the first time there were families where the wife was in work and her husband at home. A piece in the *Colchester Evening Gazette* of January 1974 noted that men forced to spend time at home were finding it difficult to avoid getting involved with the housework – but to what extent and whether this remained the case after the state of emergency was lifted is not recorded!

By the late 1970s radical women's libbers may have felt that all interaction between the sexes was so corrupted that any relationships with men were impossible, but pragmatists in the movement took another view: that male–female links were inextricable and the role for modern feminism was to build on these while challenging society's male biases at the same time. There would be no going back to the status quo of the sixties.

The freezer comes in from the cold

As women entered the world of work in increasing numbers throughout the 1970s, many new gadgets appeared in the kitchen to make life easier for them and save precious time. Electric carving knife, slow cooker, sandwich toaster, soda stream, egg slicer and lolly-maker all found their way into homes.

But one technological advance above all others helped free women from the confines of the kitchen. This was the period that found the families of Britain embracing the freezer. In 1969 a mere 3 per cent of the population had owned one, often a chest freezer kept out in the garage, as they were useful for those who grew their own fruit and vegetables either in the garden or allotment, allowing their owners to 'beat the seasons'. By the middle of the decade, nearly half of us had upgraded from our much-loved but out-of-date stand-alone fridge of the 1960s, with its tiny little icebox, either to the latest must-have, an

The home freezer helped transform shopping and eating habits for many families – now a meal could be on the table in minutes rather than hours.

upright fridge-freezer, with a special fast-freeze button on the latest models, or an under-the-counter freezer. Their popularity was driven by need: a freezer was viewed as the ultimate labour-saving device, allowing the efficient seventies housewife to home-freeze her own batch-cooked dishes, buy in bulk to save money and always have the makings of a meal in the house. It meant convenience items such as fish fingers, boil-in-the bag fish, frozen chips and frozen veg (many of which, like frozen peas, had been around for decades though the average home had nowhere to keep them frozen), where most if not all of the cooking preparation was done by the manufacturer, could easily be stored at home. Frozen foods allowed the housewife to get a meal on the table in minutes rather than hours, as well as to cater for different tastes within the family, to serve out-of-season foods all year round, and they offered reliable quality and greater flexibility. More expensive luxury items, such as seafood, that seventies staple the cheesecake, frozen gateaux (with the Black Forest the cake of choice) and Findus Crispy Pancakes also started to find a place in the family freezer. By the mid-1970s a third of households owned a freezer and this figure had risen to 50 per cent by the end of the decade. And the appliance had developed from a bulky, awkwardly shaped 'coffin' stored outside in the garage to a streamlined version designed to fit neatly under the standard worktop of a modern fitted kitchen.

In the early 1970s dedicated 'freezer centres' started to appear on British high streets, selling only frozen food: Bejam, Sainsbury's Freezer Centres, the Freezer Centre chain and, most successful of all, Iceland. Two bored Woolworths employees opened the first Iceland store in Oswestry in Shropshire in 1970, with just £60 in their pockets to pay the first month's rent, initially selling frozen food loose. Within four years there were fifteen Iceland shops in Wales and the north-west and by 1980 there were thirty-seven stores nationwide selling Iceland's own-branded products. Seventies Britain went crazy for frozen food. Households spent an enormous £180 million on frozen goods in 1972, and by the following year that figure had increased to £240 million.

National Food Survey records show the main foods found in the average freezer were:

- frozen peas
- frozen bacon
- frozen roasted chicken
- frozen sprouts
- frozen puff pastry
- frozen haddock
- ice cream

And there was plenty of advice for the housewife. *Home & Freezer Digest* magazine launched on a shoestring in 1974, but was soon such a success that it outsold stalwart women's magazine *Good Housekeeping*. Its editor, Jill Churchill, described her title's aim succinctly: 'It's not just what the freezer can do for you, but what the freezer frees you to do.' Cookery books from the period came with plenty of advice about what to freeze, how long to store food, how to blanch fruit and vegetables (maybe from your own vegetable patch) ready for freezing, and how to cook in bulk. Working on *Good Housekeeping* at the end of the seventies as a junior home economist, a large part of my job involved testing our recipes to see whether they were suitable for freezing or not. Most were, and came with detailed instructions for freezing, defrosting and reheating.

Another familiar face closely linked with freezing food was Mary Berry. From her days as a demonstrator for the Electricity Board in Bath, she had moved on to work as a cookery writer for *Housewife* magazine in the late 1960s, and by 1970 was food editor of *Ideal Home* magazine. She appeared regularly on lunchtime television programmes such as *Pebble Mill at One* on BBC1, giving hints and tips to housewives about freezer food. She remembers that freezers were initially viewed with suspicion and how, as a cookery editor, she was inundated with questions from women about how best to use their latest appliance. The whole idea of freezing, defrosting and reheating food was a totally new concept for most of them and created a great deal of confusion, and Mary wrote several freezer cookery books during the decade to help women understand how to freeze food to get the best from it for their families. Many people thought of frozen food as less healthy than fresh food and Mary was keen to dispel this view by encouraging people to cook their own dishes and freeze them. She advised her readers to batch-cook healthy, family-friendly dishes such as ratatouille and lasagne so that they could stock their freezers full of home-cooked food that was quick to defrost and reheat, rather than fill them up with

Magazine food editor Mary Berry (seen here with her children) encouraged her readers to make the most of their freezers to provide healthy, home-cooked meals.

more expensive and often less healthy processed foods. In her introduction to her *Popular Freezer Cookery*, published in 1972, she explains
how 'the food will remain in the condition it was frozen . . . in a state of
suspended animation' but how 'there is no magic about a freezer . . . it
cannot improve poor quality food'.

Frozen and other pre-prepared foods came into their own when
there were a large number of people to be catered for. When the Queen's
Silver Jubilee was celebrated in June 1977, the street-party throwers
had the option of simply opening the freezer, heating up the oven and
boiling a kettle or two. Oh and open a packet (and then throw away the
packaging). Although many things on the menu would have been quite
familiar to those celebrating the Coronation twenty-four years earlier
– sandwiches, jelly, trifle and cakes all appeared – important elements
reflected the changes that had taken place in what we ate since Her
Majesty arrived on the throne. Bread for the sandwiches was mostly
white, sliced and pre-packed; orange squash for the children came full
of artificial flavours and additives; elaborate ready-made gateaux, ice
creams and ice lollies appeared as if by magic from the home freezer;
and snacks such as crisps were on every table.

In the final years of the 1970s convenience food was set to reach
a new level. By this time every local shop had a chest freezer in the
corner packed with pre-prepared processed foods such as fish cakes,
crinkle-cut chips and hamburgers. Mary Berry's advice on cooking from
scratch to fill the freezer had been overtaken by the frozen ready meal,
which had by now become an acceptable option for busy dual-income
families with money but no time. It might cost a bit extra, but the convenience made it worth it. Familiar family favourites such as cottage
pie or liver and bacon, which were easy even for men to cook for themselves, appeared in freezers. Sainsbury stocked everyday basic products
suitable for bulk-buying, such as 5lb 'Home Freezer Packs' of peas,
meat and fish portions, while for the more adventurous they introduced
a range of frozen 'speciality dishes'. In 1975 these included Duckling à

l'Orange, Beef Bourguignon, Chicken à la Crème and that staple of the pub menu, Breaded Scampi.

The science of taste

The period was also a breakthrough time for food science, in every area from preservation and packaging to food chemistry and engineering. Food was becoming ever more expensive, and at the same time people were worried about feeding a fast-growing world population. For many, artificial foods seemed a cheap and nutritious solution. In the 1970s the ability to extend the world's scarce supplies by the manufacture of proteins 'knitted' from artificial fibres was recognized to be vastly cheaper and less labour-intensive than producing meat from animals. But the problem with artificial foods was their taste – to make them attractive to the palate, they required an army of 'flavourists' to engineer artificial and 'natural' flavours chemically. The industry was so significant to modern food development that the British Society of Flavourists was founded in 1970 to promote the interests of individuals working within the 'flavour' industry. By the 1980s an estimated 6,000 flavours were being regularly added to our food, and the industry wouldn't be fully regulated until 1984, when European law brought in the 'E number' scheme. As a result, all chemical flavouring and colour now had to be tested thoroughly before being assigned an E number and being deemed safe for consumption. In the 1970s and early 1980s, the bases for most savoury snack foods were salt, monosodium glutamate (MSG) and hydrolysed vegetable proteins (HVP) in conjunction with artificial flavours. Artificial coal tar-derived colours were also the norm.

Flavourists had a wide palette to work from and the tools of their trade read like something from a science-fiction novel: single-note natural essences such as lime or hazelnut; oleoresins; concentrated solvent extractions (taken from natural ingredients like paprika, black pepper and celery); 'sea-slics' or liquid savoury flavourings, which represented 'total flavourings' for bland products such as pâté and sausage. Some flavourings needed 'flavour adjuncts' before they could be added to food. 'Extenders' like cellulose could make a flavour seem richer and last longer in the mouth – 'tomato extenders', for example, drastically cut down on the number of real tomatoes manufacturers needed to use to get the right depth of taste. Flavour enhancers like MSG and suppressors like sucrose could mask unpleasant flavours and magnify desirable ones, while spray-dried emulsified oils gave texture and richness to soups and sauces that were little more than powder and water. In this brave new world of taste, the possibilities were exciting and endless. TV presenter Magnus Pyke (author of *Synthetic Food*) likened the flavours coming from the food scientist's lab to a Beethoven symphony.

But as is so often the case, these factory-produced foods, with their promise of liberation from want, had a downside. As early as 1972 artificial food dyes were suspected of triggering behaviour problems in children and within a couple of decades, though most chemical food additives were judged completely safe, several of the range introduced in the 1970s came with a health warning. Artificial sweeteners such as aspartame, some artificial food dyes – used in countless foods including cereals, snacks and fizzy drinks – and partially hydrogenated fats have all given cause for concern as carcinogens and triggers for ADHD.

The one product that summed up the technology of the time more than any other, perfectly representing not only the 1970s consumer's love of convenience but also their trust in food science and technology, must be the Pot Noodle. In an article for *The Times* in 2010 Heston Blumenthal named the seventies 'the decade that good food forgot' and, recalling the period in which he grew up as the culinary 'dark ages', none the less remembered the Pot Noodle (along with Smash and Angel Delight) with great fondness, so much so that he re-created a version – Pot Heston – with melting noodles and edible sachets for his 2010 TV series, *Heston's Feasts*. Launched by Golden Wonder in 1977 as 'the king of easy, quick, tasty, instant, no-faff food', the Pot Noodle divided the nation. With more than 4g of salt and ten different E numbers in its original form, it was made from dried glucose syrup, chicken flavouring and E635 – a flavour enhancer that is up to four times stronger than MSG. It swiftly became a staple of the budget kitchen cupboard and a student late-night essential. Still around in the twenty-first century, in 2004 it was voted the UK's most hated brand! But as Rosalind comments when the Robshaw family encounters the start of the snack culture: 'Four minutes and then you've got a meal!'

Sunshine and snacking

The year 1976 was one of economic gloom for Britain. The pound plunged on the currency markets, Harold Wilson resigned as prime minister and the country entered a new financial crisis as the IMF came to bail us out. But for most of us that year is remembered for

---

Top cookery books

- Mary Berry, Ann Body, Audrey Ellis, *Hamlyn All Colour Cook Book*, 1970

- Delia Smith, *How to Cheat at Cooking*, 1971

- Katie Stewart, *The Times Cookery Book*, 1972

- Richard Mabey, *Food for Free*, 1973

- The Reader's Digest, *The Cookery Year*, 1973

- Jane Grigson, *English Food*, 1974

- Delia Smith, *Complete Cookery Course*, 1978

---

just one thing – sunshine, and lots of it! The summer of 1976 has gone down in legend as the hottest and driest in the UK since records began. The heatwave started on 22 June and lasted more than two glorious months before finally breaking with thunderstorms on Bank Holiday Monday, 26 August. For an unprecedented fifteen consecutive days, from 23 June to 7 July, the temperature reached 32°C (89.6°F); no previous or subsequent heatwave has produced more than five such days in a row. The hottest day of all was 3 July, when a temperature of 35.9°C (96.6°F) was recorded in Cheltenham. Coming on top of a prolonged nationwide drought that had begun in April 1975, the hot weather added to the country's woes. For a short time parched parks and countryside, sleepless nights and, for the worst-hit areas such as Yorkshire and East Anglia, standpipes in the street became the norm. With no such thing as air conditioning, working conditions in offices became almost impossible, and dozens of people collapsed from heat exhaustion at the Wimbledon tennis championships. For those mums forced to go out into the street to fill containers from a tap, it made cooking and washing up a real chore, while farmers struggled to feed animals as grass shrivelled in the fields and heath and forest fires raged in southern England. Failing crops meant food prices rose in response. The consequent shortage of potatoes saw a rise in prices that in turn would lead to a decline in Britain's traditional potato consumption that would prove irreversible.

One sector of the food industry did thrive, of course, as the ice-cream man became everyone's best friend. There were over 25,000 ice-cream vans in the UK in the 1970s, compared to around 4,500 today. Even then, there were strict regulations over attracting customers. The 1974 Control of Pollution Act meant all mobile vans were limited to playing their jingles between 12pm and 7pm only; in the 1980s regulations were tightened further to limit tune-playing to 4-second bursts.

Ice-cream vans of the period tended to serve soft ice cream pushed through a nozzle into a cone and often topped with a chocolate flake – the iconic 99 – and what the ice-cream business calls 'hand-held confections' but the rest of us call ice lollies, which were targeted specifically at children. The latter had first emerged after the Second World War and by the 1970s accounted for half of all ice-cream sales. The two big brands of the seventies were Lyons Maid (since then absorbed by Nestlé) and Walls (now owned by Unilever). Both had been around for decades but this was their heyday – Lyons Maid launched over fifty new products during the 1970s, including Haunted House, Orange Maid and the Cola Rola, as well as numerous film- and TV-character-inspired lollies (Dalek Death Ray, Mr Men and Star Wars), while Walls were so powerful that Roy Hattersley, the minister for prices and consumer protection, investigated them to see whether they were a monopoly. He concluded in November 1976 that they were, but a 'fair' one!

The 1976 heatwave aside, the vagaries of the British climate made running an ice-cream van an unpredictable affair. But our love affair with ice cream was in full flow and, with a freezer finding a place in an increasing number of kitchens, take-home ice-cream desserts were one of the fastest-growing product areas for supermarkets. Ice-cream manufacturers responded with a wealth of creations that offered the housewife an ice cream for every occasion, from family meals to the fanciest dinner party. And of course lollies such as Lyons Maid Dairy Maids – milk ices on a stick – were sold in take-home packs of twelve so that children didn't have to wait for the ice-cream van for a treat.

It wasn't just ice cream that children were developing the habit of eating regularly at home. Other snack foods, often marketed directly to them on children's TV, were finding their way into daily diets. More hectic lifestyles meant traditional meal patterns were changing as the decade went on – and, with the move away from the 1950s model of three formal cooked meals a day mainly eaten at home, a significant development was the increased amount of snacking and 'grazing'.

In part this was a consequence of more and more mothers being out at work when their children came home from school – a phenomenon which some saw as a return to the 'latchkey children' for which the war years were known, when children as young as five, with mothers out doing essential war work, returned after school to an empty house. Whereas once they would have had a meal very soon after arriving home, now they had to wait until their mothers came back from work to prepare the family dinner, which was eaten later in the evening. To quell their hunger in the intervening hours, children would help themselves to snack foods kept in store cupboards and freezers.

And so in the 1970s the snack came of age. More than twenty new brands of crisps were launched in the period, while the UK chocolate industry more than tripled in size in six years, all supported by massive TV advertising campaigns. Chipsticks, Frazzles, Wotsits, Discos, Hula Hoops and Monster Munch (in the most lurid artificial flavours), Curly Wurly, Club Biscuits and Creme Eggs were all creations of the seventies. The kitchen cupboard became home to a range of sweet and/or high-fat treats, and whereas previously no child would have dreamt of helping themselves without asking, now with parents out at work they had leave to treat themselves. The NFS log books show crisps beginning to be bought on a regular basis by families across the country, signalling the start of a snack obsession that would grow and grow over the coming decades, making Britain one of the biggest crisp-consuming populations in the world.

Another factor that kept children indoors and snacking was a perceived lack of safety outside, which meant that instead of playing out of doors as they would have done in the past, many more children remained inside their homes. Social changes such as modern high-rise estates and the clearing of Victorian terraces had led to the loss of extended family and neighbours close by who might have kept an eye out for children as they played. No one on hand meant opportunities for preying adults and, though statistically these were rare, shocking cases such as the Moors murders in the previous decade still loomed large in the public consciousness and, along with a number of stranger-danger campaigns run in the 1970s, meant parents were less willing to let their kids roam free. In reality the rapid rise in car owner-ship and road traffic proved a far greater threat to children's safety and the Green Cross Code Man (actor Dave Prowse, who would go on to play Darth Vader though famously not voice him) appeared in a series of iconic ads that promoted road awareness by encouraging children to 'Stop, Look, Listen, Think'. As traffic accidents steadily increased, the use of the street as a playground necessarily stopped. These changes led to a reduction in freedom for children, who now spent much of their time indoors in front of the television – munching as they watched their favourite programmes and simultaneously absorbing the adverts that promoted the latest snack foods designed with them in mind.

Adverts aside, this period saw children's TV enter what is now seen as a golden age, and children were more than happy to oblige their worried parents by staying inside in front of the box. *Blue Peter* and ITV's *Magpie*, both launched in the 1960s, remained popular. For younger children the BBC replaced its dated *Watch With Mother* format with colourful animated series such as *Mr Benn*, *Bagpuss*, *The Magic Roundabout* and *Play School*. ITV responded with *Rainbow*. Programmes like *Rentaghost*, *Jackanory*, *Playhouse*, *Grange Hill* and *Catweazle* catered for older children, while *Tiswas* and *Multi-Coloured Swap Shop* transformed Saturday mornings for many families.

From cheating to impressing: entertaining, seventies-style

In the early 1970s not even the seriously competitive business of enter-taining was impervious to the nation's love affair with convenience. With more women working than ever before, they had less and less time to spend in the kitchen, so books, newspapers and advertisements encouraged them to play dirty. In fact, the title of the very first book from new food writer Delia Smith, then known for her column in the *Daily Mirror*, was *How to Cheat at Cooking*. Written following her marriage to a successful magazine editor and publisher, the book was a very personal story. Her role as his wife was, in part, to entertain a lot of his clients and, discovering how demanding this was, Delia set out to write a book that would make it easy for other women to entertain confidently – with more than a little help from convenience foods.

The book commences with Delia's 'Cheat's Charter', in which she declares: 'There are more important things in life than cooking.' She goes on to suggest you 'create an aura of good cooking in the home with serious-looking accoutrements and jars half full of herbs and spices and bay leaves hanging . . . If anyone asks you for a recipe tell them you're one of those cooks who never measure anything or write things down'; and she recommends the use of convenience foods in a way that your guests and even your husband wouldn't spot: 'Using canned and frozen vegetables, tinned soups, frozen fish . . . so skilful is she in disguising shop and supermarket specials with a dusting of herbs, a dash of wine, a spoonful of cream that even the most discriminating husband won't realize how little time the cook has spent in the kitchen.'

The trend for encouraging deception was widespread. In the classic TV ad for Birds Eye Chicken Pie from 1970, June Whitfield plays a vicar's wife who guiltily claims, 'It's my own recipe,' when complimented on her pastry at a dinner party. Four years later, Shirley Conran would famously declare that 'life's too short to stuff a mushroom' in her bestselling book *Superwoman*. She too encouraged women to cut down on domestic tasks by tarting up dreary store-cupboard foods, but to do it out in the open. But as author and cookery writer Carole Wright commented at the time: 'there will be no emancipation for women until boys are instructed in home economy'.

Ingredients list for Delia's 'How to cheat' Cottage Pie

15oz can of savoury minced beef

1 tablespoon of dried minced onions

1 small green pepper, chopped

½ teaspoon of dried mixed herbs

15oz can of Italian tomatoes, drained

1 packet of instant mashed potato

2oz grated Cheddar cheese

And with the cheat's dinner party the seventies couple (or Brandon and Rochelle in their psychedelic 1970s kitchen) was likely to have served their guests wine – chilled, sweet German Blue Nun, or maybe a distinctive round-bodied bottle of lightly sparkling pink Mateus Rosé, or Hirondelle (named by one *Guardian* journalist twenty years later as 'the Jacob's Creek of its time'); in 1979 a bottle of Hirondelle cost £1.39. Whereas previously wine had been bought to drink at home only by aficionados and experts – mostly men – from specialist wine merchants and suppliers, the 1970s is when ordinary British families began to develop a taste for drinking it as a treat. M&S started selling alcohol in 1973 with eight wines, four sherries and a selection of beers, and it was such a success that the range was expanded very quickly. Other supermarkets followed suit. Wine was certainly not an everyday drink, consuming it was essentially a middle-class activity and it was served only on special occasions, but with advertisers increasingly presenting wine drinking as modern and glamorous, and British tourists developing a taste for it on their two-week break to Spain, millions started to enjoy a glass or two. By 1973 annual consumption of wine per head stood at 9 pints (5 litres) and by 1980 this had more than doubled to 20 pints (11 litres). In 2014 it is over 26 litres, having doubled again in the last twenty years; we now consume 1.6 billion bottles a year (not counting those we drink when we go abroad); and wine has changed from being a middle-class luxury to an everyday part of life for many people.

Another seventies obsession, but definitely one for the man of the house, was home brew – beer conjured up in a bucket under the sink as an alternative to the pints of Double Diamond drunk down at the pub. But whether churned out by cash-strapped students or middle-aged dads, home-brewed beer never really enjoyed the best of reputations. In most cases the emphasis was definitely on quantity rather than quality and the kits on sale from places such as Boots in this period, when home brewing reached its peak, were not very professional, with low-grade equipment and ingredients. In most cases the results were barely drinkable and gallons of the stuff ended up being poured down the drain rather than into a glass. Much of the beer served in pubs was little better and 1971 witnessed the start of the Campaign for Real Ale (CAMRA), which was set up in response to the perceived power of the big breweries and the poor quality of their products.

By the end of the decade, however, there was something of a backlash against the growing domination of the convenience culture, particularly when it came to entertaining. Cooking had become, and remains, essentially a schizophrenic business. On the one hand, for mums struggling to work, run homes and feed families, quick and easy was the mantra, but come the weekend or when trying to impress, then all the stops were there to be pulled out. The arrival of convenience foods had freed women from the drudgery of cooking from scratch every day, which allowed them to be even more experimental when guests came over. Even though 60 per cent of married women were working by 1979, when it came to entertaining many had good kitchen skills and rarely turned to convenience foods for help. Cheating was definitely no longer an option: the evening was a chance to impress and show off your sophistication with the latest fashions and foods. Entertaining at home had become a spectacle, fuelled as ever by the continuing growth in foreign travel. Visits to France, Greece and Austria were all part of the package-holiday boom that had kicked off in the sixties, and by the end of the seventies even schoolchildren were going on school ski trips and educational cruises around the Greek isles. Skiers of all ages brought back the tastes of the mountains on their return, and fondue sets appeared on wedding-present lists across the country. A cheese fondue (adopted by the Swiss in 1930 as their national dish) required audience participation, as everybody round the table dunked their cubes of bread into the bubbling pan (often Le Creuset orange enamel) of hot melted cheese and white wine, and paid forfeits (usually downing a glass of wine) for every dropped chunk. Other versions featured pieces of raw steak cooked by the guest in hot oil, or, to finish the meal, the fondue might be chocolate served with fresh fruit and marshmallows for dipping. And dinner was dangerous at the end of the seventies! Whether speared by a fondue fork, burnt with piping-hot dripping cheese, eyebrows singed as you flamed the crêpes suzette, or injured during a spot of plate-smashing after the taramasalata, stuffed vine leaves and pitta bread, you had to be prepared for drama.

Magazines and cookery books of the late 1970s focused on entertaining, with ideas of what food to serve, the wines to accompany the menu, and how to dress the table and prepare the cocktails. Many hostesses kept detailed dinner-party books with lists of guests and menus recorded to avoid the horror of serving the same person the same dish twice. Wedding-present china was on display, glasses polished and drinks tray set out ready with nibbles such as Ritz crackers topped with soft cheese, sausages on sticks, vol-au-vents and the classic cheese-and-pineapple-chunk hedgehog so beloved of the hostess in *Abigail's Party*. Prawn Cocktail or Avocado with Crab might start the meal; the main course could be Beef Stroganoff or Coq au Vin; and there would always be a choice of desserts, maybe a Baked Alaska, Peach Melba, Black Forest Gateau (I did a step-by-step version for *Good Housekeeping* magazine in 1978) or Chocolate Mousse. And a hostess trolley in fake wood would have been on hand in the dining room to keep all the food warm for a couple of hours (but not for too long, or it risked drying out). These too are all the rage again and in 2013 John Lewis reported an increase in sales of trolleys of 50 per cent!

A more elaborate menu suggestion for a 'Celebration Dinner Party' to serve twelve from the *Reader's Digest Cookery Year* of 1976 features Melon and Prawn Basket, Duck Breasts en Croute, followed by Crème Brûlée, Coffee and Petit Fours. Wines suggested to accompany the meal are Chablis and Red Burgundy, along with Champagne, Brandy and Liqueurs. Alcohol would flow and drink-driving was still common.

Saturday Dinner Party
Menu for eight

Dressed Avocado

Walnut Rolls

Beef Steak and Wine Pie

Courgettes with Lemon

New Potatoes in their Jackets

Chilled Apricot Sabayon

Hazelnut and Chocolate Meringue

Petits fours and Fudge with Coffee

Wine: Choose a robust red, Côtes du Roussillon or Rioja

Fifties Britain placed the housewife at the heart of the home – at the cooker, smiling and fully made-up to welcome her husband home, while the kids search his briefcase for treats.

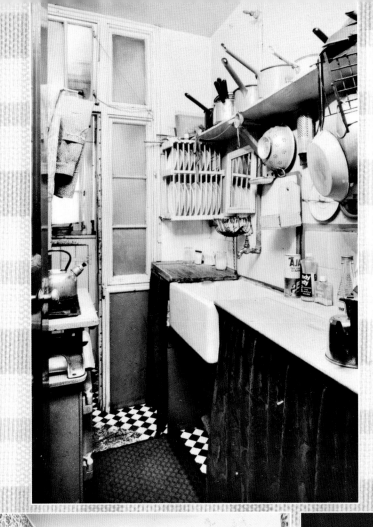

In half a century the kitchen has been transformed from a cramped, utilitarian space with no frills to the most important room in the house, where even Dad feels at home. Along the way it was fresh and fitted in the 1960s and cheerful, welcoming – and orange – in the 1970s (decade of the eye-level grill), followed by a more retro country style in the 1980s, when everything was on show.

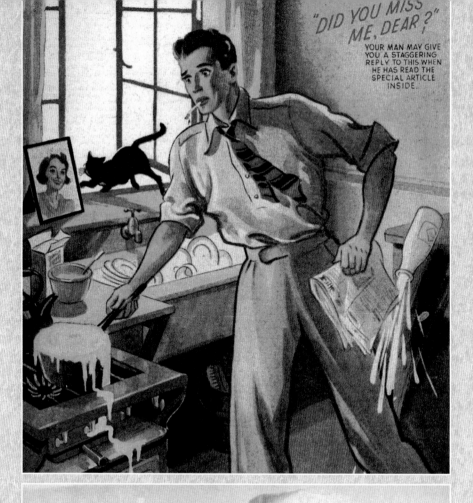

Changing trends have seen men embrace the kitchen, where once they feared to tread – whether Len Deighton-style in the 1960s or with Jamie in the 1990s. Now they are at home teaching their kids new cooking skills.

JAMIE OLIVER
pukka tukka

ACTION COOKBOOK
BY LEN DEIGHTON

Thriller writer and cook extraordinary turns from guns to gastronomy

Selected by Sainsbury's products on offer, offer end dates vary, see instore for details
Selected stores and availability. Some items available in larger stores only.

for DINNER PARTIES

The discriminating hostess coaxes the palates of her guests with the delicate fresh flavour and tempting appearance of Country Market fresh-picked Garden Peas. Specially selected and picked at the moment of perfection and cooked immediately, they retain all their natural tenderness and sweetness.

Packed by
UNITED CANNERS LIMITED,
1 PRINCES STREET,
HANOVER SQUARE, LONDON, W.1

COUNTRY MARKET GARDEN PEAS

"...with Clark Gable and Marilyn Monroe..." It's next Saturday evening, the telly's on, and the two of you have got a bit of peace and quiet. Could be just the right time to give him something a bit different. A Vesta Chow Mein.

A Vesta meal always makes what would be just an ordinary mealtime into something rather special. Think about it.

VESTA

Chow Mein with soft noodles, crispy noodles, red peppers, green peppers, beef, onions, soy sauce, green beans.

Back in the 1950s entertaining at home might demand a black tie, but tinned peas were perfectly acceptable and sausages on a stick were de rigueur for parties. In the 1960s and 1970s the exotic Vesta curry was a favourite meal in front of the TV. Social gatherings in the style of *Abigail's Party* still entailed ties and long dresses and more cocktail sticks. Now entertaining has become a competitive sport, with contestants going to great lengths to impress . . .

Supermarkets have transformed our lives and the way we eat – from self-service, convenience and a welcome escape from queues in the 1960s to miles of aisles and endless choice in the 2000s. And now the discounters are tempting us through their doors with value and quality with no frills . . .

In 1979 while I was working at *Good Housekeeping* we created a whole weekend-entertaining plan of menus for the May issue that year, with almost every dish cooked from scratch, making use of the freezer and planning ahead: 'Guests for the weekend don't have to mean more work than play. GHI shows you how to entertain with ease.' Detailed menus for each meal came with a 'countdown' plan, shopping list and wine suggestions.

This type of party was time-consuming to prepare and serve, and busy souls interested in the more upmarket aspects of food and cooking, who looked askance at the new wave of convenience foods but still wanted to save time and display their sophisticated knowledge of foreign flavours and ingredients, increasingly turned to the specialist deli for inspiration and help. These had first arrived in the country with Italian immigrants in the nineteenth century. Terroni of Clerkenwell have been selling their range of Italian foods and provisions, speciality wines and cured meats since 1878, while Valvona & Crolla have been a stalwart of the Edinburgh food scene since the 1880s. These had mainly catered for local Italian communities, but with the interest in all things Italian that boomed in the 1950s and 1960s the demand for ingredients such as aubergines, olive oil, Parmesan and garlic grew. By the 1970s there were delis springing up in market towns with middle-class residents and city areas with ethnic communities. Their success was, of course, noted by the supermarkets, who in the next decade would start to imitate their chilled counters, selling quality prepared foods and authentic ingredients and offering their own interpretations.

Curry and chips

The 1970s saw a continuation of our taste for foreign foods in the growing number of Indian restaurants. In 1970 there were around 2,000 in high streets across Britain. Walthamstow, in north-east

London – home to the Robshaws, our *Back in Time for Dinner* family – saw its first Indian restaurant open in 1971, and by 1978 the area boasted no fewer than five curry houses. This increase was mirrored in the rest of the country: by 1980 the number had grown by 50 per cent to 3,000. Much of the expansion in the south of England was due to the arrival of refugees from Bangladesh in 1971 following the war of independence from Pakistan, while the majority of restaurants further north were run by Pakistani and Kashmiri owners, and in Scotland, Punjabi owners. Today, Bangladeshis own 65–75 per cent of the 8,000 Indian restaurants in the country, and the industry is worth a staggering £2 billion a year.

The popularity of Indian establishments had a lot in common with that of Chinese restaurants. Each offered a touch of the exotic but with tasty food that was affordable for the whole family. Service was quick and friendly, the atmosphere was informal, and the food served was adapted to the British palate. And they remained open for long hours, which made them the perfect destination for students in search of a meal after pub closing time, those living in bedsits and young workers on a night out. What's more, the popular new drink of the time was lager, cheap and the perfect partner for the spicy food.

The food served in a 1970s Indian restaurant was rather different from that on offer today and in itself bore little resemblance to traditional Indian cooking practices on the sub-continent. On the average menu only about 30 per cent of the dishes were 'Indian', and these tended to be heavily anglicized, such as chicken (or other meat) with masala sauce. That national favourite, chicken tikka masala, was in fact specially created for British tastes; food writer Charles Campion has since dubbed it 'a dish invented in London in the Seventies so that the ignorant could have gravy with their chicken tikka'. Most Indian offerings were based on one basic recipe cooked up in large batches and then sauced just before serving to create a wide variety of dishes. Indian names on the menu, derived from traditional dishes but bearing little similarity to the original, gave customers an easy shorthand by which they could recognize what to expect – anything 'korma' was sweet and creamy; 'madras' was hot and spicy; while ordering the notorious 'vindaloo', the hottest dish on the menu, became the ultimate proof of macho credentials on a drunken lads' night out. The rest of the menu was filled out with omelettes, chips and the like. More authentic regional food, such as tandoori (Pakistani street food), which we eat more of today, was still viewed as pretty innovative in the 1970s. The very first *tandoor* (clay oven) had appeared in London in 1966, but, as these were an expensive investment for proprietors, in the seventies restaurants serving this type of dish were viewed as more upmarket, patronized by a wealthier, more discriminating clientele.

In the early part of the decade cooking your own Indian food at home was practically unheard of, practised only by expatriates returning from living in India or by those who had followed the hippy trail to the sub-continent in the late 1960s. And even for them, getting hold of the ingredients could be tricky. Most British supermarkets stocked a very limited range of dried herbs and spices, which would have included a generic curry powder (a British invention in itself, as Indian cooks don't use just one spice mix but prepare their own – called a *masala* – which varies from region to region), a tub of which found its way into many kitchen cupboards, where it loitered at the back, to be brought out very occasionally for use in dishes such as Coronation Chicken.

It was in the 1970s that US-style restaurants too really arrived in the capital, brought across the Atlantic by entrepreneurial young Americans. The Hard Rock Café opened in 1971 on Piccadilly, just off Hyde Park Corner, and was a regular haunt of rock gods such as Eric Clapton and members of The Who, many of whom donated the music memorabilia that became a feature of the restaurant along with the burgers, lengthy queues and glasses of iced water that arrived at the table when you finally got a seat. Bob Payton, who brought the first deep-pan pizzas to London in 1977 at his Chicago Pizza Pie Factory off St James's, also gave us other simply themed restaurants that reeked of cowboys and redneck food in the form of Rib Shacks and Meatpackers, all with the Chicago tag. As we lapped up burgers and beans we watched Mel Brooks in *Blazing Saddles*, Clint Eastwood in *The Outlaw Josey Wales* and *High Plains Drifter* and Dustin Hoffman in *Little Big Man*, and we read Dee Brown's *Bury My Heart at Wounded Knee* and embraced the ideals of the Native American. For a more everyday style of celebrating the 'special relationship' we made do with a Big Mac at McDonald's and fell for the Fonz in *Happy Days* on television. The first McDonald's opened here in Woolwich in 1974 – now there are 1,200 across the UK and Northern Ireland.

Grow-your-own and wholefoods – the counter-culture begins

By the middle of the decade, it wasn't just the plunging economy, industrial disputes and soaring inflation that were causing concern. Thirty years of post-war growth, the desire for cheap convenient food (which has informed the way we shop ever since) and the development of industrialized agriculture had transformed the British landscape, and concerns about the cost to the planet were becoming hard to ignore. In the previous decade books such as Rachel Carson's *Silent Spring* had warned about the dangers of pesticides to wildlife, and the impact of rapid population growth was widely debated. The disappearance of hedgerows, woodlands and wetlands to intensive farming practices, alongside environmental disasters such as the wreck of the oil tanker *Torrey Canyon* off the Scilly Isles in 1967, fiction such as the rabbit epic *Watership Down* and BBC series like *Doomwatch* in the early 1970s created an atmosphere of general pessimism about the future of the world. This was the decade when the 'green' movement found its feet and one of its offshoots was a re-examination of what we ate.

National Food Survey Menus 1975

Tuesday
Single mother in Brighton with three children: 10, 6 and 5

Ready Brek
Oat Krunchies
Golden Nuggets
Tea
Sugar/saccharin
Milk

■

No midday meal

■

Baked Beans
Toast
Margarine
Cheese
Cake
Biscuits

Chicken
Mushrooms
Peas
Orange squash

■

No evening meal*

Ask most people what they remember about the green movement of the time and they will probably answer *The Good Life* – and it is true

---

* Note the range of breakfast cereals served, and Mum eats chicken and mushrooms with the kids who have beans on toast when they get back from school.

that the sitcom did bring the concept of self-sufficiency into the heart of the mainstream. The first series aired in 1975 and within a couple of years it was watched by a staggering 21 million. But the success of the TV show was far from the only reason people became interested in growing their own vegetables. Food prices were subject to massive inflation – they went up by a shocking 10 per cent in the first nine months of 1973 alone, rising to over 20 per cent, and the impact on household purses is clear from entries in the National Food Survey. One fifty-year-old mother from Brigg, South Humberside, is recorded as saying: 'Budgeting for the family's food every week is my problem and each week prices seem to rise – penny on this, two pence on that, this has been going on far too long – I long for stability in food prices as one who has only one wage coming in and two growing boys to feed as well as a man who works in the heavy industries.' Another mother writes: 'Cost of living is too high – prices have gone up out of all proportion.' The idea of total self-sufficiency portrayed in *The Good Life*, or advocated in John Seymour's seminal book *Self-Sufficiency*, published in 1976, which explained how to slaughter a pig and build your own house, might have been a step too far for most families, but in economically straitened circumstances, growing some of your own food took the pressure off household purses, so a trip to the allotment made good economic sense.

When 1976 dawns in television land, we find the Robshaw family harvesting fruit and vegetables at the allotment, just as Brandon and Fred had done at the start of the series – 'we were doing this twenty years ago'. They're part of one of the biggest trends of the mid-seventies: growing your own had become popular once again. In the 1970s there were around 500,000 allotments in England (years of steady decline had reduced the number from 1.4 million in 1943). After a brief surge in the 1970s, numbers levelled off and then went into further decline in the next decade, as high land prices meant cash-strapped local authorities sold off ground formerly used for allotments, but by the end of the century the desire for home-grown produce free from chemicals – part of the growth of the organic movement – witnessed another resurgence in allotment applications. In 2008 the *Guardian* reported that there were 330,000 allotments in use in the country with a waiting list of 100,000, and with the recession and increased interest in local food and home-grown food in the new millennium this number is expected to continue rising.

At the same time people were beginning to question the benefits of the advances in technology that had created the convenience and fast-food cultures. Preservatives, hormones and intensive-farming methods were being seen as dangers rather than progress. Hormones in meat were suspected of causing cancer and reducing male sperm counts. Factory-farmed meat was high in the saturated fats that were being associated with coronary thrombosis. In response, vegetarianism grew in popularity. In 1945 rationing records show 100,000 registered vegetarians; by 1975 that had risen to 1 million. People from all walks of life embraced the vegetarian way of eating, but it wasn't an easy path to follow even with the arrival of all kinds of new wholefoods. Famously, Paul and Linda McCartney and their children gave up eating all meat and fish in the seventies. In an article in the *Daily Telegraph* their daughter Mary recalled that growing up as a veggie in the period was 'quite an alien thing'. She continues, 'None of my friends were vegetarian, it felt like we were a different sect of people.' In this period of traditional meat and two veg, eating at home was just about manageable if you were vegetarian – though challenging for mums faced with a veggie child in an otherwise meat-eating family – but having a meal in a pub or restaurant usually meant a bowl of chips, cheese sandwich or that eternal veggie standby, the omelette. Cranks, which in the previous decade had set the tone for vegetarianism with its pine tables and earthenware bowls of lentil and carrot salad or homity pie, had opened a branch outside London in Totnes in Devon, but vegetarian restaurants were still a rare breed.

Alongside vegetarianism, the 1970s saw the idea of 'wholefoods' enter the mainstream, helped on its way by two key players, American-born brothers Craig and Gregory Sams. Back in 1967 the pair had opened Seed, an organic macrobiotic restaurant in London and then expanded the same principles into Whole Earth Foods, launched in 1970, with the aim of bringing organic and natural foods that were 'better for body and planet' to customers increasingly concerned about where the food they ate was sourced and how it was produced. The pioneering business brought hard-to-find ingredients such as tahini, wholegrain rice, wholewheat pasta and aduki beans to a wider audience. (Craig went on to found Green and Black's chocolate, and is currently chairman of the Soil Association, while Greg was responsible for coining the word 'vegeburger' when they opened Seed and put them on the menu.) One commentator called the seventies the Brown Decade.

The Wholefood Cookery Book by Ursula M. Cavanagh was published

Emerging concerns over intensive-farming methods, increasing use of food additives and levels of processing saw the development of the wholefoods movement in the 1970s.

in 1971, with an introduction by renowned violinist Yehudi Menuhin, a yoga-practising environmentalist and vegetarian, who wrote:

> Too long have we followed the fashion of convenience, buying not really what we choose, so much as what the supermarket, the food embalmers and the distribution systems wished to get rid of on their all too trusting and gullible shoppers. We are being persuaded that for our convenience we must buy devitalized, harmful and often poisonous food, because it is processed, or packaged, beautified or treated . . . We learn nothing of the many thousand makers of chemicals, fertilizers, colourings, preservatives, bleaches, plastics, refrigerators and transport who have profited from that poor blanched asparagus tip long before you, the buyer, will have released it from its tin or plastic prison.

One of the first 'wholefood' menus to be found in the NFS diaries appeared in 1975 from a thirty-year-old housewife in Cambridge:

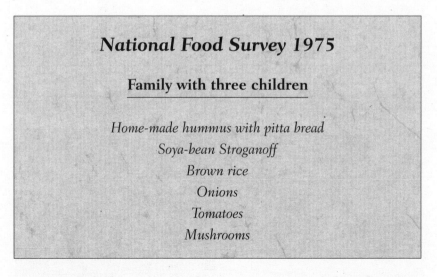

National Food Survey 1975

Family with three children

Home-made hummus with pitta bread
Soya-bean Stroganoff
Brown rice
Onions
Tomatoes
Mushrooms

Even with the greater sophistication in eating habits that came with more foreign travel and more eating out, hummus would have seemed extraordinarily exotic to the average housewife of the 1970s.

In 2014 we consume £60 million of the stuff, bought ready-made from supermarkets and corner shops, and hummus is now found in 41 per cent of British fridges.

Backwards and forwards

During the 1970s, the ground was also being prepared for a new food movement in home cooking that would finally emerge among chefs at the end of the next decade: traditional British food. Many home cooks would say it had never gone away, despite two decades of obsession with all things foreign. The Women's Institute had never stopped supporting traditional recipes in its magazine and cookery books and was instrumental in preserving many of the old traditions that might otherwise have been lost. Elizabeth David praised them in her scholarly *English Bread and Yeast Cookery* of 1977: 'owing to the initiative of the ladies of the Women's Institutes . . . recipes have

been preserved, recorded and published'. British cooking was also being championed by food writers such as Jane Grigson with her seminal *English Food*, published in 1974, and Michael Smith, popular with women at home from regular appearances on BBC's *Pebble Mill at One* and described in his obituary in the *Daily Telegraph*

The members of the Women's Institute recorded traditional regional recipes and skills, which might otherwise have been lost, in cookery books of their own.

as a 'champion of English cookery in the Mrs Beeton tradition'. Smith's *Fine English Cookery* was reviewed by the *Times Literary Supplement* in 1973 as containing 'recipes which represent the very best of English food . . . methods are "translated" to suit today's equipment . . . so-called "convenience foods" are not spurned where these can lighten a cook's task . . . without impairing the flavour of the dish'.

The food of the seventies, with its opposite extremes of wholefood and convenience food, home-grown food and lab-produced food, mirrored the contradictions of the decade in the rest of society. It was an age of deep austerity and mass aspiration; a time that saw both the struggle for women's liberation and gay rights set against the ultra-conservatism that brought about the election of Margaret Thatcher. As the decade progressed, we had moved from the hope and innocence of the sixties boom years represented by the early Beatles to cynicism and consumerism, perfectly represented by those intensely self-conscious 'New Romantics' with their bouffant hair, fancy dress and 'post-punk' New Wave pop, with its focus on style and use of synthesizers, who would lead us on into the eighties. The corrosive anger of the punks, take-home pay falling for most people, the Winter of Discontent of 1978/9 with its 'industrial and social chaos' – ports closed, rubbish in the streets, even the dead unburied – led to a kind of revolution. It all paved the way for the fast-moving eighties, with food as 'lifestyle' and the arrival of a gadget that would really transform the way we ate – the microwave.

But most of all it brought us one woman who would be inextricably linked, for better or worse, to the years of the new decade. In March 1979 Margaret Thatcher – already dubbed the Iron Lady by the Russians in 1977, and with the backing of a raft of image-makers and advertising men such as the Saatchi brothers – became the first woman to lead the country, bowing in a decade of 'Thatcherism' whose principles would be equally lauded and reviled at home and around the world in the years to come. The battle lines were set for taking on the challenges of the unions, inflation and high taxation. A Grantham gro-cer's daughter, Mrs Thatcher set out her stall early, announcing in 1980 'the lady's not for turning'. The beleaguered middle classes welcomed her with open arms.

CHAPTER 5

Only Fools and Horses: the 1980s

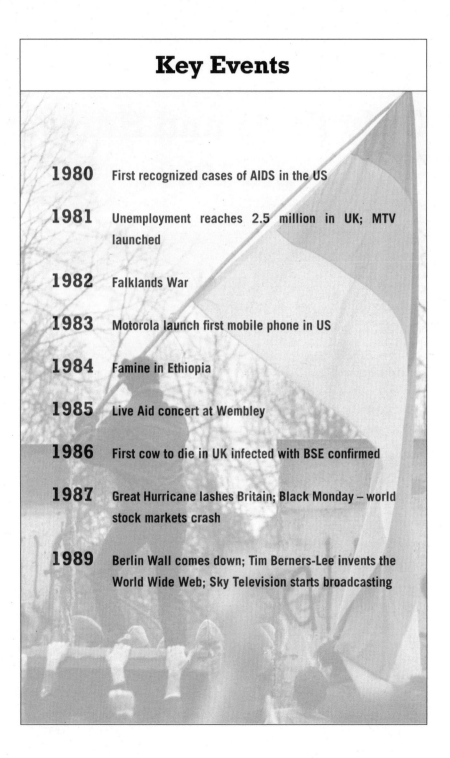

Key Events

1980   First recognized cases of AIDS in the US

1981   Unemployment reaches 2.5 million in UK; MTV launched

1982   Falklands War

1983   Motorola launch first mobile phone in US

1984   Famine in Ethiopia

1985   Live Aid concert at Wembley

1986   First cow to die in UK infected with BSE confirmed

1987   Great Hurricane lashes Britain; Black Monday – world stock markets crash

1989   Berlin Wall comes down; Tim Berners-Lee invents the World Wide Web; Sky Television starts broadcasting

COWABUNGA, AWESOME, COUCH POTATO, space cadet, 'greed is good', city slickers, yuppies and foodies – slang terms that all entered our consciousness in the 1980s. This was a decade of hedonism, credit and consumerism or, as writer Jonathan Meades later described it in an interview, a time of 'pleasure without guilt'. And oddly, this period of excessive consumption was overseen by Margaret Thatcher, who held the post of prime minister from May 1979 to November 1990 and whose main aim was to create a nation that embraced what she saw as Victorian values of self-reliance, traditional marriage, good neighbourliness and, of course, hard work.

But Britain in the 1980s was deeply divided, and as the rich got richer, the bottom 10 per cent of society saw their incomes fall. In 1982 unemployment topped 3 million, and for the first years of the decade miners throughout the country were striking in a desperate bid to save their jobs and communities – an action that fiercely divided public opinion. At the same time, deregulation of the financial markets saw the birth of a group of people who wholeheartedly embraced the free market and everything it stood for: the yuppies, or young, upwardly mobile professionals. Margaret Thatcher promised a bright new world for those prepared to strive for it; she undertook to create a fertile climate for go-getters and high achievers, offering the opportunity for thousands to become home-owners for the first time through the right-to-buy scheme for council homes, and bringing in lower taxes for high earners. As the miners lost their bitter battle with Mrs Thatcher, the decade saw the City of London take the helm as the driver of the British economy. Old rules went out of the window as the country reinvented itself and witnessed huge economic, cultural and demographic change. All this was played out against the backdrop of the Cold War, with Britain standing side by side with the United States – and happily adopting yet more aspects of American culture and habits along the way.

And, as ever, food and the way we sourced, prepared and ate it provides a fascinating indicator of what was happening elsewhere in society, as 1980s attitudes and social behaviour created huge changes in what we ate and how we ate it. Appliances and food technology evolved rapidly, keeping pace with the speed that the decade's fast lifestyle seemed to demand. And despite Mrs Thatcher's championing of the family, that institution was also in flux, with the 1980s witnessing the end of the traditional family unit for increasing numbers of people. Divorce rates rose, marriage rates decreased and more babies were born outside marriage, up from 12.5 per cent in 1979 to 29.8 per cent by 1991. Consistent with the rise of individualism in society, this trend was mirrored in the way the family ate and interacted at meal times. The social bond of sharing a home-cooked meal began to

Bombarded with advice on what made a healthy diet, the conscientious 1980s mum forced on her reluctant children a diet of lentils and muesli.

loosen; and this, alongside the isolating technologies of the decade – computers, computer games and personal stereos – underlines the fact that families seemed to spend less time together. With food ever more accessible, even children could get their own dinner, so there was no need for Mum to be there to greet them and serve a family meal that brought everyone together at the end of the day. Convenience food and a move to more 'grazing' paired up with the latest technology to take Mum's place in the kitchen.

For women, the Equal Pay Act of 1984 saw rates of pay begin to rise. More of them were entering high-paying managerial and professional jobs – this was the decade of 'power-dressing' women with big shoulders and hair. In fact, the growing number of women in the workplace was a critical factor in the UK's economic success in the 1980s. But for most women jobs were still in the 'feminine ghetto' of service industries and the public sector with their low rates of pay, and a large proportion of these women were mothers. In the eighties for the first time talk of a glass ceiling for women began, and although many more wives were out at work full time it was still not typical for men to get involved in domestic chores at home. It was still Mum doing the planning, shopping and cooking – but now on top of working longer hours.

Enter the microwave

The 1980s was the decade in which cooking was transformed into a social activity rather than just a functional one, and the kitchen reflected this trend. Better ventilation and improved extractors meant food smells would not travel all through the house, so open-plan design that integrated the kitchen into other living space became the fashion. Guests sat in the kitchen and ate a meal there for the first time, which meant your kitchen (and you cooking in it!) was now on show. Display was all-important, with the chance to show off your affluence and cooking skills. The psychedelic look of the 1970s was replaced with a more conservative style: natural woods in warm hues, a ceramic hob, built-in oven, modern laminate worktops and vinyl flooring. Asymmetry was all the rage – everything from clothes to make-up to kitchen design. Electrical appliances were an integral part of the kitchen for the first time rather than just slotted in between the units, while the ends of the cupboards became open shelves to house items like teapots and tea caddies (but not gadgets!); as *Good Housekeeping* magazine put it, you should 'utilise a shelf for good-looking odds and ends'. Utensils emerged from drawers to hang on racks. Everything was highly patterned and matching, from tiles to kettle to wallpaper, down to the mugs hanging on the obligatory mug tree.

New electrical gadgets continued to proliferate in this bright new space – the four-slice toaster, food processor (the Magimix processor had launched in the UK in 1974 and was quickly beloved of caterers

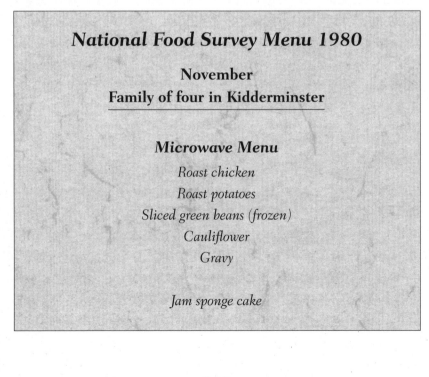

National Food Survey Menu 1980

November
Family of four in Kidderminster

Microwave Menu
Roast chicken
Roast potatoes
Sliced green beans (frozen)
Cauliflower
Gravy

Jam sponge cake

but took a while to trickle down to the average kitchen), filter coffee machine, juicer and blender. By 1981, 54 per cent of British families had a freezer in the kitchen, now for most people a fridge-freezer, and as the decade progressed it was transformed from a luxury item into a day-to-day essential; by the mid-1980s it was a vital part of the 'integrated' kitchen, hidden with the other appliances behind matching 'cupboard' doors. A smaller item, the electric sandwich-maker, was also hugely popular. This was a gadget that was specifically used to make a 'snack' rather than a nutritious, balanced meal. Now it was easy to eat whenever you were hungry rather than waiting for a meal time.

But without doubt the defining appliance of the decade was the microwave, which would come to dominate the kitchen. Paired with the freezer, this was an alliance that, more than any other kitchen development, would be responsible for completely transforming the way we ate, both in the home and outside it.

The first commercial microwave had gone on sale in Britain as early as 1958, but it wasn't until 1974 that a domestic model finally appeared in the shops. However, it was the 1980s that saw sales really take off and by the end of the decade 50 per cent of British kitchens had one. These days a microwave is to be found in over 90 per cent of British homes, and it has been voted our favourite kitchen gadget. Nowadays the appliance is mainly used to heat up a supermarket ready meal in a hurry. On most packets the microwave heating instructions take precedence over those for any other method of cooking. But when the ovens launched, no supermarket sold ready meals to put in them. Instead the microwave was championed as a means of transforming the way you cooked from scratch by saving that precious commodity, time. The marketing message was that it was possible to cook conventionally in one but faster, and the cost of your new appliance was as high as a conventional oven. In 1984 a microwave cost £229.95, the same as a gas cooker.

At the outset it was believed that the microwave could actually replace a conventional oven altogether, but as the introduction to the special microwave section in the revised 1985 edition of *The Good Housekeeping Cookbook* reveals, the reality was different. Although 'cooking [in a microwave] is quick, clean and easy', *Good Housekeeping* does admit 'there are certain foods it cannot cook, such as Yorkshire puddings, deep-fried foods and meringues . . . meat, pastry, cakes and breads do not brown, so it is best used in conjunction with a conventional oven'. Probably the biggest disappointment when you first used your new purchase was the look, texture and taste of what emerged from it. Food ended up pale and unappealing, with a rather insipid taste. And the cooking process itself was complex and unrewarding. As *The Good Housekeeping Cookbook* advised: 'Cooking in a microwave is very different from cooking by other methods and does require practice and special techniques.' Working at *Woman & Home* magazine as deputy cookery editor in the mid-1980s, I had to come up with microwave recipes to be cooked up on a whole range of the latest ovens sent in to us by manufacturers. It was like learning how to cook all over again. Food had to be carefully positioned on plates, with the thinner end towards the centre; items had to be covered with cling film or kitchen paper; standing time was needed to even out cold spots in the food. But most frustrating of all, the more you put in the oven the longer it took to cook, so items had to be put in and taken out separately, turned, prodded and stirred. Planning the cooking of a meal assumed the proportions of a military campaign, and in the end the whole business took longer than using a traditional oven and with poorer results. What's more, it was all too easy to burn yourself, as the plates and dishes used for cooking got extremely hot in the process. As Brandon comments when heating up a meal for the family, 'They're savage – you'd be surprised how hot these microwave things get!'

For many people it was soon back to the conventional oven for home cooking, but what the microwave did do was transforming in an unexpected yet decisive way. Apart from the useful facilities of defrosting food in a hurry when you got back from work (ovens started to come with automatic thawing controls), melting chocolate, softening butter or warming the baby's milk, once the flood of new chilled ready meals arrived in the supermarkets (see below) and sales rocketed as the eighties advanced, every member of the family was able to heat up an individual meal in minutes, ready to eat at a time that suited them. And family life changed as a result.

The microwave oven was also instrumental in altering catering methods, opening the floodgates for fast food such as burgers, which could be heated up on demand in cardboard or polystyrene boxes, and greatly broadening in scope the food served in pubs and high-street restaurants. Chilled pre-prepared dishes cooked in centralized commercial catering companies could now be transported to places across the country, popped in the microwave and sold to the customer as 'home-made'.

The supermarket takes control

In a 2013 article for the *Financial Times* looking back at the Sainsbury's range of cookbooks launched in the late 1970s and 1980s, *Back in Time for Dinner* presenter and food historian Polly Russell wrote of the period: 'British supermarkets were set to become the most powerful players in shaping the culinary habits of the nation. Technological developments, sophisticated distribution systems and consumer curiosity created the perfect environment for supermarkets to expand their product ranges.'

Since their arrival here back in the 1940s (beginning with those purpose-built by the Co-op), supermarket success had been fuelled by the rise in women working, growing wealth and broadening cultural horizons. As we have seen, an increase in car ownership from 11.5 million vehicles in 1964 to 20 million in 1980 had encouraged the move towards out-of-town shopping. The decrease in manufacturing in the

1970s and 1980s meant land was freed up on the edges of towns and cities; at the same time planning laws were liberalized and large out-of-town supermarkets sprang up like so many mushrooms in the new retail 'parks'. In 1974, the average size of a supermarket was 2,800 square feet, but by 1990 they had grown to a massive 10,000 square feet. In 1972 Tesco had only five 'superstores' of over 25,000 square feet; by 1980 there were sixty-six (and by the mid-1990s this number had grown to 264). With the growth in size, supermarkets were able to offer more and more choice, at even more reasonable prices. With more control over their supply chains, economies of scale in operating costs and a proportional reduction in the labour that had been needed to run smaller shops, they set the standards for quality and product range. Many smaller shops struggled to compete and either closed their doors or were bought up by the big players. The multiples increased their market share from 44.5 per cent in 1971 to 66.8 per cent by 1983.

In the 1980s, another piece of technology arrived that cemented the power of the supermarkets even further, as it meant they could respond to what customers wanted even more accurately – the barcode. Supermarkets were now able to track every product a customer bought. They could monitor exactly what people were buying, how frequently and from which store, and, because they were able to amass this information on a nationwide scale, it gave them an enormous advantage over other, smaller food retailers and manufacturers. As they could now second-guess what people might want, they were able to take bigger risks and so began to make huge investments into convenience-product development, packaging and taste, often bypassing traditional wholesalers and dealing with manufacturers directly to develop innovative product ranges, manage supply chains and control quality.

As retailers increasingly recognized the power of the information at their fingertips, they also developed their store design and associated services – such as in-store bakeries, fish counters and butchers – to reflect the way people shopped and to encourage them to spend more.

Aisles were enlarged and choice of products rocketed. And whereas once supermarkets had provided a passive display of goods from which shoppers picked up what they needed, they were now actively telling shoppers what to consume and driving what was manufactured for them.

One of the most important innovations was the introduction of the cold chain. This technology enabled manufacturers to manage every step of a temperature-controlled supply chain from manufacture into the store (but this careful control disappeared once the product was in the shopper's basket!). By the early 1980s the public's attitude towards frozen food, which had been wavering in the 1970s, had hardened into active disdain. Frozen products were seen as second best and even of dubious quality. Instead, customers wanted freshness, speed and ready meals that tasted as good as home-made food. Marks & Spencer had pioneered the cold-chain distribution system back in the early 1960s, for the first time allowing its stores nationwide to sell chilled poultry – at the time whole fresh chickens and chilled chicken breasts – as opposed to frozen or pre-cooked. And once again the company led the field with the introduction of chilled ready meals at the very end of the 1970s.

M&S began with the launch of its chicken kiev in 1979, brought out under the St Michael label. The dish was aimed at customers with a higher level of income, working women with sophisticated tastes who were used to eating the classic dish in restaurants. The first kievs were hand-made and flash-fried before being chilled and packed in foil-lined trays. A pack of two would have set you back £2, the equivalent of about £8 today, but they were so popular they sold out in days. The M&S board was initially concerned about the levels of garlic in the recipe, but product developer Cathy Chapman knew it would be wrong to cut such an inherent part of the dish. 'It isn't kiev without the garlic,' she told the directors, and she was right. Such was the product's success that in the 1980s Cathy went on to develop the country's first ready-made lasagne (beef lasagne was and continues to be one of

M&S's bestsellers and held the top spot from 2003 to 2010), then chilli con carne, spring rolls and that essential of the Friday-night shop on the way home from work, the chicken tikka masala. Waitrose launched their own version of this last in 1983 and in 2001 British foreign secretary Robin Cook declared chicken tikka masala to be a true British national dish and 'a perfect illustration of the way Britain absorbs and adapts external influences'. By 2014 Marks & Spencer was selling over 10 tonnes of chicken tikka masala in their UK stores every week and we eat our way through three times as many ready meals each year as people in most European countries. Today, chicken kievs are popular once again as we embrace the trend for retro dishes from our pasts. In November 2014 Aldi reported that the sales of their version had increased by 43 per cent in just a year, while Ocado has reported the same jump in sales of Angel Delight, and Heston's take on the classic prawn cocktail, with added vodka in its 'Bloody Mary' sauce, is flying off the shelves at Waitrose.

With microwave at the ready and a supply of ready meals in the fridge, a family of four could sit down at the table together but eat dishes from four different corners of the world. Middle-class shoppers had come to believe that chilled, pre-cooked food, with its short sell-by dates and fresh ingredients, was healthy and desirable. By the early 1990s all the supermarkets were in on the act and the sector was worth £300 million a year.

Why were they so popular? With the rise in female employment, a greater number of households where both parents worked, the continuing domination of the microwave and, sadly, a rising divorce rate (divorced men who had never really learned to cook were considered a key ready-meal market and targeted appropriately), the traditional family meal prepared from fresh ingredients was vanishing into the distant past. The growing number of one- and two-person households, paired with long working hours, fuelled demand for meals that could be prepared in minutes rather than a frozen ready meal that took at least half an hour to heat through. More men took on the role of cooking (or reheating) as in many households the job now fell to whoever came home first. In the majority of families, however, women still took the lion's share of providing meals.

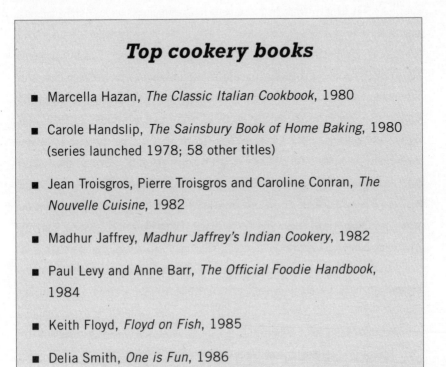

Top cookery books

- Marcella Hazan, *The Classic Italian Cookbook*, 1980

- Carole Handslip, *The Sainsbury Book of Home Baking*, 1980 (series launched 1978; 58 other titles)

- Jean Troisgros, Pierre Troisgros and Caroline Conran, *The Nouvelle Cuisine*, 1982

- Madhur Jaffrey, *Madhur Jaffrey's Indian Cookery*, 1982

- Paul Levy and Anne Barr, *The Official Foodie Handbook*, 1984

- Keith Floyd, *Floyd on Fish*, 1985

- Delia Smith, *One is Fun*, 1986

Another important development which helped in the sales of ready meals, as well as other product lines, was in the area of packaging – a change that has come back to haunt us in the environment-conscious twenty-first century. The 1980s saw huge leaps in packaging technology, and food manufacturers and consumers embraced them. The amount of packaging on food exploded, as did the waste we were throwing away. Ready meals now came in pre-formed plastic trays that were microwavable (the first ones became available in 1986); shoppers filled their trolleys with wrapped vegetables that used to be sold loose, and with plastic yogurt pots and squeezable plastic bottles instead of glass. Controlled-atmosphere packaging (controlling the oxygen levels within a plastic container or bag) allowed more delicate, perishable vegetables such as broccoli to be stored and kept fresh for a lot longer, while everything from baby tomatoes to doughnuts came in clear plastic cartons.

Now, almost three decades later, processed food is seen as one of the contributors to the obesity epidemic. It isn't just the high levels of fats, sugars, salt and additives – even higher back in the eighties than today; it is also the speed with which food can be cooked and eaten, which encourages us to graze and snack at all times of the day. It's small wonder that since 1980 levels of obesity in the UK have trebled. Had we traded speed and convenience for health? The debate rages today.

Also evidence of the supermarkets' power to shape what we eat was their role in driving a boom in exotic ingredients that soon became mainstream. A shopping list for a typical family weekly supermarket shop in the 1980s might have included all kinds of new ingredients presented and packaged in ways unthought of by the previous generation:

Chilled microwavable meals (different for each family member)
Tomatoes in plastic punnet
Guinness in cans
Plastic bottle of ketchup
Doughnuts in plastic box
Yogurts
Wrapped broccoli
Mangetout
Packaged pears
Packaged kiwi fruit
2-litre bottle of coke
Party food for entertaining

All change – new ways of eating lunch

During the 1980s outside influences were starting to have an effect on what everyone ate, particularly at midday. The 1980 Education Act changed school lunches, making it no longer compulsory for local authorities to provide them universally (only a small minority on Income Support still received free meals), while also reducing their nutritional requirement and making them more expensive for those not on benefits. A rise of over 40 per cent from a fixed price of 35p to about 50p a day was the immediate impact in most schools. As a result, school-meal take-up, which had stood at around 70 per cent in the early 1970s (6 million pupils ate them in 1973), had dropped to just over 40 per cent by the late 1980s.

For most mums this meant that the task of preparing a packed lunch became a regular and much-resented part of the already time-squeezed morning routine. And now it was also down to all parents, normally mums, to make sure that their children had a healthy midday meal – a responsibility that they had been able to hand over to the government since the expansion of the school-meal service during the war. Food manufacturers and supermarkets responded quickly to the opportunity to give busy mums a helping hand with this new chore. The 1980s witnessed the launch of a huge range of lunchbox-sized treats, and the NFS records of the time show just how many parents were happy to put them on their shopping lists. This one from a family of four in south Dorset shows that sweets and treats to go in packed lunches were now a regular feature in families' shopping baskets:

Crisps (Riley's)
Mixed biscuits
5-pack Milky Way
5-pack Club biscuit
6 Twix bars

Nowadays the internet is brimming with ideas for packed lunches, especially at the start of the school year; back in the 1980s it was magazines and newspaper supplements that leapt into action with ideas to help mothers take on this task. The supermarkets also offered advice – Sainsbury suggested that lunches for children aged between five and eleven might include:

1 chequerboard sandwich made from:
   1 slice of white bread/1 slice of brown bread/chicken/mayonnaise
1 raw carrot
1 orange
½ pint of chocolate/strawberry milk

And for those aged from twelve to seventeen:

2 slices of brown cob bread with egg and cress
2oz of peanuts
1 raw carrot
1 portion of apple and blackcurrant crumble
½ pint of lemon squash

But as is often the case, the reality revealed by the NFS was that the average schoolchild was more likely to tuck into:

white-bread meat sandwiches
crisps
chocolate biscuit

Mums who packed healthy choices for their child's lunch often found them left untouched and squashed at the bottom of the schoolbag at the end of the day, as even if you sent your child off with a well-balanced pack there was (then as now) no way of ensuring that is what they ended up eating. In many secondary schools, self-service snacks and the vending machine soon replaced the ordered discipline of the hot school lunch, eaten under the eye of a prefect or teacher who monitored both what was consumed and the table manners of those doing the consuming. Gone were the days so vividly remembered by many who are now parents themselves and whose memories of school dinners in the 1960s are of being made to eat everything on the plate before you could leave the table.

But it wasn't just school lunches that were being transformed. While our children tucked into the contents of their lunchboxes (or swapped them with friends), working parents too would see their midday meal change for ever as the pre-packed sandwich arrived on the high street. It makes me wonder what I ate for lunch before they took over. Well, on the occasions when I wasn't working in a kitchen, there was the work canteen, which served up meat and two veg along-side such delights as baked beans and baked potatoes, shepherd's pie and pizza, or something from the ubiquitous salad bar. And I paid with Luncheon Vouchers. On London's South Bank in the early 1980s there were few places to go out for a meal, but I could have got a sandwich made freshly for me at a local café or sandwich shop, sat down in the only restaurant near enough to get a meal in the hour-long break – a traditional Italian trattoria in The Cut, just opposite the Old Vic – or trekked over the River Thames to a wine bar for the traditional journalist's lengthy 'liquid' lunch of the period.

But by the end of the decade, like many other office workers, I was joining the queue in Marks & Spencer for a prawn mayo sandwich (still their bestseller). Sandwiches first appeared in M&S in 1980, made fresh on the premises in five stores. The first pre-packed version was salmon and tomato, followed by prawn mayonnaise which was introduced the following year. By 1987 they had twenty-five varieties, compared to over seventy today. Other retailers quickly followed suit. Sainsbury's first pre-packed sandwiches, introduced in 1983, were cheese and tomato, egg mayo, chicken and lettuce, salmon and cucumber, prawn mayo and pâté and salad. Initially seen as a luxury, this soon changed. By 1992 the Moorgate branch of M&S in the City was selling 3 million sandwiches a year, with fillings including chicken tikka, BLT and bacon and avocado. Today the sandwich market is worth more than £6 billion a year.

The ciabatta – the term means 'slipper bread' – was born in 1982 when it was invented by an Italian baker in order to compete with the French baguette, as Italians had developed a taste for sandwiches made with the import. Soon many regions had their own version. Its launch into this country by M&S in 1985, as one of their new 'continental-style' breads made with extra-virgin olive oil, propelled it into the big time and the *Guardian* called it 'the Mother's Pride of the middle classes'. Now, thin, crusty and full of more holes than bread, it is a staple of British bakeries, supermarkets and sandwich shops, and an essential part of our love affair with Italian food.

The early 1980s saw the dawn of the modern working lunch, cold and quick to consume, either on the move or at your desk. This emphasis on speed – both in the technology for producing fresh sandwiches in huge numbers and in lunchtime itself – made the meal far less social than in the 1970s, as food on the go meant there was no need to set time aside for a meal in the middle of the day. Now, 60 per cent of us eat lunch at our desk and the average lunch break is just 20 minutes. And although they might look insubstantial, a sandwich – especially if it was full of mayo (and salt), and accompanied by crisps and a can of fizzy drink – could pile on the calories; if eaten while remaining sitting at your desk, none of these was burned off with a lunchtime walk. Just like the new-style school dinner, the working lunch wasn't getting any healthier.

Video dinners

Even though the amount of time had decreased from what it had been in the middle of the century, in the 1970s and 1980s children still played outside for more than two hours a day on weekdays and for over nine hours at weekends whatever the weather. Today the figures have dropped to just one hour a day on weekdays and five hours at the weekend. A recent report by campaign group Play England revealed that 42 per cent of children aged between six and fifteen have never made a daisy chain while, incredibly, a quarter have never rolled down a hill. In the 1980s children still had plenty of good reasons to get out and about – whether to walk to the library to research a school project or, as BMX bikes replaced the Chopper of the previous decade in the hearts of boys and girls and the craze for breakdancing hit the streets, to muck about outside with their friends. And no mobile phones meant children could head off unsupervised and without being checked up on. But the temptations that were emerging indoors with the advances of technology meant outdoor games were starting to be seen as 'uncool' and the winds of change that would affect the way children spent their free time were continuing to blow. With Mum and Dad both working late and the kids home alone, a whole new swathe of time-saving and leisure-improving technology arrived with the promise of making life easier for everyone. The first video cassette recorders had gone on sale in 1978, so for the first time people could watch films and television programmes at a time of their own choosing. In 1980 Science of Cambridge (later Sinclair) launched its new affordable home computer, the ZY80, while the Nintendo Family Computer or video console arrived in 1983, with the result that cult computer games such as Space Invaders, Pac-Man and Donkey Kong that had taken off in arcades, pubs and bars could now be played at home.

It might not cook anything, but the VHS player would transform TV dinners for teenagers such as Miranda and Ros nationwide. Sitting on the sofa, watching telly and eating at the same time quickly became the easiest thing for children to do. With Mum and Dad out at work, friends could be invited round for a video party with no-effort food from the freezer or store cupboard; they could snack on pizza and watch TV while playing with a Rubik's Cube and reading *Smash Hits* magazine. Another typical meal might be burgers, chicken nuggets (McDonald's launched the chicken McNugget in 1983 as a so-called 'healthier' alternative to burgers and in the 1990s many people switched to eating them after the BSE scare) or Bernard Matthews' 'bootiful' crumbed Turkey Drummers, served with some of the new oven chips which could safely and easily be cooked by kids on their own, and, to finish, that *pièce de résistance*, the Vienetta, introduced by Walls in 1982 and instantly a classic, all washed down with cola made in a soda stream. Meanwhile, *The Young Ones, Only Fools and Horses* and soap operas such as *EastEnders* and *Neighbours* (both of these arrived in 1985) played on the video in the background. This was the decade that saw children move from watching programmes made specially for them to viewing adult television shows.

And if they didn't want to heat up the oven to feed their friends, they could pop out for a bucket of fast food. When it came to eating, speed had taken over from taste and nutrition as the most important feature in meal choice, and American-style fast-food restaurants such as McDonald's really exploded in popularity in this decade; English competitor Pizza Hut also opened its doors on the high street in 1982. Home deliveries soon followed, making it even less necessary to move from the sofa.

Health versus the couch potato

'It's 6.30, Monday 17th January 1983. You're watching the first edition of BBC TV's *Breakfast Time*.'

Several key social changes of the 1980s would see the transformation of weekday mornings in many households. As a meal, breakfast had stayed essentially the same for the previous twenty years – NFS entries show tea, toast, cereal and milk remained the staples – and, apart from the arrival in middle-class homes of the filter coffee machine, popular in offices for nearly a decade but only now starting to make an impact on domestic life, this was still the basis of the meal for most families. In 1983, however, mornings were about to change yet again as breakfast television arrived in the home. The BBC started the ball rolling with Frank Bough, Selina Scott, Debbie Rix and Nick Ross sitting cosily together on a sofa, plus Francis Wilson forecasting the weather, Diana Moran – the Lycra-clad 'Green Goddess' – getting the nation fit over their cornflakes, and Russell Grant, in a brightly coloured jumper, giving horoscopes. It was unrelentingly middle-brow – the BBC had unexpectedly gone for a light-hearted and friendly approach that it felt fitted with the mood of the sleepy morning viewer rather than the widely expected serious news format – but it worked. Two weeks later ITV countered with its own version, the ill-fated TV-am's *Good Morning Britain*, but it was seen as too intellectual for the breakfast audience and by the summer had to be rescued by Roland Rat and his 'rat fans'.

Breakfast TV tapped into the huge paradox of early-eighties lifestyle: at a time when the nation was consuming ever more snacks and sugary food, simultaneously health and fitness were becoming a media obsession. Perhaps for the first time in the country's history, as the result of a series of reports on the risks of dietary factors in contributing to disease, the general public became aware of some of the consequences of an unhealthy diet and lifestyle. So whether it was the Green Goddess on the BBC or TV-am's 'Mad Lizzie' Webb, breakfast television had a fitness guru all ready to help the nation limber up, don a pair of leg warmers and get physical. And, as the decade went by, TV's early-morning health kick was being replicated on British breakfast tables.

The National Food Survey has ample examples of people becoming

'Let's get physical' – as waistlines bulged and working hours lengthened, women donned leg warmers, bought low-fat convenience foods and read diet books to try to keep things in check.

more health-conscious in their eating habits. All Bran, wholemeal bread and cartons of orange juice appear on shopping lists and in meals. Orange juice had appeared on the NFS as far back as 1950, but in those days it was a medicinal 'nip' prescribed by the doctor for children under the age of five. In the 1970s frozen orange juice, which you diluted with water, was all the rage, although it was more likely to appear as a starter on a restaurant menu than to be consumed at home. By the 1980s it was being marketed not just as part of a healthy diet but as a key component of a stylish, modern lifestyle. With the advent of flash pasteurization (rapid heating then cooling), which meant that imported orange juice didn't need to be mixed with water once it arrived in Britain, companies could produce chilled versions. They used the infrastructure of the dairy industry to distribute the new juice, and milkmen began to deliver it in milk bottles alongside the doorstep 'pinta'. However, most people bought their juice from the supermarket in aseptic packaging (that's Tetrapak to most of us). The man from Del Monte in his white suit and Panama hat, who travelled to the furthest corners of the world to select the best oranges for his juice, appeared on our screens in the middle of the decade. And he got his message across. Orange juice is one of the big success stories of the 1980s: consumption rose from 97ml per person per week in 1981 to 225ml per person per week by 1990.

For the expanding sector of the population concerned with health, one item was becoming a particular problem: sugar. As we had got larger over the past couple of decades, healthy eating had focused on fat as the main culprit and the food industry had responded by taking the fat out of their processed foods and replacing it with sugar, from the mid-seventies in the form of high-fructose sugar syrup. In liquid form, this could be added to all kinds of everyday foods – cakes, biscuits and fizzy drinks, but also less obvious items such as pizza, coleslaw and even meat-based ready meals. Growing awareness of the dangers of sugar saw the sales of table sugar (sold in packets) halve during the 1980s, but, ironically, our consumption of all these processed foods meant that sugar intake actually exploded: it was what we were consuming unaware that was feeding the seeds of the obesity crisis already sown in previous decades.

As waistlines grew under the onslaught of fast and convenience food high in fat, sugar and salt, and of much more sedentary modern lifestyles, another huge growth area of the period was dieting, which became a multi-billion-pound industry in the eighties. A raft of diet books hit the bestseller lists as people increasingly worried about how to eat healthily. Changing diets and lifestyles had completely transformed body shape since the war and by the 1980s British women were continuing to develop the classic British pear shape as the average woman of the period had added 2 inches (5cm) to her hip measurement compared to the 1960s. Constant snacking had taken over from three regular meals a day, making following a balanced diet even more of a challenge. Even new supposedly 'healthy' foods such as yogurts and breakfast cereals were high in hidden calories. Unlike the war and post-war years when state control was exercised through rationing, little dietary advice now came from the government. Responsibility for what they ate had been handed over to individuals, and it was the food and diet industries themselves that stepped in to fill the information vacuum.

Fad diets have always found followers, from the vinegar-and-water diet popularized by Lord Byron in the 1820s to the cabbage-soup diet of the 1950s (there was even a tapeworm version advocated by opera diva Maria Callas in the 1960s). More sensibly, people had turned with relief to Weight Watchers when the organization launched in 1963, or they tried the Slim Fast diet range of meal-replacement shakes when it appeared on supermarket shelves in 1977. More food companies jumped on the diet bandwagon in the 1980s. Findus launched its Lean Cuisine range of frozen ready meals in 1985, with twelve 'recipe dishes' from spaghetti bolognese to chicken à l'orange and zucchini lasagne all coming in at under 300 calories and supported by a TV ad campaign featuring a lithe girl in bright keep-fit clothes. The voice-over promised less fat and more taste as 'Hey, good lookin', what ya got cookin'?' played in the background. The 1980s saw twenty-four diet books enter the bestseller lists, including the *F-Plan Diet*, *Fit for Life*, *The Complete Scarsdale Medical Diet* (published in 1978 but a big seller in the eighties) and *The Beverley Hills Diet*. Fitness gurus such as Jane Fonda launched exercise videos, hers with its frankly terrifying (for most of us) catchphrase 'No pain, no gain' in 1982.

Food as lifestyle

As well as being a factor in our health and well-being, food now became a hobby rather than just a chore. In the 1980s food on television, previously the domain of sensible, reassuring Delia Smith and Marguerite Patten, was transformed into entertainment, presented by flamboyant, lively personalities such as Keith Floyd, who chatted with the camera crew and knocked back red wine as if he were cooking for friends at a great party. Floyd changed the way we watched food on television with a single (often entertainingly drunken) stroke. He was the first chef to transform food presenting into a kind of perform-ance art and the shows he fronted often seemed to be more about Floyd than the food itself. After his death from a heart attack at the age of sixty-five in 2009, his obituary in the *Guardian* described him as a 'natural cook of great skill . . . and effervescent charm', and his cooking style as 'cheerful mayhem'. His approach was viewed by many as a welcome departure from the 'prissy, controlled' character of pre-vious cookery programmes. His first series, *Floyd on Fish*, aired on the BBC in 1985 and food shows would never be the same again. Thanks in part to Floyd, they became must-watch television as new lumi-naries appeared on screen to guide viewers through all kinds of fresh experiences.

This was cooking for enjoyment, with all the sensuality of exotic ingredients and destinations, as the types of food people had become used to eating in restaurants were brought within the domain of the home cook. *Madhur Jaffrey's Indian Cookery* series, shown on BBC2 in 1982, inspired the nation to such an extent that Jane Grigson dubbed her 'the Elizabeth David of India', as she did for that nation's cooking what Mrs David had done for the food of the Mediterranean. The day after Madhur – also an award-winning actress – used fresh coriander in a dish, greengrocers were flooded with requests for 'flat parsley that tastes of liquorice'. The power of the television chef to influence sales of ingredients was born. The book accompanying the series sold out rapidly.

Two years later it was the turn of another style of cooking much loved by the nation's diners, when a young Chinese chef from Chicago inspired British families to try something different at home. *Ken Hom's Chinese Cookery* encouraged people to try the dishes they'd previously only eaten in restaurants or 'taken away'. The companion book became one of the best-selling the BBC had ever produced; and though woks had been on sale in shops since Habitat first introduced them in the 1960s, thanks to Ken they became a standard piece of equipment for most kitchens, and stir-frying – quick, easy and, what's more, seen as healthy – an increasingly popular way of cooking. Since that first series Ken has sold 1.7 million books and more than 7 million of his own-brand woks.

Ken had another impact on British kitchens, as he encouraged men to start cooking more. Brought up by his widowed mother, he says, 'I've never seen why men shouldn't take an equal role in the kitchen with women.' As he grew up he never knew a man who *didn't* go into the kitchen, and was always encouraged to break the rules by his mum – when he said he didn't like the school food on offer, she packed him a lunch of hot rice and stir-fried vegetables.

This engagement with what had previously been viewed as 'difficult' food was the start of a major revolution in British eating habits. In the thirty years since Ken's programme first aired we have embraced everything from Thai to Mexican and the evidence of this change is nowhere more clearly demonstrated than in supermarket aisles. One of the challenges of cooking these dishes back in the 1980s was locating the ingredients. People trekked across country to visit specialist oriental supermarkets, and items such as beansprouts and even fresh ginger, which we now view as everyday ingredients, were seen as impossibly exotic. Ethnic shopkeepers, many of whom had arrived and set up shop during the boom period of immigration in the 1960s, initially catering for their local communities, not only offered authentic ingredients alongside more everyday essentials but also stayed open for long hours. Wing Yip was one such example; initially a family restaurant business set up in the sixties, they opened a specialist Chinese grocery store in

Birmingham ten years later, at first to supply Chinese restaurants but before long catering to home cooks searching for the right Far Eastern food products. The company now runs four 'superstores' across the country, each stocking more than 4,500 specialist products, with two more stores in the pipeline. Another hard-working family, the Pataks, came over from Kenya in 1956 and within a few years had opened a small Indian grocery store near Euston station, selling among other ingredients their own spice pastes. By 1978 their products started to appear in supermarkets to much acclaim, and by 2000 they had opened the world's largest food factory producing Indian ingredients in the world. Supermarkets also rose to the challenge of providing specialist ingredients to satisfy their demanding customers, often working with these new entrepreneurs and sending their product developers around the world to source authentic ingredients for their stores. During the decade the diversity of their ranges increased dramatically. In 1980 Sainsbury carried 7,000 lines of products, but by 1989 the figure was 17,000.

But this period also saw another pattern emerge, one that still resonates with many of us today. Once the initial burst of enthusiasm following a food series was over, many of us simply put our special purchase, such as the pasta machine or jar of black bean paste, away at the back of a cupboard, quite possibly to gather dust and never be used again. Like children at Christmas, we played with the new toy for a while but soon returned to old habits. For busy 1980s cooks it was time-consuming to make exotic dishes, as supermarkets were not yet stocking the pre-prepared ingredients and ready-made sauces we find today, so the draw of that old fallback, meat and two veg, was still strong – but it was in the process of changing. Stir-frying, whether we used an authentic wok or just our regular frying pan, was a really useful, quick cooking technique that fitted with our busy lifestyles and desire for healthier food. As a result, slowly our meat and veg transformed into dishes such as a chicken stir-fry with rice that could be cooked and set on the table in minutes rather than hours.

By the mid-1980s, as excessive consumption became the norm and food developed into a leisure activity, a shocking parallel world was thrust to the forefront of many British people's minds. October 1984 brought harrowing images to the country's televisions as the BBC's Michael Buerk reported on the devastating famine in Ethiopia. The response from a sector of the entertainment business, using its celebrity to raise awareness, transformed fundraising for ever. Profoundly shocked at the reports on the BBC, Bob Geldof and Midge Ure gathered together a 'super group' of stars christened Band Aid to make a fundraising Christmas single. And to the strains of 'Feed the World', the country united in supporting aid to Africa, raising an astonishing £65 million. But as the decade went on, Britain itself seemed to be becoming ever more divided.

A nation divided

As the 1980s progressed, inequality between the haves and the have-nots in British society was beginning to make its presence felt. While those in work were indulging themselves as never before, at the other end of the scale were those families who weren't out shopping for unusual new ingredients but were wondering how to feed themselves at all. The miners' strike, which began in March 1984 and ended almost a year later, saw families struggling with no strike pay, a recent cut in benefits and only a small daily allowance for picket-line duty. Throughout the strike most survived on a weekly food parcel, made up from donations from the union and the general public. Across the country a large network of support for the miners emerged, which raised funds of an estimated £60 million, set up kitchens to provide meals and distributed food parcels; Kim Howells, then a NUM official and later a Labour minister, called it 'the alternative welfare state'. A typical parcel might contain two tins of beans, a tin of tomatoes, a tin of fruit, sixteen teabags, four eggs, 8oz of sugar, six potatoes and an onion, and was the same for a family with four children as for a couple. Every striking miner's family relied on the food donations to survive. Once the strike ended in March 1985, the closure programme that had triggered the dispute was put into action and by the following year thirty-six mines had closed, with massive job losses. With little local employment to take the place of the pit jobs, the miners' families again bore the brunt. Now they faced even more uncertain times, and within ten years 90 per cent of the jobs in mining that existed at the start of the strike had gone for good.

The strike had one unexpected consequence for the wives and mothers who rallied to the support of their menfolk. Many became politicized by the dispute – they joined in picketing, travelled to London on rallies, set up soup kitchens in their communities. They stopped being the traditional housewives so many of them had been before the strike began. Children, too, were affected; many learned to cook for themselves while their parents were out on the picket line. When the strike was over, the dynamics in the household had changed as a result.

During the miners' strike, women set up soup kitchens to feed their husbands and families.

Marriages broke down, and even in those that didn't the women were no longer prepared to be stay-at-home wives. Many families had no choice in this anyway, as the jobs that were available in the community tended to be in the female-dominated service, caring and catering areas and were often part time. And the corollary was that more men entered the kitchen for the first time, several never to retreat back out again.

In stark contrast, those in work were enjoying an unprecedented disposable income and unequalled opportunities to spend it. Just like the newly affluent under-twenty-fives in the early 1960s, the young middle classes were embracing all that was on offer – but, unlike the sixties generation, they were doing so with ostentation. This was the age when it became acceptable to flaunt your wealth in a way that would have hitherto been deemed vulgar. The talk was of 'conspicuous consumption' and, in this period of infinite choice, what could be more conspicuous than choosing to pay a fortune for a meal that left you, and your guests, still feeling hungry?

'Nouvelle cuisine' arrived on these shores from what was then still the food capital of the world, Paris, at the end of the 1970s. A group of young French chefs, led by the Troisgros brothers, Roger Vergé, Michel Guérard and Paul Bocuse, had rejected the heavy, over-sauced, complex dishes that epitomized their country's classic cuisine in favour of less meat and more fish; lighter, reduction-based sauces; and colourful fresh ingredients that suited simpler cooking methods and shorter cooking times. British chefs embraced the principles and jumped on the nouvelle bandwagon, while a host of aspirational glossy food magazines, such as *Taste* and *A la Carte*, as well as the Sunday colour supplements, all embraced the trend with enthusiasm – although in many cases they really rather missed the point and the food seemed to become more about appearance than about taste. But fashion can be a fickle mistress and, when taken to extremes by over-enthusiastic chefs and over-ambitious home cooks, 'nouvelle cuisine' soon became

"If I'd wanted a Picasso I'd have gone to an art gallery, wouldn't I?"

As the craze for nouvelle cuisine with its minute portions swept the nation, many diners finished meals hungrier than when they started.

a bad joke. Due to the amount of work needed to prepare and serve it, this food was really only suitable for restaurants. It would arrive at the table 'plated up' by the 'artist' working in the kitchen. Enormous white platters were theatrically set down before each diner with, at their centre, exquisitely arranged but in miniature, a mouthful or two of fish or meat accompanied by a smear of sauce, a perfectly 'turned' baby vegetable, a scattering of pink peppercorns and maybe an artistically dribbled purée of something mysterious – and all topped off with a slice of that vital component of an eighties dinner plate, the kiwi fruit. Oh, and of course the dessert came with the obligatory coulis.

One of the most celebrated chefs working in 1980s Britain was Swiss-born Anton Mosimann, who in 1976, at the tender age of twenty-nine, had become the youngest head chef ever to be appointed at the Dorchester Hotel. He went on to win the accolade of two Michelin stars for his work and has cooked for five prime ministers and four generations of the royal family. He followed (and still follows) the maxim of Auguste Escoffier, the great chef of the early twentieth century, that good food is food that tastes of what it is. He adopted the basics of nouvelle cuisine with its principles of the finest ingredients cooked simply and lightly, and concentrated his skills on developing the flavours of the foods themselves in dishes that were almost free from fat and cream. As such, Mosimann preferred the term 'cuisine naturelle'. And, though he believed in lighter, simpler, smaller dishes, he served them in up to six courses in order to give his diners more 'joy'. And fuller tummies!

As Mosimann showed, the original principles of nouvelle cuisine were sound and fitted well with modern, lighter ways of eating. Today, the term is defined in an online dictionary as: 'a modern style of French cooking that emphasizes the use of the finest and freshest ingredients simply and imaginatively prepared, often with fresh herbs, the artful arrangement and presentation of food, and the use of reduced stocks in place of flour-thickened sauces'. And as the impact of this approach worked its way into the mainstream consciousness, thanks to chefs such as Mosimann, its key principles of fresh ingredients, enhancing rather than masking flavour, technical excellence and innovation became watchwords for chefs that hold good today. Even more importantly, it also changed the way we bought the food we ate at home, in a perfect example of the 'trickle-down' effect on our eating and drinking habits.

Few of the general public were eating at these high-end restaurants in the 1980s, but all of us were affected by what was happening in their kitchens. Delis and supermarkets began to stock the new ingredients, helped enormously by changes in food retailing brought about by modernized production methods in developing countries, air freight and much cheaper sea freight, and the broadening tastes of the British public, who were travelling abroad more than ever. As consumers, we began to expect strawberries in winter, asparagus all year round, 'speciality' bagged salads such as radicchio and oak-leaf (the first was shredded iceberg, introduced by M&S in 1986), and all kinds of exotic fruits such as the tasteless but artistically useful star fruit. Sales of kiwi fruit went through the roof, from around 16,500 trays in 1984 to nearly 320,000 trays in 1985, a rise of an astonishing 2,000 per cent!

The Big Bang

Enter the yuppie, who in the second half of the decade came complete with aggressive attitude and lavish lifestyle – oh, and a love of fast cars and gadgets. He/she was always to be seen talking into the most enormous mobile phone while checking an overstuffed Filofax, when not quaffing magnums of champagne in City wine bars. Like so many other imports, the term had arrived over here from the US, where *Newsweek* magazine had declared 1984 'the year of the yuppie'. In Britain, we embraced its tenets with enthusiasm. At the same time, 1986 witnessed the Big Bang, a raft of deregulation that transformed the City of London from a class-divided, carefully delineated cartel as the multinational finance houses arrived in force. As is still the case today, London, with its advantageous time zone, language, political stability, cultural heritage and relatively safe and prosperous lifestyle, was ideal for foreign investment houses. The cosy days of patronage and nepotism were over, and the unbridled greed that has become indelibly associated with the City today was unleashed. The changes provided an opportunity for bright young people to break into a world previously dominated by old-boy elites. Until then most women in the City had been in clerical jobs, but as the decade advanced more of them could be found in investment and broker positions.

Extravagant eating out was seen as an ideal way to enjoy the benefits of the boom, an opportunity to 'flash the cash'. Chefs became superstars, if at times very badly behaved ones, and their status rocketed. The customer was definitely no longer king, no matter how large his wad, and the new rich queued up to be insulted at huge expense – told they couldn't add seasoning to their food, didn't understand the basics of a good meal, and on occasion even asked to leave if they didn't follow the direction of an irascible chef. The yuppies arrived in their hordes to be seen at these temples to gastronomy, parking their flash cars outside restaurants run by well-regarded chefs such as the Roux brothers, Nico Ladenis, Raymond Blanc, Simon Hopkinson and Marco Pierre White (not all of whom were temperamental!), and splashing out on extortionately priced bottles of rare wines and fine champagnes. Menus featured the finest ingredients – luxuries such as foie gras, wild turbot, langoustines, beef fillet and caviar. *Coeur d'Artichaut Lucullus* at Le Gavroche was a dome of artichoke mousse with a wonderfully rich foie gras and chicken mousse hidden inside, studded with black truffle; *Truffe en Brioche*, served by Raymond Blanc of Le Manoir aux Quat' Saisons, was a brioche-encased parcel of black truffles and Bayonne ham sauced with madeira, port and more grated truffle. Individual hot soufflés were another speciality that showed off the skills of top chefs – Gruyère and cream in a *Soufflé Suissesse* at Le Gavroche, or the famous broccoli version served at Langan's Brasserie, one of London's most fashionable haunts in the mid-1980s, which came with a little jug of warm anchovy sauce, which, crust broken, was poured by the diner into the luscious depths of the dish.

A more regular hangout, though, was the wine bar, a more female-friendly and sophisticated alternative to the traditional male-dominated 'boozer', and the ideal location to see and be seen in after a hard day at the financial coalface. The long, liquid-lunch habit of the old-school financiers, who had entertained clients and closed their business deals over a bottle or two of fine wine in a dark and discreet establishment such as Corney & Barrow at 118 Moorgate or Davys' Boot and Flogger at London Bridge (both companies were long-established wine merchants to the City before expanding into wine bars) was vanishing. In the early part of the decade the City was deserted once working hours were over, and a trip to the Barbican Centre for a concert or play was like visiting a ghost town. But that was about to be swept away. In response to changing customers and working practices, established wine bars now stayed open beyond 6pm to encourage after-work drinking, and a generation of stylish bars appeared, catering

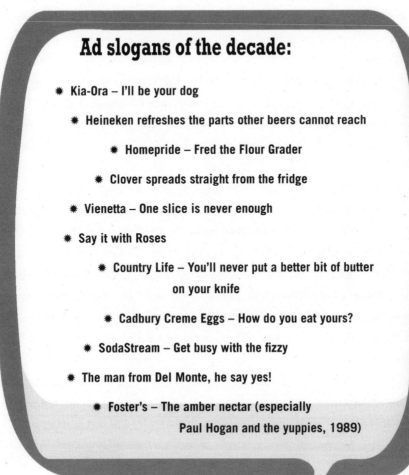

Ad slogans of the decade:

* Kia-Ora – I'll be your dog

  * Heineken refreshes the parts other beers cannot reach

    * Homepride – Fred the Flour Grader

  * Clover spreads straight from the fridge

* Vienetta – One slice is never enough

* Say it with Roses

  * Country Life – You'll never put a better bit of butter on your knife

    * Cadbury Creme Eggs – How do you eat yours?

  * SodaStream – Get busy with the fizzy

* The man from Del Monte, he say yes!

  * Foster's – The amber nectar (especially Paul Hogan and the yuppies, 1989)

for the new customers. With Simply Red or Sade crooning over the stereo system in the background, and serving a range of reasonable wines by the glass or bottle rather than the small, acidic glassfuls of something dubious that had likely been open for days on offer in pubs, these bars sprang up in cities across the land. The first Slug and Lettuce opened on Islington Green in 1984, designed to appeal to a young clientele with a fresh, modern look, large light windows, plenty of standing room and a better quality of simple food. At the time Islington was in the process of rapid gentrification and, with its easy proximity to the City, was becoming home to lots of City workers. They needed places to eat, drink and meet colleagues after stressful days spent making money. The wine bar's iconic status in this decade was reinforced in January 1989 when an episode of *Only Fools and Horses* sees Del Boy out to impress in one, trying to act cool before disappearing through a missing bar hatch. So adored is the scene that it still regularly wins the vote for the most-loved comedy moments on British TV.

The period also saw the arrival of the first generation of a current phenomenon – the tapas bar. Spanish waiters and chefs who had come over to work in restaurants and then set up on their own began the trend. Living in Stockwell, south London, at the time, I was lucky enough to enjoy some of the earliest and best establishments, which became regular haunts with friends for convivial, relaxed evenings of good wine and interesting plates of food. Meson Don Felipe in The Cut, near Waterloo, was one of the first, if not *the* first, tapas bars in London, and Rebatos in Vauxhall was another favourite – plates of chorizo, *albondigas* (meatballs), perfect ham *croquetas* and *Pimientos Padron*, all washed down with excellent Spanish wines and sherry, set the style for the little plates of food that fitted well with our grazing habit.

The number of wine drinkers in Britain rose by a quarter between 1983 and 1992, from 25 million to 31 million (the number of regular wine drinkers rose from 3 million to 10 million). This was due to a combination of factors, including the lowering of tax on wine and beer within the EU and the emergence from the recession at the start of the decade, but the main reason was that wine was really being taken seriously by the supermarkets, which demystified the whole wine buying and drinking process. Wine had become fashionable – and in those years image was everything. With the help of TV programmes such as the BBC's *Food and Drink*, whose Jilly Goolden changed the way we tasted and described the wines we now sniffed, sipped and swigged (in one classic Jilly moment she enthused over a 'bouquet of a soft flannel

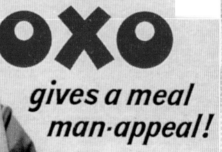

Katie says...

OXO

gives a meal man·appeal!

Changing family life as viewed through the Oxo ads: while Mum cooks the meal, Dad is there to be pleased in the 1950s; he's tolerated in the 1980s and completely absent by 2000.

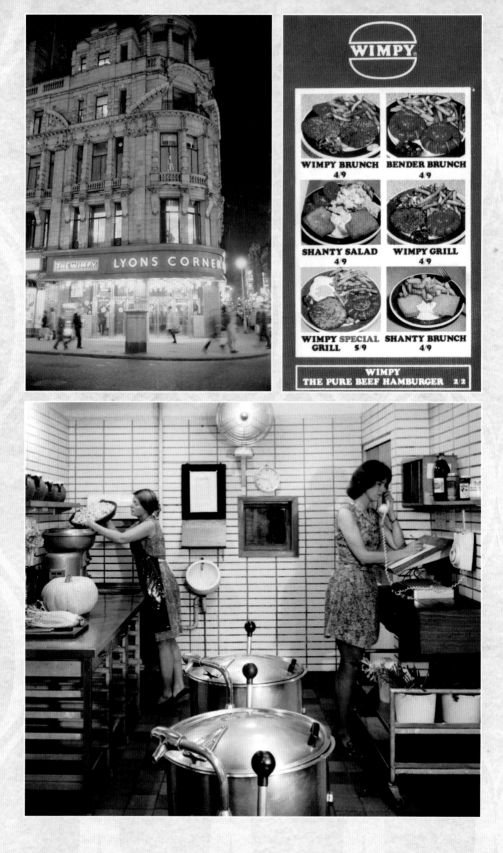

In fifty years of eating out we've come full circle: after the war, afternoon tea and a snack at a Lyons Corner House was an occasional treat; for the adventurous young, there was a Wimpy in the 1960s and 1970s, or meat-free wholefood at Cranks; on through nouvelle cuisine with its stacks and smears, and back to British dishes and nose-to-tail eating with Fergus Henderson at St John in London's Smithfield.

From the post-wartime wisdom of Marguerite Patten via The Galloping Gourmet (seen here with Cilla Black) and sensible Delia in the 1970s, through to flamboyant Keith Floyd in the 1980s, TV chefs have guided our faltering steps through the food jungle. By the end of the century, Nigella was turning us on to eating as a sensual pleasure, while we explored new horizons for both ingredients and dishes with adventurous individuals like Rick Stein.

If you love your children, butter them up.

It takes the cream from 18 pints of milk to make one pound of butter. The best taste in the world–for just a few pennies more than margarine.

We're all a lot better for butter.

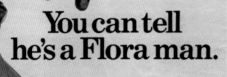

You can tell he's a Flora man.

What goes into crisps goes into you.

Some crisps contain 33% cooking oil. bhf.org.uk

COOKING OIL

It's *Kellogg's* Sweet-eatin' carnival **time!**

Buy any two packets of these cereals and ...

Kellogg's will send you a BRAND-NEW SHILLING!

Kellogg's are sure you will enjoy these sugar-sweet cereals—they are making this special offer so that you can try them. This is all you have to do:—

1 Buy any two packets of these cereals and cut off the tops.

2 Write your name and address on the back of one of them.

3 Mail the two tops in an envelope to Kellogg's, Dept. S, Stretford, Manchester.

Kellogg's will send you a brand-new shilling!

Offer closes August 31st, 1961, so send for your shilling quickly. Offer limited to one per family.

SUGAR SMACKS
the Yogi Bear cereal. Honey-sweet puffs of wheat.

FROSTIES
crisp, sparkling flakes. Tony the Tiger says, they're SCR-R-R-umptious!

ALL STARS
the new star-shaped oat cereal with a hole in the middle and sugar on top. The Wizard of Oats brings *magic* to breakfast!

SUGAR RICICLES
Little Noddy's favourite breakfast. Crunchy sweet, light and crisp.

COCO POPS
chocolate-flavoured puffs of rice. Coco the Monkey's "anytime" cereal.

FUN MASKS FOR YOUR CHILDREN!

There's a "dressing-up" mask on each packet: Yogi Bear and his T.V. friends—all ready to cut out. So let your children choose and change—for the fun of it. And for the goodness and energy too, in Kellogg's pre-sweetened cereals.

Make it a sweet life for your children

BUY *Kellogg's* SUGAR-SWEET CEREALS TODAY!

The Official Snackfood of the British Olympic Team.

In less than fifty years, we've gone from boosting our boys with lashings of butter to judging our men by their waistlines. At the same time, sugar has morphed from the sweetest of treats to serve to kids at breakfast in the 1960s, via a role in developing Olympic athletes, to being a hidden poison that we now unknowingly feed to our babies.

SHOCKING ISN'T IT? YOU PROBABLY DO IT EVERY DAY.

IN THE AVERAGE BOTTLE OF SQUASH THERE'S OVER ½LB OF SUGAR. LOOK AFTER THEIR TEETH. CUT DOWN ON THE SUGAR.

FOR MORE ADVICE CONTACT YOUR HEALTH VISITOR OR DENTIST.

As we head further into the new millennium, educators such as Jamie champion the lost skills of cooking everyday foods to our young as they embrace new ingredients and trends such as insects and lab-grown meats. Deep-fried crickets, anyone?

of oak and Maltesers'), the baby boomers got into wine – and the wine market exploded in return.

French and Italian wines dominated British taste in the early 1980s and we lapped up trends such as Beaujolais Nouveau, which became a world-wide phenomenon, supported by a huge marketing campaign, with its wine 'race' to get the first bottles of the new vintage into bars and shops at a minute past midnight on the third Thursday of November. As the decade advanced, cheap and simply labelled new-world wines arrived on the scene, transforming our wine-buying habits again. But not everyone was following the latest trends in wine drinking – sales of 1970s favourite sweet tipple Blue Nun reached their peak in the mid-1980s with nearly 2 million bottles sold (and it's still Britain's bestselling German wine today!).

Alcohol isn't recorded on the NFS, but sales figures show that the 1980s was the first decade in which wine made a sizeable impact. (In fact, the NFS itself changed format between 1985 and 1990, because it was realized that there were large quantities of foodstuffs that people had started consuming that weren't on the original list – such as alcohol and confectionery.)

While beer consumption had increased only a little since the Second World War, sales of spirits also soared. On top of catering for our growing wine habit, bars ran happy hours serving lurid cocktails with the most innuendo-laden names, made fashionable by the 1988 film *Cocktail* and consumed on holidays run by the sometimes notorious Club 18–30. Sex on the Beach, Between the Sheets and the Harvey Wallbanger were colourful and stomach-churning. Consumption of alcohol as a whole rocketed in the 1980s, doubling since the 1960s.

Dining to impress

While the new breed of restaurant chefs were cooking food that, despite the recipes appearing in glossy coffee-table books and magazines, was really way beyond the capabilities of the average home cook, another trend was emerging from the nouvelle cuisine melting pot that offered something a little more accessible. Interest in food and all its minutiae was being embraced as a hobby – increasingly, eating was no longer just a case of convenience responding to hunger, but 'eat to live' was transmogrified into 'live to eat' for members of the latest in-crowd, the foodies. In 1984 authors Ann Barr and Paul Levy used their *Official Foodie Handbook* (subtitle: 'Be Modern – Worship Food') to propose that food was now fashion: 'Couture has ceded the centre ground to food.'

The foodie was a different animal to the gourmet. The latter was concerned with eating the very best of everything, but the foodie was far more democratic, wanting to know everything about the food they consumed whether it be humble or high-class. Or as *The Official Foodie Handbook* put it: 'Foodies consider food to be an art, on a level with painting or drama. It's actually your favourite art form.' Or, more simply, the foodie is 'a person who is very, very, very interested in food'! With tongue firmly in cheek, the authors identified different types of foodie such as the Olive Oil Bore, highlighted the appeal of items such as chefs' knives and gas hobs, and bemoaned the terrible quality of much of the food in the mainstream.

But though more laid back than the gourmet approach, with an enthusiasm for all things food, the foodie still set the stakes high for home entertaining. Some of the pillars of the nouvelle cuisine move-ment had entered the foodie's lexicon, but tempered by information gleaned from food programmes on TV, new technology such as the Magimix and the innovation of the supermarkets when it came to sourcing ingredients. While the labour-intense preparation, techniques that needed an army of sous-chefs and the serving of tiny portions might be left to the starred chefs, the foodie still embraced display and, in this decade of showing off and excess, culinary aspiration was everything. Over-sized dinner plates, fashionable ingredients carefully sourced, such as monkfish, mangetout and goat's cheese, the Magimix food processor – all were grist to the foodie mill; and what's more, for almost the first time it was men as much as women who were responding to this call to action. Men tapped into their hunter-gatherer roots and enjoyed the quest for food knowledge, the thrill of the chase when it came to tracking down ingredients and the finer details of choosing the right equipment.

In the 1986 book *Take Twelve Cooks*, which came out to support two successful ITV series, a dozen leading chefs and cooks set out the framework for the home cook to follow 'to enable you to create your own professional meals for every occasion'. The introduction advises 'the recipes should act as a guideline, a stimulant to your own imagination. Rather than choosing a dinner-party menu and then shopping for it, it is far better to discover what is good and fresh that day, and only then consider your dishes and create your menu.' And as one of the chefs, Pierre Koffmann, is quoted as saying: 'The smell of cooking is the smell of life.' In the series each chef provides recipes for one course of a menu – Prue Leith and Raymond Blanc take on hors d'oeuvres, Anton Mosimann and Joyce Molyneux offer fish, and so on. A dinner-party menu taken from the book might run like this:

Prue Leith's Twice Baked Soufflé

Richard Shepherd's Cream of Cauliflower Soup

Joyce Molyneux's Salmon in Pastry with Ginger and Currants served with a Herb and Cream Sauce

Jane Grigson's Peas in the French Style

John Huber's Parfait au Praliné

These dozen chefs (or are they cooks? – the book seems unclear) represented a wide range of cookery styles, but were agreed that there was a move away from nouvelle cuisine towards 'French bourgeois cooking'. But as Raymond Blanc warns in the series, 'if you start cooking to a fashion you are in trouble'.

A meal like that would have taken some planning and preparation for even the most accomplished home cook, but I know myself how good the recipes are once you get your head around the processes. Joyce Molyneux's salmon dish is still a classic, I use Prue Leith's Twice Baked Soufflé recipe on a regular basis, and the series was a big hit at the time. The dinner would have been completed with coffee (made in a percolator), served with home-made chocolate truffles, and of course a round of the 1980s dinner-party game *du jour*, Trivial Pursuit (launched in 1982) – you could have a bite of the dessert only when you had answered a question correctly and earned your little plastic piece of pie!

The world turns

While here in Britain we were wrestling with the challenges of life in the fast lane as the decade sped by, the world outside these shores was changing beyond recognition as well. And maybe more than in any other era since the war, Britain in the 1980s was profoundly affected by world events. Ronald Reagan's election in 1980 (and his cosy love-in with Mrs Thatcher) was followed five years later by the emergence of Mikhail Gorbachev at the head of the Communist Party in the USSR, which would prove to be an initial step in the break-up of the Soviet Union. In 1986 the explosion at the nuclear power station in Chernobyl was the worst such disaster up to that time, and though those within close proximity suffered the most, sheep farmers in several parts of Britain continued to be affected by the contamination of grass for over a year. This contributed to a rising interest in ecological issues, in abeyance since the early days of the seventies counter-culture, and a growing awareness of the impact of man's actions on the planet; terms such as 'global warming' and the 'greenhouse effect' were heard commonly for the first time. Over the decade we transformed into a global society, and we watched in awe in November 1989 as, after three decades separating East and West, the Berlin Wall was pulled down.

What we ate and how we ate had also undergone a revolution in the 1980s: the microwave, pre-packed sandwiches, ready meals and junk food had all arrived in our lives, affecting the way families and friends spent time together and apart. Convenience and speed had arrived to ease the burden of preparing endless family meals, but this had come at a price. The emphasis on speed – both in cooking and eating – was to have a profound effect on our lifestyles, and even more so on our waistlines. More choice was liberating, but it came with a sting in its tail.

If we look back to the last years of the 1980s, with their pattern of excess set against stubbornly high unemployment (higher levels than at the start of the decade) and rising concerns about the unequal nature of society, the whole period can feel rather like a scene from the classic 1985 film *Back to the Future*. As the yuppies dined out on their huge bonuses, shouted into their giant mobile phones and ordered magnums of the most expensive wines in flashy restaurants, the possibility of recession was back in the news. It all feels so familiar – we've been there again in the twenty-first century and are still dealing with the consequences now.

So much had changed over a period of just ten years, as rapidly developing technology and changing social orders liberated us, giving us more choice in everything from technology – computers to car telephones, CD players to satellite dishes – to holidays, to food. The way we spent money had changed – easy credit saw us begin to buy today what we would have saved up for yesterday. You no longer needed to queue in the bank on a Friday afternoon for cash for the weekend; machines now dispensed notes at any time of the day or night in most towns and cities, and if you couldn't find one there was always the credit card. This trickle of credit would become a flood in the following decade with all kinds of consequences.

Meal times had been transformed by the microwave and ready meal. Weekday eating was done on the move for many families, who ate separately more frequently as the years went by. But Sundays were still special and the roast meal cooked at home and shared with the whole family continued to be seen as an important ritual for many, even if in some families it had moved to the evening to allow for sports, hobbies and other commitments. Another option for the Sunday family lunch that would have been a rarity at the start of the decade was a visit to a pub or family-friendly restaurant chain. This traditional meal was big business, and menus and venues had changed in recognition, with kids' menus, small portions and high chairs for babies. Cooking for friends had also been transformed as the foodie effect filtered down to the man (and woman!) in the street. Now when we had the opportunity, mostly at the weekends, we were happy to spend our leisure time in the kitchen, cooking up all kinds of exotic dishes. This was true of men in particular, especially singles, who often pushed out the boat and pre-pared elaborate menus from scratch for their mates. At the same time, with so many high-quality chilled dishes in the supermarket, unlike the cheat's dinner served up back in the 1970s, there was now no shame in wheeling out ready-made food for your guests. Your friends recognized that, like them, you were busy and that short-cuts and convenience needn't mean a loss in quality or that you were short-changing them as host or hostess. Entertaining had become more relaxed, more flexible and less stressful if that was the route you chose to follow.

On the whole people were better off than they had been at the start of the decade – wealthier, with better food, bigger cars, more gadgets, more TV channels and more choice for holidays and enter-tainment. And this was the decade that saw the growing dissociation between what we were frequently being told made up a healthy diet and the reality of what we actually ate. People knew fats and sugars were bad for them, crazes such as the F-Plan diet and aerobics showed that health was on people's minds, but what we actually consumed seemed to indicate either that we weren't listening or, more likely, that we were too busy to look after ourselves. If the 1970s had started our journey towards obesity, the 1980s had turned up the dial and ramped up the pace towards diabetes and heart disease.

CHAPTER 6

Keeping Up Appearances: the 1990s

Key Events

1990 Nelson Mandela released after 27 years in prison; BSE a cause for public concern; Aldi and Netto open their first stores in the UK

1991 Collapse of the Soviet Union

1992 Black Wednesday – Britain exits the European Exchange Rate Mechanism; first SMS message sent

1994 First Tesco Express store opens

1995 WWF announces Asian tiger is facing extinction

1996 BSE crisis – EU bans British beef imports

1997 Blair elected as prime minister; Birth of Dolly the sheep, the first cloned adult animal

1998 Good Friday Agreement brings peace to Northern Ireland

1999 Devolution of Scotland and Wales; arrival of the BlackBerry

IN 1990, AS BRITAIN rushed headlong towards the millennium with all its apocalyptic associations, what kind of nation were we? What were the issues that we discussed over our dinner tables – or, more's the point, did we even use our dinner tables any more? As Giles Coren, who bought his first flat in the 1990s, comments at the start of the episode, 'The nineties isn't that long ago, is it? Surely it wasn't very different from now.' But, boy, have things changed in the twenty-five years since the decade burst upon us.

After thirteen years with one leader and political party at the helm – a period that saw us increasingly spending today what we would have to pay back tomorrow – this new, more unsettling decade would find Britain living under three prime ministers, Margaret Thatcher until 1990, then John Major until 1997, and finally Tony Blair, as the country experienced a period of economic and political turmoil. As recession bit, unemployment – already at a high level through the eighties – reached 5 per cent of a population of 57 million in 1990 and would continue rising for the next three years. The same year saw household debt stand at £347 billion, with soaring interest rates of 14 per cent (they reached 15 per cent in both 1989 and 1992). With mortgage payments rocketing and recession hurting through wage freezes and job losses, property prices dived. New property owners, who had been tempted by Margaret Thatcher's right-to-buy, were stuck with negative equity and repossessions reached record levels (75,000 in 1991). The crashing property market meant household spending was scaled back. By the 1992 general election – which saw the re-election of John Major, who had taken over from Mrs Thatcher in 1990 – the recession would officially be the longest since the Second World War, 1,200 businesses were going under every week and the amount of credit owed had doubled in ten years. It would be the second half of the decade before the good times really returned.

The mood across the country was bleak. Not even the royal family was immune. The Queen declared 1992 her 'annus horribilis' – within those twelve months the Prince of Wales separated from Diana, the Princess Royal was divorced from Mark Phillips, and the Duke of York's recently estranged wife Sarah graced the front pages of the tabloids top-less while having her toes sucked by an enthusiastic 'financial adviser'. And on top of all that Windsor Castle caught fire. Then in August 1997 the unexpected death of Diana, Princess of Wales, at only thirty-six, would change the way the nation related to the royal family yet again. Their popularity slid to a new low, but at least we could see that really they were just like us after all.

These unsettled years saw a kind of national nostalgia, a yearning for the security of the past which was manifest in the retro styles that we introduced to our homes. But the 1990s was also a decade that looked forwards, with technology, and communications in particular, taking a big leap into a new world. Not only did more people have per-sonal computers – enabling the growing trend towards working from home – but on 3 December 1992 British engineer Neil Papworth sent the first SMS (Short Message Service, otherwise known as text mes-sage) to his client at Vodafone. Typed out on a PC as mobile phones didn't have keyboards at the time, it simply read: 'Merry Christmas'. By the late 1990s, when phones were able both to send and to receive on different networks, their popularity had exploded and now, in the UK alone, we send millions of texts every day. They even affect the way we shop: supermarkets and stores use SMS to announce their online-shop delivery times, and as customers we can text the driver to ask him to leave our purchases in the shed or with a neighbour.

On the beach or in bed we were consuming *Wild Swans*, *Fever Pitch*, *Captain Corelli's Mandolin*, *Diana: Her True Story* (1.5 million copies sold by 1998), *Bridget Jones's Diary* and 'Aga sagas' such as *The*

Rector's Wife by Joanna Trollope. We tried to understand the opposite sex with *Men Are from Mars, Women Are from Venus!* At the same time we were laughing at *Ab Fab*, *The Vicar of Dibley* and *One Foot in the Grave* on TV, envying the coffee-house lifestyle of the crew in *Friends* and hiding behind the sofa as *Cracker* and *The X-Files* scared the living daylights out of us. And then there were those *Teletubbies* – everyone say 'Eh oh!'

Time, or rather the perceived lack of it, looms over this decade, and the trends in the way we lived set up in the eighties expanded exponentially – families spending less time together than ever, eating on the hoof, relying on convenience foods and preparing fewer meals from scratch. The Institute of Grocery Distribution reported that sales of raw ingredients for cooking fell in the ten years between 1988 and 1998. But interestingly, time to cook was not really the issue at all, despite the marketing message of cash-rich, time-poor modern living. Although average working hours had risen during the previous decade, reaching 42 hours per week for men in 1990, from that point onwards they fell again, giving most people more leisure time. By 2012 official data from the OECD would reveal that the length of the working week had actually decreased to its lowest level on record – the vast majority of British people work fewer hours than they did in 1990. As journalist Joanna Blythman pointed out in 2006 in her book *Bad Food Britain*: 'It is not so much that Britons do not have the time to cook, than that they no longer see cooking as a good use of their time'!

Home comforts

How would the kitchen, the heart of the home, have looked in 1990? Well, there was a lot more going on here than previously – no longer was the space just for cooking and eating. As the decade developed we were all in the kitchen watching TV (digital TV recorders arrived in 1999), playing Nintendo, gossiping over coffee, doing homework,

National Food Survey Menus 1990

Sunday
Family of seven in Bury
Mum: 31; Dad: 32; children: 10, 9, 6, 3 and 8 months

Poached egg on toast
Juice
Tea
(Baby breastfed)

■

Chicken
Boiled potatoes
Yorkshire pudding
Peas
Carrots
Gravy
Juice
(Baby breastfed)

■

Corned-beef sandwiches
Angel Delight
Tea
Milk
Juice

■

(Baby breastfed)

DIY or – in a new development – working from home. The number of people working at home doubled between 1981 and 1998, and many of them were doing this work on an Apple Mac computer, which sat in the corner of the kitchen or on what had been the dining-room table – the dining room itself transformed into an office/relaxing room while we now ate in the kitchen.

The look of the kitchen itself was somewhat schizophrenic – modern but at the same time with a retro feel – as it underwent this role change, and these opposing trends were replicated in the food issues we faced in the 1990s. Rather as in recent years, recession saw us turn to home comforts and look to the past for reassurance as we abandoned the lavish eating-out style of the 1980s. But at the same time, with a whole world of food opening up to us on television and in the shops, we also embraced change and headed boldly on towards the millennium and all it promised.

Compared to its predecessor, the 1990s kitchen was minimalist and clean-lined, taking inspiration from a raft of über-cool designers and the trend for warehouse and loft living, as we cleaned up our lives in anticipation of a fresh beginning symbolized by the new century. The effect came from pale colours, granite counters, bleached wood and a wash of previously much-derided magnolia on the walls (now renamed as some kind of 'white' – ivory or oyster – by trendsetting paint companies). Home makeovers swamped the television schedules; when you weren't watching a chef, it was the turn of a flamboyant interior designer on a tight budget (*Changing Rooms* was first broadcast in 1996) creating design magic – or the opposite – in some hapless victim's home.

As the kitchen began to morph into a family room, it became, thanks to the television, a more welcoming habitat for men. At the same time, the garden was transformed from utilitarian to leisure space and came into its own as a fashionable extension of the home. Alan Titchmarsh and his team got on with the makeover process in our gardens (*Ground Force* arrived in 1997) and soft borders were swapped for hard landscaping (decking), banana plants and all kinds of barbecue paraphernalia dear to male hearts.

With credit card ready and waiting, the model that was your home had to be dressed and accessorized with all the latest gadgets on display

– Bodum cafetière and Alessi storage jars; Philippe Starck's seminal Salif juicer; Global stainless-steel knife set (darling of nineties chefs); and, hidden away in the drawer, one of the most useful objects: a swivel-headed fruit and vegetable peeler. Simple Shaker style or, as the decade progressed, stainless-steel professional were all the rage, with bookshelves to display the flood of cookery books from TV's latest generation of chefs. Swedish furniture retailer IKEA, which had opened its first UK store in Warrington in 1987 with a café serving good-quality, low-priced Swedish dishes, such as meatballs with chips and redcurrant sauce, or hotdogs (by 2012 IKEA estimated it had sold 11.6 billion Swedish meatballs and 1.2 billion hotdogs to its British customers since it first opened in the UK), bought Habitat in 1992 and with DIY (supposedly!) made accessible and easy, people could transform their homes regularly and cheaply. Huge numbers took up the challenge as DIY boomed again on the back of IKEA flatpacks.

If you were very lucky and had the budget and space, a large breakfast island appeared in the centre of your kitchen, around which family

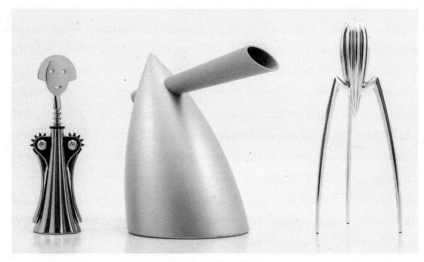

Cutting-edge design and professional gadgets from innovators such as Phillipe Starck and Alessi were on display in the 1990s kitchen.

and friends congregated, as the new music system played Britpop or the Three Tenors in the background. Kitchen appliances were fully integrated and hidden away, as now that everyone had one there was no requirement to show off. There was still, however, seldom a dishwasher; in 1990 only 15 per cent of households owned one. There might, though, be a 'tall-boy' larder, stuffed with all kinds of ingredients unrecognizable to previous generations – but they would have felt at home with the retro look of the Dualit toaster and enamel bread bin that found their way into many 1990s kitchens, revealing a hankering for the security of the past.

The supermarket reigns supreme

During times of hardship consumers naturally cut back on unnecessary spending, and National Food Surveys of the early nineties reveal that, just as in previous recessions, during this downturn eating out was one of the first things to go for families watching the pennies. As has been the trend again since the late noughties, we went out less and entertained at home more. In response, the food industry plugged into our desire for ever more convenience and choice of food to eat at home. This was a pivotal time for the supermarkets, which consolidated their domination of our shopping trolleys with all kinds of quick fixes, short-cut ingredients and irresistible items specially created in their development kitchens to tempt us and to take the work out of food preparation: chilled and prepared oven meals, all kinds of quick cook-in sauces, pre-prepared vegetables – even, to my and my colleagues' amazement, the ready-to-heat baked potato and mash. A 2003 report for the food industry looking back over the latter half of the 1990s sums up the trends, reporting that the best-performing sectors overall from 1997 were bread, cakes, cereals, biscuits and – interestingly, as we moved away from meat – fish and fish products. Ready meals, pizza and cooking sauces also performed well; with more women

Announcing the Instant Lunch.

At home or at work, **Lean Cuisine** Light Meals in a pot give you more than a snack. Full of delicious ingredients, they're ready in 5 minutes from frozen, and can be eaten straight from the pot, with no messy washing up.

Choose from Chicken & Prawn Creole, Chicken & Broccoli Pasta, Smoked Ham & Mushroom Tagliatelle and Vegetable Tikka Masala. Priced at 99p.

So, next time you want real food in an instant, reach for a **Lean Cuisine** Light Meal.

NEW

light meals in a pot.

As the decade progressed, fast food got even faster as manufacturers came up with all kinds of ways to help us eat on the go.

working or opting not to have children, households had more money to spend on food but had less time to prepare it, so these items were popular. Even more interestingly, fruit and veg as a sector accounted for 27 per cent of the market, outselling meat for the first time.

Food turned increasingly global as we snapped up out-of-season goods flown in to us from across the world. The volume of imported foods into the country soared as consumers began to expect all-year-round availablity of certain fresh foods, and ever wider variety and choice. French beans from Kenya, strawberries from Spain and mangoes from India all found their way into our baskets, along with more traditional imports – lamb from New Zealand, but now chilled rather than frozen, bananas from the Caribbean and frozen prawns from Thailand. The supermarket was at the cutting edge of the changes to the way we shopped, cooked and ate in this decade, and we lapped it all up. But a bit like the prevailing view of the US troops stationed here during the war as 'over-sexed, overpaid and over here', it could be argued that what we were buying was becoming over-packaged, over-processed and over-transported. And the way we shopped for all this new food changed too.

The NFS reports show that by the 1990s the gradual shift in our food-shopping habits from several trips during the week to a single mega-shop once a week, or even fortnightly, had become the norm. What's more, with both parents in many families working long hours, at last the family shop was no longer the responsibility of the housewife alone. What was going into the trolley was shifting too. As in previous decades, changes to what we were buying and eating for breakfast were indicative of an overall pattern. For a more sophisticated, well-travelled public (the Channel Tunnel was opened by the Queen in 1994 and Easyjet launched with cheap flights the following year), cereal had been abandoned in favour of the latest in breakfast fashion. During the week many of us opted for a cereal bar on the move, but at the same time the 'continental breakfast' with croissants, pain au chocolat and baguette – previously a treat to be enjoyed on the family holiday in Europe – now arrived in supermarkets ready to be heated up at home. Although for many it was more of a weekly treat than an everyday occurrence, the appearance of the continental breakfast on British tables signalled the more adventurous turn taken by our national palates during the 1990s.

Continental-style Breakfast

Chilled orange juice

French-style croissants

French butter (or, for the healthier-minded, Olivio spread)

Bonne Maman jam

Ground coffee from a foil pack

The coffee was made in a glass cafetière – Bodum had launched its first cafetière shop in London in 1986 – and now we could buy our own coffee beans from supermarkets or delis and grind them specially to suit our chosen coffee machine. UK orange-juice consumption doubled between 1990 and 2000, with the average person drinking 13.9 litres each year by 2000.

The time we spent on meal preparation over this decade declined from one hour each day on average in the 1980s to 45 minutes by the start of the 1990s. All kinds of 'added value' foods appeared, helped by the latest advances in packaging. Modified-atmosphere packaging, first introduced in the 1930s, evolved to extend the shelf life of prepared salads by more than 50 per cent. We had already developed the habit in the previous decade of buying more unusual salads, but this new packaging allowed us to buy a broader range of imported exotic leaves, such as rocket and lamb's lettuce, that could be eaten all year round, all tossed with a ready-prepared bottled salad dressing. And we seized the opportunity: the value of the UK salad market grew by 90 per cent between 1992 and 2002. The trend has continued, bringing with it its own problems. In 2013 Tesco revealed that of all the bagged salads produced in this country, a truly staggering 68 per cent are never eaten. Instead, the leaves rot in the fields, are thrown away in the packing warehouse, or languish in the salad drawer of our fridges before being thrown out, often unopened. We also started to buy ready-made fresh pasta, cook-in sauces, pre-prepared salad dressings and, of course, hummus (first stocked by Waitrose in the 1980s). But all this convenience came with growing worries over what happened to the packaging after we had discarded it, as treatment of waste was linked to pollution and a wide range of environmental problems, such as the escalating amount of food waste and non-degradable packaging materials going into landfill. We were right to be alarmed. Though the decade saw a move towards the use of recyclable materials, today the UK still produces more waste per head than any of our European neighbours *and* lags behind in recycling.

One particular fashion that would come to encapsulate all these concerns was increasingly taking up space in our baskets at the start of the decade and neatly summed up the way we lived. The French company Perrier single-handedly introduced us to a whole new phenomenon – bottled water. It was a triumph of advertising, creating a brand that was to define a generation. In a 2010 item for BBC2's *Money Programme*, Richard Wheatley of Leo Burnett ad agency, who oversaw the iconic 'Eau' advertising campaign, was quoted as saying: 'Perrier popularized bottled water, it made it acceptable, more than acceptable, it made it . . . desirable.' In 1990 only 5 per cent of households were buying mineral water, but NFS records show consumption soaring during the decade, with marked increases in 1991, 1995 and 1997. Perrier persuaded us to buy something that came out of our taps for free and saw annual sales increase from 12 million bottles in 1980 to 152 million at the end of the 1990s. And we continue to be hooked on water. According to the *UK Bottled Water Drinks Report 2014*, UK sales of plain (i.e. non-flavoured) bottled water by volume surged by 10.4 per cent in 2013 to an astounding 2,539 million litres.

Already by 1990, 80 per cent of our food came from supermarkets and their reach was extending all the time. In 1991 there was a rapid expansion of out-of-town shopping centres throughout the country, from fewer than fifty in 1986 to 250 five years later. The building of out-of-town superstores, which had started to expand in the 1980s, rocketed, bringing them within reach of a larger percentage of the population and setting the framework for modern food shopping. Overall the number of supermarkets across the country reached 4,500 by the end of the decade, up from just under 2,000 in 1965. And there were not just more of them, they were much bigger too – the average store was now 2,300 square metres (25,000 square feet) and carried 8,000 separate lines. And as the scale of the supermarket ballooned, so did everything else – the amount of preparation done for us by the food companies, the size of the packs and the degree of choice, with whole aisles dedicated to yogurts, crisps or biscuits. The supermarkets are now so powerful that they are able to drive down costs by insisting on still greater industrialization of food production by their suppliers. And their complicated supply chains mean we, the customer, have become further and further removed from the source of our food.

In the 1990s Tesco, which had been growing steadily since its beginnings as a market barrow in the 1920s, continued to tighten its grip on the UK with more stores opening and an intense marketing campaign as it attempted to overtake Sainsbury as the UK's leading grocer. A look at Tesco's history on its website reveals the overwhelming power of the brand and store through the second half of the century:

- 1961 Tesco Leicester enters the *Guinness Book of Records* as the largest store in Europe
- 1968 Tesco opens its first 'superstore' in Crawley, West Sussex

- 1974 Tesco opens its first petrol stations (it would become the UK's largest independent petrol retailer in 1991)
- 1979 Tesco's total sales top £1 billion
- 1982 Tesco's sales double to more than £2 billion
- 1992 Tesco launches its slogan 'Every little helps'
- 1993 Tesco Value range launched
- 1995 Tesco launches its Clubcard scheme, helping it overtake rival Sainsbury as the UK's largest food retailer
- 1996 Tesco introduces its first twenty-four-hour store; it also expands overseas, opening shops in Poland, the Czech Republic and Slovakia

Meanwhile, between 1991 and 1997, a total of 4,000 food shops closed in rural areas, but the distance people travelled to go shopping rose by 14 per cent between 1990 and 1995. Most of those journeys were now by car, often as part of a weekend outing for the family, and come the middle of the decade another change allowed us to spend even more of our leisure time embracing this convenience culture.

After what one MP called 'flagrant disregard of the 1950 Sunday Trading Act' by large retailers, in 1994 the Sunday Trading Act introduced legislation to allow small stores – less than 280 square metres (3,000 square feet) – to open whenever they chose, while stores larger than that could open on a Sunday for six hours continuously, between 10am and 6pm. So now we could worship at the temple of shopping seven days a week – and we leapt at the opportunity. Twenty years on, we are shopping more and more, and the argument for even longer Sunday trading hours has once again become an issue. In 2014 new data from Visa Europe showed that in the previous four years 'face-to-face' spending has grown by 50 per cent on Sundays, more than any other day of the week apart from Thursday, when spending has also grown by 50 per cent thanks to more widespread late-night opening hours. Kevin Jenkins, managing director of Visa, said in an interview for the *Daily Telegraph*: 'Even 20 years on from the introduction of the Sunday Trading Act, it's clear that the appetite for shopping on a Sunday continues to grow at a pace. In fact, according to our card transaction data, growth rates for Sunday shopping are outstripping Saturday quite significantly.' Mark Allatt, co-founder of Open Sundays, a group of retailers campaigning for reform, said the rise of online shopping means the existing law is 'outdated' and 'doesn't make any sense'. Research by the group showed that 72 per cent of people believed they should be able to shop when it was convenient for them.

The statistics tell the story of the last half-century. If the distance the 1990s family travelled to get to the supermarket, plus the steps taken down each aisle, is compared to the daily journey the 1950s housewife was making to all her local shops, we can see that, while the journey was further in the 1990s, the weekly shop itself was taking far less time. And in 1991 food prices had dropped to a level which saw food as a percentage of household expenditure lower than at any point since the war. By 2000, the standard family food shop weighed around 36kg (5 stone 9lb) – equivalent to the weight of an average eleven-year-old child! Just a year later, in 2001, 46p of every retail pound was spent in a supermarket – and by 2011 this had risen to 60p.

Sunday trading hours were relaxed in the 1990s, giving us even more opportunity to spend time and money in the pursuit of happiness through consumerism.

Food scares and the quest for healthy food

As the decade progressed and the supermarkets continued to dictate our shopping habits, the recession deepened and throughout the country people were forced to tighten their belts. Alongside the economic gloom, however, a new crisis was also making us increasingly concerned about what we were putting in our trolleys. This time it was the safety of our food.

The first major food scare in Britain had come along in 1988, when the discovery of salmonella in a number of eggs led junior health minister Edwina Currie to declare during a television interview that 'most of the egg production in this country, sadly, is now affected with salmonella'. The claim, which proved unjustified, caused widespread panic amongst the public and angered farmers, politicians and egg producers, as sales of eggs and also of chicken plummeted. Now another scare that had been brewing in the farming industry since the mid-1980s erupted and continued to rumble along throughout the decade. This was the discovery of BSE in British cattle. Standing for bovine spongiform encephalopathy, it is a neurodegenerative disease that causes severe deterioration to the spinal cord and brain of cattle – hence its common name of 'mad cow' disease. It is caused by cattle consuming the remains of other infected cattle or sheep in their feed.

BSE was first found in British cattle in 1984 and formally identified two years later. Despite government action to cull infected beef herds, by 1990 the number of cases stood at around 14,000. Over the next few years television news broadcast horrific images of infected animals staggering around and also of burning pyres of cattle; 1,000 a week were destroyed at the peak of the cull in 1992 and by the end of the decade the number of cattle slaughtered as a consequence of the outbreak in the United Kingdom was approaching 4 million. Most of them were killed as a precaution, not because they had actually developed 'mad cow' disease.

Fears about the safety of British beef rose steadily in the early 1990s. In an attempt to calm public anxiety, minister of agriculture John Gummer invited newspapers and camera crews to photograph him trying to feed a beefburger to his four-year-old daughter at an event in his Suffolk constituency, while chief medical officer Sir Donald Acheson announced 'beef can be eaten safely by everyone, both adults and children, including patients in hospital'. However, in 1996 scientists linked the consumption of certain parts of infected cattle with new variant Creutzfeldt-Jakob disease (vCJD) in humans and public alarm intensified as cases of this incurable condition made headlines. This would fundamentally change the way the government approached risk to public health. After years of secrecy, weak controls, inadequate supervision of slaughterhouses and general complacency, politicians and civil servants started to see the light. A ban prohibiting the use of possibly infected sheep remains in cattle feed had been in place since 1988 but had not been rigidly enforced. Speaking to the BBC in 1999, the British Veterinary Association's spokesman on BSE told *News Online*: 'If the ban had been enforced properly from the start, I have no hesitation in saying categorically that we should be seeing only a few cases today. But . . . contaminated feed was being given to animals until at least 1995, and possibly a year later.' Another loser in the crisis was the relationship between town and country, which became even more fractured as a result, with the feeling of alienation between those who produced our food and those eating it intensified yet again.

At the time, the media responded in its usual fashion with overly dramatic headlines and horror stories about vCJD that ramped up public fears. The *Sun*'s 'Mad Cow alert over kids' was matched by 'Could it be worse than Aids?' from the *Daily Mail*. Despite claims at the outset of tens of thousands of cases, in the end a total of 176 people in the UK are thought to have died from vCJD, with the number of cases peaking at twenty-eight in 2000. Public confidence in the British

In 1990, agriculture minister John Gummer went to extreme lengths and roped in his young daughter to reassure the public that British beef was safe to eat.

beef industry was shaken to its core, however, and sales of British beef dropped like a stone. Back then we were fundamentally still a nation of meat eaters. The NFS diaries for 1990 (by this stage encompassing 400,000 households and representing the diets of 1.25 million people) show that 43 per cent of all households were purchasing carcass beef and veal (joints and cuts) each week, while 88 per cent were buying other meat products (such as ready-made meals containing meat and processed meat such as sausages and pâtés) on a weekly basis. Across the decade, however, our meat consumption dropped from 301g per head per week to 235g in 2000 (it would not recover to 1990 levels until 2005). After the discovery of the link between BSE and vCJD, McDonald's and Burger King both stopped using British beef in their burgers, schools dropped it from dinner menus, while the EU stopped all exports of British beef. Burger sales plummeted by 90 per cent. Sales of beef on the bone were banned in this country, although die-hard fans of comforting dishes such as oxtail, beef rib and T-bone steaks found ways around the ban and names of butchers who were able to provide such contraband were surreptitiously passed between aficionados.

At the same time the numbers of people giving up eating meat altogether soared. As editor of the BBC's *Vegetarian Good Food Magazine* for the first half of the decade, I was a witness to this change, as more and more of us gave up, or cut back on, meat. In the previous vegetarian wave, during the 'brown revolution' of the 1970s and early 1980s, avoiding meat was something of a philosophical and political decision, but this time it was driven more by fear. And, as well as its perceived dangers, meat was expensive as recession took a firmer hold. By 1997, 14.3 per cent of the population polled in a RealEat survey claimed to be avoiding eating red meat, as against only 1.9 per cent in 1984, while 5.4 per cent were vegetarians, up from 2 per cent in 1984. The trend covered everything from strict vegans to 'part-time vegetarians', 'demi-vegetarians', those who still ate fish, and so on – as many types as there were diets. Vegetarian food became something that everyone could consider eating at least part of the time, and it benefited from celebrity endorsement: in 1991 photographer and Beatle wife Linda McCartney had successfully launched a range of vegetarian and vegan foods under her name, which offered meat-free alternatives such as veggie sausages, burgers and lasagne, and more followed suit. This was the decade that saw veggie food start to shake off its worthy image and became an acceptable choice for foodies.

Crises such as BSE and salmonella, environmental disasters, growing concerns about the emergence of 'super bugs' all came to a head in the nineties. The dangers posed by antibiotic resistance (a new virulent strain of MRSA first appeared in the 1990s) and controversy surrounding the high level of their use in modern industrial farming, together with the badly handled introduction of genetically modified foods (which became known as 'Frankenstein foods') highlighted just how little the British public knew about how and where their food was produced. The first commercially grown GM food, the FlavrSavr tomato, had been created by a Californian company at the beginning of the decade and a variety of it was used to make a tomato purée sold in Europe a few years later. Farmers and scientists saw the technology that created these new crops as the bright, fresh future, full of potential for solving many of the world's food problems, and millions of acres of them had been planted worldwide by the end of the millennium, half in the United States. But the backlash was just as dramatic. The public, especially in Europe, viewed the risks posed by these seemingly untested foods as too high. It was believed that their introduction threatened the purity of indigenous crops, while simultaneously putting ownership of precious seed into the hands of a few multinational companies. The companies behind the technology are still paying the price for virtually ignoring the concerns of the consumer and targeting their primary customers, the farmers, when they introduced these products. They have yet to come up with an effective marketing strategy that will persuade people of the benefits of the controversial crops.

Consequently, as we worried about our ever more anonymously produced food, the 1990s (and the early years of the new millennium) saw rising interest in organic and locally sourced produce. The huge loss of trust in our industrialized food systems and the government responsible for its monitoring saw those who could afford the price and time involved in sourcing them turn to other food networks – frequently farmers' markets and organic producers. 'Local', 'small-scale' and 'provenance' became the watchwords for customers who were looking to re-establish those very same personal relationships of trust and familiarity with small retailers and producers that had been taken for granted by their grandmothers and

'IT LIVES!!!'

Public fears over genetically modified foods and their potential dangers were not assuaged by the reaction of the food industry to these concerns.

mothers shopping in the 1950s. This nostalgia for a supposed halcyon time pre-dating one's own experience, when 'old-fashioned' values held sway, became a powerful driver in the success of these alternative food sources, which represented a romantic view of a country before industrialization. They were seen to offer the customer both transparency and accountability, which were felt to be missing in the supermarket.

The first farmers' market opened in Bath in 1996, and during the nineties sales of organic fruit and vegetables increased by between 20 and 30 per cent every year. By 2009 the number of markets had grown to around 750, according to the Farmers' Retail and Marketing Association, and remains stable at about that number today, despite the latest recession. Food writer and local-food campaigner Henrietta Green launched her book *The Food Lovers' Guide to Britain* in 1993, championing local foods, producers and suppliers. She was a key figure in the rise of the farmers' market movement and in at the start of another phenomenon which rose like a phoenix in the 1990s – Borough Market in south-east London. A market had existed on the spot since the eleventh century, but its regeneration as a speciality food market has been part of the huge redevelopment of London's South Bank since the 1970s, which saw Shakespeare's Globe open in 1995, the renovation of the derelict Oxo tower whose fancy rooftop restaurant opened to acclaim in 1996, and found Gary Rhodes cooking in a new venue at the Festival Hall for a while in the middle of the decade. Henrietta ran a Food Lovers' Fair on the site in 1998 to much acclaim, and by 2011 4.5 million visitors were patronizing stalls and retailers such as the Ginger Pig, Neal's Yard Dairy, Brindisa and the Monmouth Coffee Company, transforming the market into one of London's most popular tourist attractions. In the years since, Borough has undergone even more transformation with the expansion of the Thameslink rail service, but has withstood the upheavals, and in 2013 was voted one of the ten best fresh-food markets in the world by CNN 9 (though stallholders have complained that many of the visitors are now tourists

Ad slogans of the decade:

* Umbongo – they drink it in the Congo
* Australians wouldn't give a Castlemaine XXXX for anything else
* You know when you've been Tangoed
* Boddingtons: Put a flake in it
* I feel like Chicken Tonight
* Chewits – Do it before you chew it
* Safeway – Everything you want from a store, and a little bit more
* National Lottery – Maybe, just maybe
* Pop-Tarts: Pop-start your day
* Weight Watchers – Taste not waist
* Pukka people pick a pot of Pataks
* Tesco – Every little helps

who come to look rather than to buy).

During the 1990s we increased our spending on organic fruit and vegetables by around a quarter each year, and sales continued to soar until the latest recession in 2008 saw households rein in their spending. Now, as the economy starts to recover, we are once again buying organic and 2013 saw an increase in UK sales of 2.8 per cent as a whole, but with a healthy 11 per cent growth in vegetable-box schemes and home delivery. One of the pioneers of veg boxes launched his scheme in 1993 and it has gone from strength to strength since, defying the decline in the late noughties. Farmer Guy Watson had moved his south Devon family farm to organic production in 1988, in response to the tighter controls imposed by the supermarkets, concerns about GM foods and food scares. As he said in a recent profile, 'You should be able to eat produce without worrying about what's been sprayed on to it.' The Riverford box began when he started delivering locally to thirty friends, and by 1997 Riverford had been joined by ten (later sixteen) local farmers to form a producers' co-operative, increasing production to keep pace with the expanding scheme. The business has now grown to encompass four farms across the UK, working with local growers to deliver an astounding 47,000 boxes of seasonal produce every week. Guy believes the secret of Riverford's success is that it has remained personal. And the company also guarantees prices that are 20 per cent cheaper than supermarket-bought organic produce. He is determined that organic shouldn't have to mean expensive. 'I hate the way the term "organic" is associated with posh or poncy food,' he said in a recent interview with the *Daily Telegraph*. 'There aren't these negative associations anywhere else in Europe.'

A touch of the Med

In our search for healthy food, many of us also looked to the peasant dishes of other countries that were influencing the way we cooked – Italian, Indian, South East Asian – which were often more or less meat-free for reasons of economy and which were beginning to fit in with the way we were now living and cooking in Britain. By the 1990s the elements of the 'Mediterranean' diet, identified in the previous decade for their health-giving properties, had been recognized by the majority as a desirable model and we were all being encouraged to eat like Sicilian peasants both in the home and outside it. Dinner parties in the 1990s were about showing off the quality and provenance of your ingredients, as we learnt from the TV chefs to be lavish with the extra-virgin olive oil, freshly grated Parmigiano Reggiano, filo pastry and prosciutto, and struggled to get the pronunciation of ciabatta and bruschetta correct. Delia's *Summer Cooking* epitomized the trend with her obligatory Cous Cous Salad with Roasted Vegetables, *A Year in Provence* by Peter Mayle was required reading and we all craved a simple Mediterranean way of life. But this style of cooking could be hard work. I remember one of my colleagues on magazines at the time who would spend her weekends making her own squid-ink pasta at home. I had two small children, so home-made spaghetti bolognese was as far as I got – using good-quality dried Italian pasta of course, and reassuring myself that no Italian mama would make her own fresh pasta as the quality of the dried was actually better!

And anyway, once the supermarkets had got into the act, we could serve 'authentic' Mediterranean meals without all the hard work:

The Robshaws' Cheats' Convenience Supper (*without guilt*)

Supermarket 'fresh' pasta sauce

Supermarket 'fresh' pasta – e.g. mushroom tortellini

Parmesan

Bagged salad

Garlic bread

This was definitely cheating by our Sicilian peasants' standards, but you could easily make yourself believe you were cooking a healthy meal from scratch – even though most of the labour had been taken out of the meal and it was merely a case of assembling pre-prepared ingredients. In the late 1980s and early 1990s pasta was a small but rapidly growing market in the UK, increasing by 10 per cent to £85 million in 1991 and up to £102 million in 1992. Fresh pasta appeared from nowhere to achieve sales of almost £12 million in 1992, but the lion's share of over £100 million in sales was of dried pasta. But was this cooking? As new generations became accustomed to what the industry termed 'meal solutions', their understanding of what represented a home-cooked meal became blurred: 59 per cent of respondents to a British Potato Council survey felt that pasta and prepared sauce could be classified as such.

That sauce was more than likely to be pesto, which along with sun-dried tomatoes appeared in countless recipes from chefs and food writers (including me!) in the early 1990s. The basil-based paste had been around in specialist Italian delis for the cognoscenti since the 1960s, appeared in supermarket jars as an oddly perfumed brownish sludge in the 1980s, but now, with the help of the chiller cabinet, finally bore some resemblance to its original. Fresh, green and aromatic, it became ubiquitous, appearing in tarts, stuffed into chicken breasts, drizzled over tomatoes, even used as a sauce for pasta. It now comes in all kinds of varieties – chilli, red pepper, lemon and coriander – all totally at variance with its Ligurian origins.

To round off your meal there was also a new luxury product on the menu for dessert – with a very fashionable fusion twist. A previously childish pleasure suddenly became all adult and sophisticated with the arrival of the luxury ice cream/instant dessert. The 'pleasure' ads for Haagen Dazs were launched in 1992 and were soon absolutely every-where; with their sexy black-and-white models getting all sensual with their scoops, the ads transformed the process of eating ice cream! In 1994 Ben & Jerry's followed in their wake, arriving here with their wit-tily named creations – Chunky Monkey, Phish Food and the top-selling Cherry Garcia. This last has only just been knocked off the top spot in the UK by Half Baked in 2014, which in itself is a combination of two other bestsellers – Chocolate Chip Cookie Dough and Chocolate Fudge Brownie. This was the beginning of emerging markets created in the 1990s – the 'super premium' sector. Brandon and Rochelle serve up Haagen Dazs vanilla as a grand finale at their 1990s convenience dinner – with a 'drizzle' of that other nineties icon for the trendsetting cook: balsamic vinegar.

The new face of the pub

Back in the 1970s the pub was the place to which the man of the family could retreat to meet friends, play darts and drink beer. If he was lucky he might find a pan of sausages cooking or a scotch egg with greying yolk served with a pickled onion to go with his pint. As we have seen, pubs gradually morphed into places to take the family for a traditional Sunday lunch, or for a microwaved mass-produced meal. Much pub food was notoriously bad quality and by the 1990s there was still a clear distinction between pubs that served food and those that didn't. Out in the country growing awareness of the risks of drink-driving saw more pubs turn to serving food in order to survive as drink sales dropped.

Perhaps surprisingly, as the decade went on the meal of choice for many of us couldn't have been further from the traditional pub dishes we were used to. Workers from South East Asia as a whole but especially from Thailand were arriving here to work in the food industry (or to marry British citizens – in 2001 the Home Office revealed that the overwhelming majority of new Thai immigrants to the UK became naturalized citizens through marriage, and this country has the largest Thai expatriate community in the world outside Asia). At the same time Thailand had opened up its borders and become more democratic, so travellers other than the standard backpacker began to visit the country and to bring an appreciation of its cuisine back home. With more Thais working in cafés and pubs, it wasn't long before they began to introduce their own cuisine, serving simple curries and soups that were viewed, especially by women, as a healthy alternative to the classic pork pie and ploughman's.

Thai restaurants and cafés opened in response. Numbering only four in 1970s London (one of the first was the Blue Elephant in Fulham Broadway), by the 1990s there were several hundred. Thai food, with its fragrant but subtle flavours, was seen as healthier and less heavy than Indian curries. The balanced yet distinct combinations of sweet, salt, bitter and sour tastes from herbs and spices such as lemongrass, fresh coriander and chilli together with tamarind, peanuts and fish sauce were very much to our taste. Served with fragrant jasmine rice, the Thai green curry (usually chicken) is these days giving the ubiquitous chicken tikka masala a run for its money. Thai cooking also took off in the home and between 1994 and 1997 the Thai food market in Britain nearly doubled in value, to £235 million.

But also in the 1990s, as the economy gradually recovered and people, especially the young, chose to eat out more and more rather than prepare food at home, the pub underwent another development. Up till then pubs that served affordable good-quality food were the exception rather than the rule, but now we saw the arrival of the 'gastropub' – these days so ubiquitous that there are specially produced guides to the best ones across the country. It all started with the Eagle in Farringdon, on the edge of the City of London, which had opened in 1991 and kicked off what original owners Michael Belben and Tom Norrington-Davies would term a food and drink evolution rather than the more dramatic revolution. Opening its doors in the depths of the recession, this was a no-nonsense establishment with a clear emphasis on top-quality, simple, seasonal food served at reasonable prices. Their first chef arrived from the kitchens of the seminal River Café and introduced the standards and techniques of that ground-breaking establishment to a new, less-affluent class of food lovers. At The Eagle, classic English dishes such as oxtail and a 'roast of the day' appeared on the short menu (which changed daily), alongside Mediterranean dishes inspired by the range of nationalities working behind the scenes in the kitchens. Portuguese, Italian and Spanish influences all featured in the eclectic mix, with dishes such as their famous steak sandwich – which came Portuguese-style, cooked with wine, chilli and garlic – *Pollo al Ajillo* (garlic chicken), Serrano ham and eggs, lamb with tzatziki sauce, and lemon and almond cake with rosemary to finish. The setting was informal and relaxed, with mismatched tables and chairs, a long counter at the back, half bar and half revealing a galley-style open kitchen. Food was ordered at the counter and, with everything on display, the customer got to see his food cooked to order more or less right in front of him. It then arrived at the table served by friendly young staff on mismatched and sometimes even chipped plates.

This was comfort eating at its best, served with wines from a short, well-judged and -priced list, or a speciality craft beer or lager with the emphasis on quality, and we still benefit from its influence today. As people more often preferred to eat convenient, pre-prepared ready meals when at home, which we consumed while watching others cook food on television rather than getting our hands dirty ourselves, the chattering classes embraced the format with enthusiasm. At the time, the Eagle concept formed a neat bridge between the wine bar of the 1980s and the high-end-restaurant scene that was way beyond the average person's budget, and it set the model for a whole host of imitators and copycat establishments – some excellent, but many more cheaper copies that sprang up everywhere from airport lounges to restaurant chains. It became part of the 'Cool Britannia' phenomenon of the middle of the decade – relaxed, trendy eateries with Britpop playing in the background, patronized by young, affluent warehouse-dwellers, who saw eating out as a 'hobby'. The simultaneous arrival of the YBAs (Young British Artists) saw Damien Hirst provide art to enhance his own restaurants, such as newly refurbished Quo Vadis in London's Soho, opened in partnership with Marco Pierre White, and Pharmacy in increasingly fashionable Notting Hill Gate.

In 1997 the *Good Food Guide* announced that 'there has never been a more exciting time to eat out'; in 2011, however, the publication would declare 'the death of the gastropub', as even supermarkets adopted the term to sell their ready meals.

Wine, women . . . and sales

As can be seen from the Thai food experience, women customers in the late 1990s were clearly recognized as a vital source of spending power and they were targeted accordingly, not least by the supermarkets. One area that saw the impact of this was the wine aisle, always ready to build on the latest trend. After levelling off in the 1980s, Britain's thirst for alcohol soared throughout the 1990s, peaking in 2000 – up from 8 litres per head per year to more like 10 litres. And much of this rise was down not just to the steady democratization of wine but also to the rise of female drinking throughout the decade. With their greater spending power, women were now drinking regularly at home as alcohol was easily purchased in a supermarket, a female-friendly environment that lacked the social stigma possibly associated with women drinking alone in pubs. More of the major supermarket buyers were also now women, while new-world wines were seen as classless and more approachable, less snobby than the French wines of old; as food became less formal there was a similar rise in a less stuffy choice of wines. Companies such as Marks & Spencer recognized that, despite the changes in working over the last half century, women still did, and do, the majority of the food and drink shopping and so have become the main buyers of wine – a fact borne out by a wine industry survey in 2009, which revealed that women were responsible for buying eight out of every ten bottles of wine drunk at home. The survey also showed that a third of British women who treated themselves to a glass at the end of the day admitted that they prefer to drink it alone – in the bath.

The 1990s also witnessed the arrival of the soon-to-be-reviled alcopops. Innocuously named 'flavoured beverages' by the drinks industry, they were specifically targeted at younger women, who were put off spirits by the bitter taste, and they made drinking alcohol more like swigging a soft drink. Where once they might have gone for bacardi and coke, whisky and lemonade or occasionally an expensive cocktail, now there was a whole range of sugary, lurid concoctions with garish labels and even more garish names to tempt novice drinkers. The modern 'ladettes' lapped up Bacardi Breezer (1993), Smirnoff Ice, WKD (1996), Hooper's Hooch and the rest, which all came with big marketing and advertising campaigns that seemed to be aimed directly at the under-eighteens. A flood of negative publicity followed and in 1996 the chancellor, Ken Clarke, increased the tax on these drinks by 40 per cent. The effects on 'the alcopops generation' who binged on these sticky beverages are being seen now: hospital admissions for those now in their thirties and forties for alcohol-related liver disease have risen by 112 per cent over the last ten years. People in their twenties are also dying from liver conditions, something unheard of in the past.

Food on the move

By the late 1990s there was a stylish new kid on the block (or on the conveyor belt) in the quest for healthy and convenient food, this time from a different part of the world – Japan. It was sushi, and its success neatly encompassed the trends of the end of the century – the arrival of women in the workplace, globalization and technology. By January 1997 women outnumbered men in the national workforce for the first time. Many of them were looking for a healthy lunch option in a hurry and they happily embraced the delights of sushi at restaurants such as Moshi Moshi, which was the first conveyor-belt sushi restaurant when it opened in the City in 1994. Yo Sushi! followed in 1997, in Soho's Poland Street (just around the corner from my office at the time), and within a week there were queues around the block (which I joined with intrigued colleagues). Fay Maschler wrote in the *Evening Standard* that she had 'seen the future and it is fun'. The concept helped to democratize and demystify a previously unfamiliar food by offering a range of good-quality dishes on tapas-sized plates. The conveyor belt allowed the diner to choose exactly what she (or he) wanted and the colour-coded dishes, priced accordingly, made it simple to work out how much you were eating and spending. Best of all, you could watch the chefs preparing and cooking each dish in the centre of the belted area. Sushi was the perfect choice for the working lunch – small, healthy, tasty and stylish.

Within a few years Yo Sushi! was the market leader and it now has over sixty-five branches in the UK – and eleven overseas – everywhere from Harvey Nichols to Bluewater shopping centre to Heathrow airport, each selling eighty different 'Japanese-inspired' dishes from sushi to tempura, soups, salmon and noodles. It helped create a whole trend and since its launch sushi has become mainstream, even to the point of being named 'Britain's new national dish' by John Walsh in the *Independent* in 2008. By that year there were 277 sushi restaurants in the capital. These days you can buy it everywhere, from supermarkets to sandwich bars, from Boots to Marks & Spencer, and even enjoy its pleasures while on holiday at Butlins (the Butlins press officer admits that the recipes have been 'slightly adapted to accommodate British tastes') – although if your

" To BE FAIR, HE WAS HAVING SUSHI FOR LUNCH BEFORE IT BECAME FASHIONABLE "

Sushi was a popular choice for a light, healthy and tasty lunch for busy workers, especially women.

experience of sushi is freshly prepared in a sushi restaurant you may well be rather disappointed, if not surprised, by the difference in taste and quality! In 2014 sales of sushi are up 21 per cent year on year, while Waitrose has seen sales of its takeaway sushi boxes increase by over 88 per cent. As the company's sushi buyer David Stone says: 'With its low calorie count and nutritional benefits, shoppers are looking for more than just bread in their lunch hour. Oily fish is rich in vitamins and Omega-3 fats, which have benefits for both body and brain, making it the perfect midday snack.' Sushi is now the country's fastest-growing food market.

Who would have thought that dishes of raw fish with fiery green mustard, boiled rice and seaweed could challenge the might of chicken tikka masala or good old fish and chips? The overall trends in healthy eating, the popularity of fish and the focus on the 'authenticity' of the dining experience reveal the British public in the twenty-first century as fundamentally adventurous in our approach to our food. The sushi story neatly encapsulates the changes that have taken place in the way the nation eats over the last half century and just how far we have come. Our fifties family would view eating sushi with much the same horror as we today would turn our noses up at the thought of Spam.

Out and about

As the decade progressed, 'Modern British Food', a style that combined top-quality local ingredients with traditional regional cooking methods and the influences of Mediterranean, Middle Eastern and Asian cuisines, gained international recognition, as did the chefs cooking it. London was named as the new restaurant capital of the world by the 2000 Finnair Travel Guide 'for its culinary diversity and worldwide cuisines', yet the proportion of the population eating in even the more relaxed pubs and restaurants remained relatively small. The rest of us were eating outside the home more and more, but mainly in fast-food establishments and 'on the hoof'. At the same time, the boundaries between food eaten out of and inside the home were blurring as retailers came up with pre-cooked dishes and foods that could be bought hot or ready to heat. Meanwhile, restaurants increased their offer of takeaways and home deliveries, which saw the fast-food sector boom in the nineties.

By 2002, according to the British Potato Council, about 35p of every £1 spent on food went on eating outside the home, while nearly 30 million of us were eating out at least once a week, with ready-prepared sandwiches accounting for an amazing third of the takeaway market. Attracted by the development of more expensive luxury ranges, but also as a result of greater affluence and time pressure, most people turned to a shop-bought sandwich for their lunch. The three-meal-a-day habit was being steadily eroded and family meal times were starting to become a thing of the past. By this time 47 per cent of adults regularly ate their main meal in front of the television, while 40 per cent sat down to their evening meal alone.

Research in 2001 identified a new pattern – the five-snack day with the key 'snacking occasions' broken down into:

- early commuter rush
- mid-morning
- lunch time
- end of school day
- return home from work

Breakfast as a meal eaten together at the table had been under fire since women began to join the workforce in significant numbers. Between 1990 and 2000 consumption of the traditional breakfast fry-up of bacon and eggs declined by 23 per cent, as croissants, bagels and crumpets took the place of toast, and more cereal and yogurt was eaten. Breakfast transformed into 'deskfast', as more and more of us bought ours on the journey in to work or school from fast-food outlets such as McDonald's, who began serving the Egg McMuffin in the 1980s, or sandwich chains such as Pret A Manger. The first Pret had opened near London's Victoria Station in 1986, catering for the yuppie who expected more from their sandwich than tired ham and cheese on white bread. This new-look sandwich shop promised better quality than the rest of the high-street offerings but at a premium price, and made us feel we could make more healthy choices with its help, even if we had given up preparing our own breakfasts. Plenty of staff, who smiled and chatted as they served you, meant busy office workers could pick up their breakfast yogurt and granola or pop out for lunch without queuing and so be back at their desks in the shortest possible time. Today only one third of British families eat breakfast together, and the number of times they do so has dropped by half since the 1950s.

Another sensation arrived on the high street in the second half of the decade, one which for the first time targeted a fresh market and, like the new breed of sandwich shop, helped change the way we ate and still eat today. As BBC *Business News* would report: 'A coffee shops phenomenon has swept Britain's high streets, and coffee is now Britain's number one hot drink amongst men and women alike; but without the influence of women it's arguable that Britain's coffee revolution might never have happened at all.' And a small family-run British company with excellent credentials would become a leader in the market.

Costa was a family business of coffee roasters, who had been supplying local caterers in the Lambeth area since 1971. Run by brothers Sergio and Bruno, its warehouse was located under the railway arches at Waterloo, where the aroma of roasting coffee was familiar to commuters into that station (of whom I was one throughout the 1980s). The brothers started selling their coffee from a store in nearby Vauxhall Bridge Road in 1978. In 1995 brewers Whitbread were looking for a way to make up revenue lost from declining beer sales in their pub businesses. Their market research had identified an important new customer, but there was a problem: as we have seen, working women, with their increased spending power, were not necessarily big fans of pubs. They wanted a venue where they could relax, one where they could meet their friends, sit at a table with some work or a magazine, or have an informal meeting. Visiting Canada a few years previously, David Thomas, Whitbread's head of leisure, had noticed the success of the Starbucks chain in Vancouver. He recognized the strengths of the concept and was sure it would work well on the British high street. Whitbread bought Costa.

In 1997 Caffè Nero and Coffee Republic launched; Starbucks arrived on these shores a year after that; and by the end of the nineties the Costa brand was rapidly expanding. With big glass windows that allowed its users to see out and be seen, the relaxed, sofa-style atmosphere (as enjoyed by the doyens of that ultimate 1990s coffee shop, Central Perk in *Friends*), free newspapers, simple snacks and cakes, they offered us a home from home, and one in which we could pick up our breakfast of speciality coffee, muffin and fruit smoothie all 'ready to go' rather than having the trouble of preparing it ourselves. We might have had to learn a whole new language to place our order – skinny, moccachino, single tall, soya latte, frappuccino – but we enthusiastically embraced the whole idea. As the trend towards flexitime and part-time working has continued to expand, the coffee shop has played its part as meeting place, office (most now offer free wi-fi) and crèche. Costa is now the largest coffee-shop chain in this country, and we increasingly grab breakfast there or at one of its competitors. By 2015 the number of coffee shops on the high street is expected to have reached 6,000 outlets, even with the recent recession.

However, as is far too often the case, convenience comes at a price. With obesity booming – especially among children – Britain's coffee revolution has been charged with playing a part. In 2013 the health minister Anna Soubry accused high-street coffee shops such as Starbucks, which are very popular with young people, of encouraging child obesity by selling highly calorific foods and drinks, such as muffins and sugar-laden coffees topped with cream, syrups and marshmallows, without any guidance as to their nutritional content. At the same time she blamed parents for failing to stop their children snacking between meals. This came as it was revealed that a third of all British children are now overweight or obese to the extent that it is putting their health at risk. A medium-sized chai latte made with full-fat milk contains the equivalent of ten cubes of sugar and comes in at 422 calories – one a day will provide nearly a quarter of the 2,000 calories the NHS suggests that the average ten-year-old boy should consume (the same that a woman needs to maintain a healthy weight). But it is perfectly possible to make sensible choices and still enjoy our coffee habit – a 'tall skinny' cappuccino from Starbucks is a far more sensible buy at 76 calories.

By this century, breakfast is even more in decline as more and more people eat it on the go. The full English is now something to be enjoyed when away on a weekend break in a country B&B – or maybe a restaurant 'with rooms' – or at a business breakfast meeting. Even the bowl of cereal or couple of slices of toast have fallen victim to our desire for food on the go. Sales of breakfast cereals are in decline, to be replaced by cereal bars such as Kellogg's Nutri-Grain, which arrived on the scene in the 1990s and promised both nutrition and speed with its strap-line 'morning fuel'. In a survey for market research company Nielsen in 2014, although fewer than 45 per cent of the 30,000 consumers questioned said they replaced meals with snacks, breakfast was the meal most likely to be missed. But the vision of these breakfast alternatives as a healthy option has been challenged. A *Which?* report in 2012 revealed high levels of sugar, fat and calories. All but one of the thirty cereal bars *Which?* surveyed (including seven aimed at children) were found to be high in sugar, with sixteen containing over 30 per cent. One bar (Nutri-Grain Elevenses) contained nearly four teaspoons of sugar (18g) – that's more sugar than in a small (150ml) can of cola (15.9g) and equals 20 per cent of an adult's recommended daily allowance. Almost a third of a Tracker Roasted Nut bar was found to be fat, though some of this comes from the peanuts and hazelnuts, which do provide some nutritional benefit.

Cooking as spectator sport

Since the 1950s food on television had always been popular and over the decades we had watched a range of professionals showing us how to cook – from Fanny Cradock to Delia Smith and Ken Hom. But in the 1990s the TV chef industry went into overdrive and for the first time featured regular Brits (of both sexes) to whom the public could relate on a more personal level, both professional and amateur. With more daytime telly adding to the hours we could sit in front of the box, viewing figures and series-related book sales soared – as did sales of chef-endorsed food and equipment. And by the end of the decade cooking had become 'cool' for men and women, inspiring many to get into the kitchen for the first time – but only as a form of leisure activity, rarely to cook a daily family meal from scratch with raw ingredients.

Back in the 1950s the government had carefully prescribed what everyone ate through the medium of rationing, with plenty of advice available, from specially commissioned advertising to targeted leaflets and campaigns. By 1990 food was plentiful, but responsibility for what everybody ate now rested with them. And with greater availability came growing confusion over what was and wasn't good for you. The question was, where to turn for advice? No reassuring Marguerite Patten, no highly respected and trusted (or at least unquestioned) government agencies such as MAFF giving us paternalistic recipe sheets and daily menus, while organizations such as the Women's Institute had been steadily (and unfairly) sidelined over the years as middle class and out of touch.

Top cookery books

- Loyd Grossman, *Masterchef*, 1990

- Rose Elliott, *New Vegetarian Cookery*, reprinted 1990

- Nigel Slater, *Real Fast Food*, 1993

- Delia Smith, *Summer Collection*, 1993; *Winter Collection*, 1995

- Simon Hopkinson and Lindsay Bareham, *Roast Chicken and Other Stories*, 1994

- Rose Gray and Ruth Rogers, *The River Café Cookbook*, 1996

- Ross Burden et al., *Ready Steady Cook: the Ten-minute Cookbook*, 1996

- Jamie Oliver, *The Naked Chef*, 1999

- Nigella Lawson, *How to Eat*, 1999

The vacuum was filled by two related phenomena. First of all, the new 'celebrity chefs', who as the years went by became more and more influential when it came to what was on our dinner plates – and with a good helping of strong language and some money in their bank accounts, some of them began to look more like rock stars than chefs. And the other group who willingly embraced the mantle of food educators was none other than the supermarkets. Where once we had turned to familiar, reliable voices such as *Good Housekeeping*, with its world-renowned Institute, which trialled kitchen equipment and came up with triple-tested recipes and food advice, or the recently launched

Good Food Magazine, which appeared in 1989 and built on the trusted brand of the BBC to offer advice and to support the burgeoning number of food programmes made by the corporation, we now had an alternative. Retailers such as Sainsbury and Marks & Spencer were not only turning out excellent-quality cookery books by well-respected food writers, but were also producing their own sophisticated lifestyle magazines, either handed out free to reward customer loyalty or with a token cover price that often undercut competing magazines available on the news-stand. Launched by Delia Smith and husband Michael Wynn-Jones, *Sainsbury's Magazine* arrived in store in April 1993, with fat, glossy pages filled with recipe features and articles by the latest and best food writers, such as Nigel Slater and Mary Berry, but most of all by Delia herself.

By the middle of the decade it was impossible to avoid the nation's favourite cook (even if you wanted to!), as she dominated the airwaves with her *Summer Collection* on BBC2, with a bestselling book in support, and the popularity of the programme saw the magazine achieve huge copy sales and critical acclaim. The combination of our most trusted cook paired up in print with a supermarket was irresistible, and as a result of her ubiquity across the media we all succumbed to the 'Delia effect'. This was so intense that it has earned a place in *Collins Dictionary*, which defines the 'Delia effect' as that which 'occurs when millions seek out an ingredient or piece of equipment she has recommended' – as people did when she used cranberries or a particular omelette pan in one of her recipes.

And it wasn't just Delia we were lapping up. Food as entertainment was the order of the day. The amount of time dedicated to broadcasting cookery programmes had increased slowly but steadily during the 1970s and 1980s until it stood at about three hours a week on each of the four main channels. The trend continued into the 1990s, which saw us glued to everything from the weekly magazine format of *Food and Drink* (1982–2001) to the 'cogitations' of Loyd Grossman (with guest judges) presenting *Masterchef* from 1990, and the ever-dependable Delia herself, who was hardly off our screens throughout the whole decade. From Christmas 1990 through the *Summer Collection* in 1993, *Winter Collection* in 1995, then her *Red Nose Collection* in 1997 and, to round off the decade, her *How to Cook* series (the first part broadcast in 1998), she was unstoppable. Then we had more Keith Floyd; Rick Stein's *Taste of the Sea* in 1995 (followed by two more seafood series by the end of the decade); Sophie Grigson's *Eat Your Greens* on Channel 4; spiky-haired Gary Rhodes cooking *Around Britain* (1994); Raymond 'Blanc Mange'; *Junior MasterChef*; the *Two Fat Ladies* (1996); and, by the close of the decade, Jamie Oliver and Nigella Lawson. Chefs dominated our viewing hours, and fleets of them were roped in to fill the schedules. One notable effect of all this screen time featuring increasing numbers of male chefs was to encourage more ordinary men into the kitchen, allowing them to show a 'passion' for cooking. Brandon – now comfortably and happily back home in the 1990s kitchen – says as he cooks up one of the winning menus from the first series of *MasterChef*, 'It's good to be doing something ambitious again . . . and great to be back in the kitchen together'.

One of the most popular series of the 1990s amongst mums at home, students and the unemployed was BBC 2's *Ready Steady Cook*. It was the BBC's first regular cooking programme on daytime television and introduced such a successful format that it would go on to be sold to twenty-five countries overseas. The show, which first aired with Fern Britton at the helm, saw over 3 million viewers tuning in to see what professional chefs could cook up with a £5 bag of mystery ingredients. And by the time it came off air in 2010, it had become the country's longest-running cookery show, with twenty-one series and almost 2,000 episodes. The original format was simple and aimed to show that cooking to a tight budget didn't have to be dull. Every week two members of the public would provide the two chefs, who came from a stable of about thirty regulars, with a bag of ingredients they had brought in, usually to a set budget of £5. The chefs then competed against each other to come up with several dishes using all the ingredients within a very tight 20-minute time frame. Dishes were then voted for by the studio audience. Brian Turner was one of the first chefs to take the challenge in what was essentially the first food game show, often pitted against fellow chef Antony Worrall Thompson in an entertainingly personal contest. The show made chefs into household names, helped spawn the 'celebrity chef' phenomenon and gave birth to regular daytime schedule fillers that we enjoy today, such as *Come Dine With Me*, *Great British Menu* and *What's Cooking?* Recipes Brian created for the show ranged from Vegetarian Toad in the Hole to Sashimi of Halibut and Honey Cheesecake, reflecting the wide-ranging dishes that the inventive chefs came up with. Unlike many other cookery shows, the dishes were seen being made from start to finish, using everyday budget ingredients taken from the new value ranges that were appearing in supermarkets. As one fan on the BBC's *Ready Steady Cook* food blog wrote on the show's closure in 2010: 'I think *RSC*'s legacy to me is that it opened my eyes to the fact that food doesn't have to be "proper food" as my parents would've made – you could make anything out of anything! (Beefburger curry anyone?) It made meal times great fun when you sampled your latest experiment! I learned far more about food than I ever would have had I never watched it! It was really liberating too! I can only hope its legacy lives on and food never returns to the boring stodge it once was!'

Cookery programmes and chefs were not just filling the television schedules but, on the back of their success, were also selling books by the thousand. Cookery books moved out of the kitchen and on to the coffee table (bought of course from IKEA) as people showed off their knowledge and trendiness. For the first time, in the 1990s cookery books entered the bestseller lists – and since then there has never been a time when they have not featured. Delia stormed into the position of the nation's number-one cookery writer, and not just through the books that went with her many television series: her *Complete Cookery Course* alone, revised and reissued in 1992, remained on the bestseller list for 202 weeks. At the same time, diets and dieting continued to obsess the nation – two other books that became bestsellers were Rosemary Conley's *Hip and Thigh Diet*, which would go on to sell over 2 million copies, and a name that would be familiar back in the fifties, Doris Grant, whose *Food Combining for Health* followed a system of eating that separated food into three groups to be consumed at different times. Devised over a hundred years ago by American doctor William Howard Hay (it was also known as the Hay Diet), the new version was seized on and followed avidly by the growing number of people concerned about the effect of the food they ate on their health. (Studies have in fact discovered no clear evidence that food combining either affects weight loss or improves digestion.)

How to boil an egg

All the food shows on our screens were there, of course, to entertain us rather than to educate us in what had once been regarded as essential food skills. But as the 1990s drew to a close and we ate more and more meals away from home, heated up ready meals in the evening and watched celebrity chefs on television, a new fear gripped the nation. Cooking a meal from scratch to feed oneself and/or one's family had become the exception rather than the rule, and the worry was that a significant proportion of the population no longer knew how to do so. Two generations were now growing up without acquiring the knowledge of what had once been regarded as an essential skill – cooking.

At a time when more parents were working and had little or no time to teach their offspring how to cook, it seemed that schools were the only place where children would be able to learn. But in 1988 National Curriculum changes had taken home economics out of the classroom and replaced it with food technology, so now children were more likely to learn how to design packaging for a pizza than to pick up any practical skills. By 2003 the Guide Association would reveal research that showed that four in ten British schoolgirls had never cooked. The nation's youth were growing up lacking the basic skills needed to cook a meal and feed themselves. And it's not just our young people – as the previous *Back in Time for Dinner* decades have shown, by the end of the twentieth century it was still mainly women who did most of the cooking at home.

In the late 1990s the Focus on Food campaign identified the cooking skills that *all* adults should know as:

- knife skills for chopping
- how to grill food
- how to make a salad
- how to cook veg
- how to use fruit
- how to make a smoothie
- food safety and hygiene

Once again it was Delia, the nation's favourite cook, who arrived to save the day. In her 1998 series *How to Cook* (Parts 2 and 3 aired in the new century) Delia aimed to remind people of skills they had lost, including the, for some, surprisingly basic one of boiling an egg. To many, she was teaching the skills to enter the kitchen confidently for the first time – yes, to men and children, but also plenty of women as well. Delia's back-to-basics approach was a phenomenon and the first book was, like her others, one of the biggest sellers of the whole decade, fiction and non-fiction.

But her wise words have fallen on deaf ears: we are still in thrall to convenience and speed today. A Sainsbury's poll of 2013 revealed that, even with the 'Jamie Oliver effect', which has seen his 'distinct-ive brand of enthusiasm and desire to encourage people to eat simple, hearty food' inspiring more of our young to have a go at cooking, one in three students arriving at university still doesn't know how to boil an egg, while a third can't manage to bake a potato and less than half attempt a spaghetti bolognese. We seem to be faced with a generation of young people whose main experience of cooking is operating the microwave. Admittedly, the survey was of their parents (934 parents of children aged eighteen to twenty-five were questioned), who might have a somewhat jaundiced view of their offspring's talents, but their ability to carry out the most basic household tasks is still a concern.

Food as government policy

At the same time as the middle classes enjoyed their weekly boxed deliveries of organic fruit and veg, eating out more and having an ever-expanding range of dining choices, the delights of experiencing cuisine from around the globe while fretting about the provenance of everything from apple juice to poultry was not a luxury that all could afford. In 1998, as Tesco launched its upmarket Finest range of foods – luxury versions of popular dishes using 'superior' ingredients and what the company now refers to as 'artisanal' foods – the vast majority of the public were still buying and eating value ingredients and couldn't afford to eat out more than once a year. And for many, meals were primarily focused around getting value for money from a tin or a packet. It was a different picture from post-war Britain when, in the 1950s, the whole country was eating pretty much the same diet and the same foods were available to all, with the odd exception.

Simultaneously, growing concerns about the unhealthy nature of our national diet saw official agencies offer more and more information on what we should and shouldn't be eating. The UK had been leading the field in nutritional research since the late seventies, and since the eighties two official bodies – the Committee on Medical

Aspects of Food Policy and the National Advisory Committee on Nutritional Education (COMA and NACNE) – had published reports that were instrumental in raising awareness of the importance of diet in maintaining good health, concentrating in particular on the link between diet and cardiovascular disease. The media picked up on all of these and as a result we began to be (and remain) continuously bombarded with advice on what kinds of foods we should be eating to maintain health. As much of this information has been and still is inconsistent and incomplete from both expert and lay sources, confusion reigns.

In 1994 a COMA Report issued specific guidelines on what each adult should consume each day in order to protect against cardiovascular disease: six portions of fruit and vegetables (though 'Five a Day' was the number officially adopted in 2003), two of potatoes, pasta or rice, and four and a half slices of bread. A couple of years later, in 1996, an official publication called *Use Your Label* was the first in the UK to provide Guideline Daily Amounts (GDAs) for five key nutrients – fat, saturated fat, sodium, fibre and sugar – now commonly used in food labelling in an attempt to help consumers to make better food choices. Even then it was realized that reducing salt intake was not really about avoiding adding salt when cooking at home (which accounted for only about 20 per cent of what we consumed); changes in the amounts contained in processed foods were recognized as key. And in 1996 fat and saturated fat became the focus of government policy on diet and nutrition with targets for intake.

But the challenge of getting people to change eating habits to fit in with these guidelines was as hard twenty years ago as it is today. While the Delia effect continued, showing that plenty of people did enjoy cooking at home, there was still soaring demand for quick fast food, much of it high in the fat, salt and sugar that these reports identified as bad for our health, and during big sporting events such as the 1998 World Cup more and more of this food was being delivered straight to our door. In the wake of the BSE crisis, pizza was considered a fast and safe alternative to burgers, and as the World Cup approached pizza outlets capitalized on the potentially huge football market by casting footballer Gareth Southgate in adverts, clearly targeting a male audience. It was boom time for pizza, for both supermarket sales and home-delivery companies. World Cup fever sent Domino's pizza sales soaring by 100 per cent and in the year 1999 alone that chain's outlets rose from 175 to 201, with a turnover for the business of £63.5 million.

Naked and naughty – towards a new millennium

As we headed towards the twenty-first century, nothing would quite sum up how far we had moved on over ten years, let alone fifty, in our view of domestic duties than the cookery programme. From the prim and proper *MasterChef* at the outset of the decade to Jamie Oliver's *The Naked Chef* (BBC2) in 1999 and Nigella Lawson's *Nigella Bites* (Channel 4) a year later, we had progressed from middle-class house-wives and dinner-party menus aimed primarily at women on daytime television to food as mainstream, prime-time entertainment for the urban and young, taking visual inspiration from music videos and set in the presenter's home (or a representation of it) as they cooked for family and friends. Cooking was now shown as a lifestyle choice – relaxed and 'post-modern'; it came with laddish banter and a helping of sexuality on the side, and the programmes allowed men to take it up as an enjoyable masculine activity. Now, as traditional boundaries broke down, the two sexes embracing the domestic environment together could be seen as something pleasurable and altogether legitimate.

Jamie and Nigella established food as fun and cool – a group social activity but also a kind of sexy foreplay that set us up for the noughties, the decade when we would continue to gorge on cookery shows, from the re-booted *MasterChef* in its various incarnations through wall-to-wall

Jamie, all the way up to the cosy pleasures of *The Great British Bake Off* and Mary Berry's rise to the hallowed position of 'national treasure'. And yet we continue to cook less and less, and as the new century gathers speed there is an increasing acknowledgement of a tension between the idealized vision that Jamie and Nigella presented to us, with their achingly trendy gatherings relaxing over fashionable spreads of food, and the reality of what families are really facing at meal times. The problem of squeezed time will find both chefs embracing speed and convenience in the noughties. Food is now faster, cheaper and more or less nutritious and tasty, and we still tend to take the enormous choices we have for granted, but we also face burgeoning food-related problems – hidden salt and sugar in our food is contributing to the rise in obesity and diabetes, and the changes in the way we produce, buy and cook food over the last half century have affected every aspect of family life.

As we look towards the future, many of the food scares of the 1990s are seemingly behind us, but industrialized processing continues apace, as does the driving down of costs as we continue in our quest for the holy grail of cheap food. Despite sales of organic produce being on the rise again, we all fear what lies ahead in the way of horsemeat and other scandals yet to surface, such as campylobacter, and the ongoing battle to counter the amount of food we discard, let alone its packaging. Yet as food journalist Joanna Blythman would write in 2003, our wasteful food culture is more about the structure of working lives than it is about people trying to cook like Heston Blumenthal or Jamie Oliver. 'You're always being steered towards a processed-food choice,' she says. 'If you're the person who is still in the office at 6.30pm, and you start thinking, "What shall I eat tonight?" you'll most likely find yourself in the supermarket an hour later picking up some over-packaged food.'

As our family celebrates the millennium (and Ros's birthday – she was born in 1999) and the end of the *Back in Time for Dinner* experience, with Jamie recipes cooked by Brandon on that modern take on masculine caveman cooking, the gas barbecue, while Rochelle makes a Nigella chocolate cake drenched in cream, they will find they have come full circle as they head once more into recession in the new century, and once more the talk is of 'austerity' Britain.

CHAPTER 7

Britain's Got Talent: where we go from here

As our *Back in Time for Dinner* family, the Robshaws, party 'like it's 1999' to round off their journey across five decades of dining, we see the country facing the twenty-first century full of hope. But the vision of a bright future was soon tarnished. Foot and mouth disease, which struck Britain's cattle in 2001, once again brought distressing images of the countryside into our homes as great pyres of slaughtered animals were burned, and we saw the plight facing our beleaguered farming industry and felt the restrictions on our own visits to the countryside. That same year, the shocking events of 9/11 changed the world in a day. At home the chancellor, Gordon Brown, had promised us back in 1997 'no more boom and bust', but it was not to be. The financial crisis of 2007–8 drove many of us back into our homes and caused us to re-evaluate our priorities. By 2009 we were once more in deep recession, as the years of excess immediately following the millennium celebrations (which in many ways echoed those of the mid-1980s) came to an abrupt end and we began to pay the price for what many viewed as a decade of unsustainable growth and spending.

With the recession came rising food prices, while wages dropped or remained frozen year on year. Consumers began to budget far more carefully for their weekly shopping and to cut back on extras. Meanwhile the supermarkets themselves were struggling, with price wars, internet ordering, the move to automated checkouts, competition from discount stores and scares such as the horsemeat crisis of 2013. Loss of trust in big business has led to disillusionment with anonymous manufacturers – but are we prepared to turn away from them altogether and deal with the loss of convenience and cost savings that the giants offer us?

Eating habits themselves changed dramatically during the recession as people curbed their spending, making packed lunches to take to work and, as was the case in previous times of hardship, cutting back on eating out in restaurants. Our interest in food remained unabated, however, with cookery programmes continuing to dominate the television schedules. In stressful times we yearn for comfort, a return to the way we think our parents cooked and ate; this, combined with a re-emergence of the make-do-and-mend spirit, saw baking, sewing and gardening programmes become even more popular. This has combined with the nation's enthusiasm for reality shows to bring ordinary people into the world of television cooking and accounts for the enormous success of *The Great British Bake Off* (with its growing number of offspring – allotments, sewing, what next?). An astounding 13 million viewers tuned into the final of the programme in October 2014, while home cooks and celebrity novices are also eager to try their hands on the newly minted *MasterChef*.

We are also buying ever more books linked to television programmes: 117,911 copies of *Jamie's 15-Minute Meals* sold in just one week in the run-up to Christmas 2012. The internet abounds with recipes, both on websites and social media. We pore over them, we go on cookery courses and we regard cooking as a hobby. Yet despite all this, we are cooking less and less. The sandwich is now the most frequently eaten meal, with 6.4 million consumed each year, according to a 2014 survey into the eating and cooking habits of 4,000 British households. The same research reveals that, where in 1980 we spent an hour preparing the average meal (dropping to 45 minutes in 1990), now we spend half that time – a mere 34 minutes. Interestingly for a nation that has supposedly transformed itself into one of adventurous eaters, roasts are the most popular evening meal, followed by pizza, then sandwiches, and Indian food in fourth place. We are also ever more hooked on fast food and convenience. Obesity is on the rise and we seem to have no clear way to halt its progress.

New-century chefs

Blamed in part by doctors for adding to our waistlines with their high-calorie, high-fat cooking, Jamie and Nigella eased our journey into the new millennium, showing us how to embrace our inner domestic goddess, cook fast food faster (first in 30 minutes, then in 15 minutes – but you had to cook like Jamie to achieve that), budget better as the recession took hold, improve our school dinners and cook everything outside on the latest must-have toy for foodie chaps in this second decade of the century – the brick-built, domed, wood-burning oven. A study in 2012 found that, for both chefs, an average dish came in at 605 calories as opposed to an average supermarket meal at 405; both, though, would probably say that they never intended most of their meals to be eaten every day of the week.

As the millennium opens up, diversity is the hallmark of the food sensations we are enjoying. In the tussle for the crown of world's top chef, Britain's Heston Blumenthal competes with René Redzepi at Noma in Copenhagen, voted best restaurant in the world several years running, and the talented chefs following the trail blazed in Spain by elBulli founder Ferran Adrià, winner of three Michelin stars and best restaurant award a record five times up until its closure (with huge losses) in 2012. Here at home we've embraced the food and home-spun wisdom of Yotam Ottolenghi and Hugh Fearnley-Whittingstall, and now it seems we're looking further east for our cooking inspiration – Korean, Vietnamese and even Japanese–Peruvian fusion food (known as nikkei) are all set to take the stage in London as we head into 2015, while Wagamama and Hakkasan founder Alan Yau is due to launch the first 'Chinese gastropub', Duck & Rice, in Soho. Pig products rule as we embrace comfort food in the form of American-style 'pulled' pork, the ubiquitous pork belly and every flavour of Scotch egg, all with meat from happy pigs (taking inspiration from the master who first introduced us to 'nose to tail eating', the much-lauded Fergus Henderson of St John in Smithfield, which in 2014 celebrated its twentieth anniversary).

With this food we may well be sampling savoury cocktails based on healthy vegetable juices, such as a take on the traditional Bloody Mary, the Beetroot Mary. Or we might knock back a craft beer from the new stable of quirky small breweries, or a specialist gin from one of the small distillers, interest in which has exploded in the last decade – from the Scottish-distilled Hendricks, which makes the perfect summer cooler with ice and slices of cucumber, to a gin brewed in Portobello Road and named for the street. Another trend I welcome is the one favoured by Marcus Wareing in a review in 2014 – out go the stiff, formal service and tablecloths associated in the past with fine dining, to be replaced by waiting staff with an American approach to service, as warmth and friendliness triumph over formality. Hallelujah to that, say I.

And hurray for a woman chef, the talented Angela Hartnett, with her persuasive combination of down-to-earth Welsh savvy and Italian inspiration, both inherited from her mother's family. First at the Connaught Hotel and now at her Michelin-starred restaurant Murano in Mayfair, she has been at the forefront of a welcome move away from the macho posturing of male chefs early in the century. Also part of this trend is Clare Smyth at Restaurant Gordon Ramsay in Royal Hospital Road, Chelsea, who is still the only woman in the country to hold three coveted Michelin stars. There is still some way to go for women in professional kitchens – as chef, cookery writer and businesswoman Prue Leith said in 2014, because of the working hours, 'women with families will struggle to be top chefs unless men change their attitudes to childcare'.

Cupcakes and convenience

Since Carrie and Miranda paid a visit to New York's Magnolia bakery in a 2000 episode of many women's secret noughties pleasure *Sex in the City* (it has become steadily less secret), we have all gone cupcake crazy, and the sugar high provided by these supposedly innocuous creations is feeding our love affair with the sweet stuff. In 2012 the *Daily*

Telegraph ran a piece entitled 'Why cupcakes are the new cocaine'. It quoted restaurateur Henry Dimbleby, who runs the award-winning Leon chain of restaurants and believes, like a growing number of doctors, that 'Sugar is our number one eating problem – I think 40 per cent of the population has some sort of addiction to it.' And like the drug this is a hard habit to kick. By 2013 a Mintel report showed that small cakes had become 'the icing on the UK cake market' as sales of such items as cupcakes, cake bars and sweet muffins overtook large cakes, such as fruit cakes and Victoria sponges, for the first time. Krispy Kreme Doughnuts (or is that donut?) arrived here – also from the States – in 2003 to perform the same function of feeding our increasingly sweet tooth, opening their first store in Harrods and expanding into Selfridges and motorway service stations. With the Cookies and Kreme doughnut delivering 380 calories and 17g of fat, as well as being packed with sugar, it seems they fit the bill as the perfect modern comfort food. Doughnut domination is continuing as more branches open – the company expects to have over 100 stores by 2016. The more you buy the cheaper they are, with discounts for a whole box, therefore encouraging customers to buy more.

The consumer watchdog Neilsen in the US has identified another trend in recent years – what they call 'assembling'. As has been the case over the last half-century, people continue to want time-saving innovations, and what the manufacturers call 'home meal replacements' seem to be the latest solution. Popular on both sides of the Atlantic with shoppers who want to be involved with food preparation but also to have much of the work done for them, these come as a 'meal kit' – a pack of measured, part-prepared ingredients with cooking instructions, which allow the 'cook' to feel as though they are cooking from scratch but in less time and with the tricky preparation stages removed. Thus, with the help of ranges produced by the supermarkets and food companies such as Bigham's, we can serve an authentic Thai green curry or a Moroccan chicken tagine, as Charlie Bigham promises, 'from pan to plate in 15 minutes'. The market for these 'premium' ready meals is growing (beating the overall trend in ready meals) due to more of us deciding to eat better at home and cut back on eating out during the recession. The types of dishes growing fastest in popularity are the most recent arrivals on the ready-meal scene – where once we plumped for Italian, English or Indian, since 2007 sales of Thai meals have increased 8.8 per cent year on year, Moroccan 10.6 per cent and Mexican 13 per cent, according to market-intelligence company Euromonitor. Even more impressively, in its 2012 report on ethnic foods, forecasters Key Note predicted an astonishing 45.1 per cent growth by 2016 for the UK ethnic foods industry as a whole. As it is, we now eat more ready meals than the rest of Europe: the UK accounted for 42 per cent of all sales last year, way ahead of France with 21 per cent, Germany (20 per cent), Italy (9 per cent) and Spain (7 per cent).

Alongside convenience meals, the other trend that continues unabated is the Great British snacking habit. A 2013 Mintel report entitled *Kids Snacking* revealed that snacking is now ingrained among children, with 86 per cent of seven–fifteen-year-olds snacking at least once a day, while more than half, 52 per cent, snack 'constantly' or several times a day. Although, according to this report, fruit is the most commonly chosen food, at 72 per cent, crisps come in a close second for 70 per cent of the children surveyed, with chocolate at 58 per cent and sweet biscuits at 53 per cent. Fewer than half of the children questioned (46 per cent) said they ate snacks only when they felt hungry. And when it came to snack choices, most parents are guided by their children's preference in what they buy, rather than steering them towards healthy choices.

How we shop now

A recent piece of research in the US identified new trends for shoppers that are being replicated over here – it seems we are seeking value for money, healthy living, fresh food (in the form of freshly prepared food and 'meal solutions') and, interestingly, smaller grocery stores. And online options are a key part of this way of shopping. These trends come together to point the way forward – we more frequently buy our 'staple' food (jars, cans, packets and drinks – things that don't go off) online, but it seems that buying fresh food is such a sensory experience that retailers have now recognized that shopping will never move totally into the ether. We still want to see, smell and even taste the fresh food we are buying.

As a result, we are beginning to adopt a hybrid approach to our shop and will visit several stores for the right mix of price and quality. The one-stop shop with its vast range of choice is no longer the favoured way. Why trudge down soulless aisles and queue to pay – at an automatic till, so not even a friendly face to have a moan to – when we can get the goods delivered to our door (or office) any time of the day and, increasingly, late at night? Then we can enjoy choosing specialist items at the farmers' market or deli over the weekend, or do a top-up shop on the way home from work. Smaller local stores are better able to target what we need, so instead of a one-store-fits-all approach the pendulum is swinging the other way. Discounters such as Aldi and Lidl have fitted neatly into this trend – not as large as the vast superstore 'barns' we have seen springing up over the past decade or so (some remaining open 24 hours), they offer less choice but great value. And recently they have targeted the quality issue and are now offering middle Britain a range of award-winning food and drink at enticing prices to tempt consumers to do more of their shop with them. In 2014 Aldi announced plans to double the number of its stores in the UK to 1,000 by 2022, creating 35,000 new jobs.

Feeding the nation

Since 2007 food prices have risen by 12 per cent in real terms and now stand at the same level as in the late nineties relative to other goods, while median household incomes have fallen across the board since the economic downturn in the late noughties. With a fall in real wages, shoppers are searching out bargains and buying fewer but more carefully chosen premium products, while trying to cut down on waste by buying less but more often. But food-price increases levelled off as 2014 progressed, and with inflation falling, due in part to lower food and fuel prices, our economic recovery started to feel a little more grounded, though it seems likely there are still storms ahead.

As was the case in the post-war Britain of the 1950s, our farmers and small food producers have been working harder and harder, utilizing the latest technology and innovations in the effort to feed us while struggling with the demands of a globalized industry. Farmers also continue to face the challenges of bovine TB, new viruses such as Schmallenberg, which affects both cattle and sheep, and the flooding that occurred in the winter of 2013/14. In 2010 Britain was 58.9 per cent self-sufficient in food – the lowest level since 1968 (the country has needed to import in order to feed itself since the eighteenth century, which is when we were last fully self-sufficient). With a growing population, the need now is to produce more from less while simultaneously protecting the ever more fragile environment and also dealing with the pressure on land as the nation faces the ongoing need for housing to cater for a growing population.

The government's former chief scientific adviser John Beddington has called for a 70 per cent increase in British-grown food by 2050, and another thing in the farmers' favour is the current trend to buy British. In 2013 Sainsbury's customer research showed that 78 per cent of shoppers were buying British food where available, up from 55 per cent in 2007. In an interview for *Country Life*, National Farmers' Union president Meurig Raymond said, 'There's huge demand for food . . . food security is back on the government's agenda,' and Defra secretary Liz Truss has referred to farming as a 'sunrise industry'. And there will be competition for who gets to enjoy our farm goods in this global village – British lamb is finding a market in the Far East, especially Hong Kong, with exports up 43 per cent.

The war on waste

As endorsed by a 2014 Mintel report, we have all embraced recycling over the last fifteen years, though some more reluctantly than others. This has been down to a combination of EU targets putting huge downward pressure on the amount of waste sent to landfill and the increased focus on the environment in the media, and in schools, which has made us far more aware as individuals both of the nature of the challenges and of what we can do ourselves to help. Though we may complain as we sort waste to fill our many different bins and feed our compost heaps, according to official statistics in the first ten years of the decade we increased our recycling rates faster than any other country in Europe (though we did start from a low base of only 12 per cent of all municipal waste). By 2010 we were recycling 39 per cent, on a par with the EU overall, but since then the trend has stalled, just as the government has stepped back from measures to encourage us to continue the good work. In autumn 2014 the average Briton still throws away five times their bodyweight a year – a total of 22.6 million tons of household waste. And with EU targets for recycling set to reach 50 per cent in the next five years (and potentially 70 per cent by 2030) we need to try harder.

Women in the new millennium

Rochelle, Miranda and Ros have witnessed important stages in the development of modern feminism as they've journeyed through the decades, but today it seems we are still debating feminism just as actively as we were in the 1970s. Women's role in the home, the work–life balance, and the changing roles of both sexes are as fascinatingly complex as ever. As Brandon happily takes his place back in the kitchen, cooking for his family, what is going on both inside and outside the home for his wife and daughters?

In many ways it seems we still have a very long way to go to gain the equality that Germaine Greer acknowledged in the early seventies would take a long time. Back then did she think that by the end of the century men would still earn on average 30 per cent more than women? Or that, according to research carried out in 1999 by the Equal Opportunities Commission, many women would still be choosing to work part time to enable them to juggle the twin responsibilities of family and work? As recently as 2012 the Institute for Public Policy Research think tank revealed that eight out of ten married women still did more household chores than their husbands, while just one in ten married men took on an equal amount of cleaning and washing as his wife. Half of the women surveyed were doing thirteen hours' or more housework a week – way down on the seventy-five hours Rochelle might have spent in 1950 but, when done on top of full working days, still a chore. The answer, according to IPPR director Nick Pearce, is for men to take on greater responsibility for both childcare and running homes, which means they need more flexibility from their employers and decent parental leave.

But there has been progress, even as Jenni Murray, presenter of Radio 4's *Woman's Hour* (recently called an example of 'extreme feminism' by one male listener), admits that 'feminism – known in some quarters as the f-word – has become almost too shameful to admit'. In many ways the new view of feminism that has evolved in the twenty-first century is its best hope. The whole discussion got far too serious in the 1990s and needs a lightness of touch to engage young women today. Canadian blogger Grace Chapman recently wrote in a post called 'How (Not) to React to Anti-Feminist Women' that 'in order for feminism to be truly powerful it needs to be accessible and engaging, to everyone, and at the moment it's just not, not yet'. Her words seem borne out by the success of *How to Be a Woman* by columnist and author Caitlin Moran, whose witty and irreverent approach has struck a chord with many women (it was my daughters' favourite book of the last few years). And at last it seems that the place and role of women in everything from the home to politics and the media is being properly debated, and we are starting to see a range of women from all backgrounds step into positions of responsibility (though, sadly, with some startlingly obvious omissions: in 2014 the UK dropped to seventy-fourth out of 186 countries in a league table of female representation in parliament – below Sudan, China and Iraq).

And so to the future . . .

So it seems that, compared to fifty years ago, we cook less, we're no longer cooking from scratch, women are working much more outside the home but still not catching up with men when it comes to pay (the gender pay gap widened in 2013 for the first time in five years), we're getting fatter and our food is getting ever more expensive. But what about the future? We already worry about the impact of global warming and disappearing natural resources, most importantly water, on the way we live in this new millennium, and the pressure is on to produce more food to feed a rapidly expanding global population – it is estimated that by 2050 we will have to find 50 per cent more food than we do now, as the population grows to a projected 9 billion (in October 2014 it stands at around 7.16 billion). With increased demand and climate volatility putting resources under more and more pressure, plus the impact of disasters such as the 2014 Ebola crisis which has crippled domestic food production in West Africa, where two thirds of the population work in agriculture, food prices are going up. We're going to need to become even more efficient and inventive about how we produce what we eat.

How will these issues affect our everyday lives, and what are the big changes that will impact on how we're *all* going to be eating in twenty years' time? What sort of food will the Robshaws be sitting down to (and will it still be around a dinner table) by the time Brandon and Rochelle are grandparents themselves?

Big companies spend a fortune trying to work out how we will be living in the future so that they can tap into the latest trends to tempt us into opening our wallets. One market research firm (RTS Resource) identified five key food and drink trends in 2014 to watch out for in the future – they dubbed them 'natural highs, one-step convenience, foraged ingredients, flavour-full benefits and next-generation proteins'. When we rephrase these in plain language, they seem very familiar: healthier foods that make us feel good, such as porridge, which provides slow-release energy; convenience foods but, rather than straight ready meals, dishes with an element of self-preparation to absolve us from guilt; local seasonal ingredients (including at the extreme end of the spectrum the celeb chefs' current ingredient *du jour*, foraged items); more exciting flavours in familiar foods (exotic rice and seed mixes, flavoured couscous, etc.); and more enjoyable snacks that steer away from crisps and other carbohydrate-based products to fit with the move towards high-protein diets.

These trends are, in essence, a continuation of what we have already experienced on our *Back in Time for Dinner* journey, but as series historian Polly Russell points out, we are going to have to make big changes to the way we eat as it is simply not going to be possible to sustain the diet we have today. She emphasizes that this is not just a vague warning, but a real issue that Miranda, Ros and Fred are going to be facing in their lifetimes. The times they really are a changin', and in ways our sixties family, humming along to Dylan, would barely recognize.

In response, scientists are coming up with some rather extreme alternatives that may make those of us (such as me!) who follow the live-to-eat maxim decide to turn completely vegetarian – or even wonder whether to give up eating altogether (see below)! Some of the propositions seem like something out of a 1960s science-fiction movie – maybe we really are still 'Lost in Space'. Back in that science-obsessed decade we all thought that by the end of the century we'd be eating space food. That hasn't yet come to pass, but the reality should give us pause for thought. There is a newly coined term for those who predict the trends – 'food futurologists', and what they are foreseeing for our culinary future makes even Heston Blumenthal, with all his gastronomic chemistry, seem like something from a London gentleman's club in comparison.

One of the first things we are going to have to evaluate is the place taken by meat on our plates. And this is not a problem for the distant future. Meat is going to be more expensive, and soon. Some experts estimate that the price of meat will double in the next five to seven years. Our grandparents, living through the years of wartime and post-war food shortages, would certainly be at home with the idea of meat as a luxury, to be served for high days and holidays alone. In their day they turned to cheaper cuts and filled the hunger gap with left-overs, seasonal ingredients and basics such as potatoes and bread. As more and more countries in the developing world adopt Western diets (China's meat consumption has quadrupled since the 1970s), we will have to find ways to achieve the same.

Lab meat . . . or no meat?

In the 1950s meat was also scarce (Rochelle remembers with distaste the meagre slices of liver from which she had to feed the family in that decade), and scientists and technology responded to the problem by bringing us cheap meat – the supermarket-driven mass production that transformed the poultry industry saw chicken turn from a rare treat to an everyday family choice. Meat farming, however, is an incredibly inefficient use of resources and beef is the worst offender (chicken is far more economical to produce). But many of us do still love a burger, so how can we go about tackling this problem of supply? Once again the scientists are at the cutting edge of the search for more economical, humane and environmentally friendly ways for us to continue our love affair with meat.

One possible solution is meat created in a laboratory – welcome to 'the test-tube burger'! In 2013 a group of Dutch scientists managed to produce the world's first lab-grown burger. By extracting cells from a cow then turning them into strips of muscle, they created a patty, working to replicate the natural consistency of meat by achieving the correct composition of protein and fat tissue. Its inventors believe that making meat in a lab in this way is more sustainable and more efficient than raising whole animals. It is a convenience food; Professor Mark Post, who led the team working on it, calls it 'cultured beef'. But even

With growing demand for meat worldwide, our own meat-eating habits will have to change fast. Food scientists have plenty of ideas for alternatives.

he admits that the challenge to get his burger to taste and have the 'mouth feel' consumers will find acceptable is still some way off; at the moment what has been produced is a very bland imitation of the real thing. Still, he considers it 'a good start' and, given that Professor Post believes synthetic meat could reduce the environmental footprint of meat by up to 60 per cent, there is an enormous amount to gain from pursuing its development.

If we look back to the 1950s, the Robshaws on their *Back in Time for Dinner* journey were, like most families, eating mostly carcass meat – that's raw meat rather than processed – such as chops and liver, joints, and a whole chicken if lucky. These days the trend has moved away from whole joints and the consumption of essentially the entire animal, and the prevailing fashion now is for us to eat our meat pre-prepared in portions – chicken breasts, fillets and mince – or in a ready meal. As the scientists behind the technology argue, why grow the whole animal when many of us will eat only a small percentage of it? Lab meat could offer us a more efficient way to deliver the meat we want to consume. At the moment, it's not commercially viable – in 2014 a lab-grown burger would cost you a staggering £215,000 – but inventors are hoping to be in production within seven years and are aiming to account for as much as 25 per cent of the meat market by 2025.

Other scientists argue convincingly that the best way to achieve the same end is simply to eat less meat – an old-fashioned approach that would resonate with our grandparents' generation. Molecular biologist Dr David Steele, president of Earthsave Canada, believes that, although there are definite environmental and animal-welfare advantages for this new science, plant-based alternatives offer the same opportunities to protect the planet and, what's more, don't need to be pumped full of 'antibiotics and antifungal chemicals to stop the synthetic meat from rotting'. I must say I prefer the idea of a plate of lentils, noodles and seeds to what might be the ultimate processed food, so no lab burger for me.

American writer Michael Pollan, in his book *The Omnivore's Dilemma* on the eating challenges facing us in the twenty-first century, points out that 'we are not only what we eat, but how we eat, too', and he sees this dilemma as an opportunity to escape from the blandishments of the food scientists and the marketing industry, who 'exacerbate our anxieties about what to eat, the better then to assuage them with new products'. Pollan proposes that the best way to answer the modern challenge is to go back to the very beginning of the food chains that have sustained us throughout history. For millennia, communities and cultures have followed meatless diets for both economic and moral reasons, and large segments of the world's population have thrived on plant-based diets. A return to this model seems to be an eminently sensible alternative for a sustainable future. In comparison to diets rich in animal products, those based on plants are more sustainable because they use many fewer natural resources and are less taxing on the environment.

Crispy-fried crickets and the ultimate convenience

Remember the fear and suspicion with which garlic was once viewed by large sections of the British public? Well, now the squeamish among us are facing another challenge. If you don't want to turn vegetarian or eat a laboratory-produced substitute, a further option for meat replacement that is making headlines is one that will be familiar to fans of *I'm a Celebrity . . . Get Me Out Of Here!* with its stomach-churning 'bushtucker' trials. For a growing number of trend-watchers, insects are a very promising alternative to meat, but here in the West we do need to overcome the yuck factor. Many countries are already well ahead of us when it comes to this kind of eating, and over 2 billion people worldwide already snack on bugs. In Thailand, Cambodia, Nigeria and Mexico edible insects have always been much-loved snacks, whether it's a handful of crispy fried beetles served up in the street markets of Bangkok or garlic-infused caterpillars in Mexico City. Residents of these countries have been eating such dishes since childhood and see nothing strange about the practice. This is one trend we'd do well to adopt. Insects are not only a great source of protein, but raising them emits a tiny 1 per cent of the greenhouse gases that are released rearing cattle and uses 100 times less water. And, with more than 1,400 species of edible insect in the world, there's plenty of choice! The Dutch are so interested in this source of protein that their government has invested €1 million in developing insect farms. The United Nations, meanwhile, is committed to the idea following a report in 2013 and is encouraging the world not only to develop tasty insect-derived protein products, but also to make the case to consumers that eating insects is both good for their health and good for the planet.

Even if you can't stomach eating bugs themselves, there will be plenty of alternative uses for them in what we eat. Ground insect powder will be supplementing protein in foods like burgers, or you might want to try a sweet energy bar or tortilla chip made from cricket flour? These are the kinds of products that are going to challenge consumer aversion, and young people like Miranda, Ros and Fred are exactly the sort of customers manufacturers will be targeting. So we'd better be prepared to be more adventurous! And it's not only us who will be eating more insects. They will also replace the increasingly expensive protein ingredients in feeds for the livestock, poultry and aquaculture industries, releasing the grain they currently use so that it can be channelled towards feeding humans.

If insects are a step too far, the scientists engaged in developing dietary alternatives have other answers up their sleeves. One man at the forefront of this new world is American Rob Rhinehart, who believes he has seen the future of food – and it's a powder called Soylent. It may sound like a design for a super-yacht, but it is no such thing. Visit the eponymous website and it promises what for some sounds like a utopia: 'What if you never had to worry about food again?' Soylent is a food replacement that, according to the benefits promised on the web page, is quick, cheap and balanced.

In a blog entry in 2013, Rob admitted that, as a poverty-stricken software engineer, he resented the 'time, money, and effort the purchase, preparation, consumption, and clean-up of food was consuming'. And so he decided to embark on an experiment: to create the perfect food alternative in the form of a drink that would provide all the elements the body needs for energy. He continued: 'The first morning my kitchen looked more like a chemistry lab than a cookery place, but I eventually ended up with an thick, odorless, beige liquid. I call it "Soylent". At the time I didn't know if it was going to kill me or give me superpowers. I held my nose and tentatively lifted it to my mouth, expecting an awful taste.'

The liquid, which contained all of the thirty-five nutrients human beings need for survival, was, according to its inventor, 'delicious', and

he continued to replace all his regular meals with it for the next thirty days. Dried peas, flaxseed, brown rice flour, olive and sunflower oils, sulphur powder, malodextrin, salt and assorted vitamins go into the recipe to create a drink with around 2,000 calories, the recommended daily amount for an adult. It could be called the ultimate convenience food. Rhinehart now lives predominantly on the formula and says

It's back to the lab as inventive individuals create different solutions to feeding the world. All your meals in a glass, anyone?

it has actually improved his health – he's lost weight, has more energy and generally feels great since changing his diet to Soylent. And the powder has come on in leaps and bounds in the eighteen months since it was first whizzed up in a domestic kitchen. The first mass-produced batch went on sale in May 2014, and fans can now buy a week's worth of the powder – twenty-one-plus meals – for $85 from a purpose-built website. Rhinehart says people can live on it exclusively, but the real question is, would anyone want to? Let's hope not, though in many ways Soylent does seem the logical end to the journey we've been following from the 1950s towards the ultimate convenience food. As a fast alternative to fatty, over-processed, sugared and salted convenience foods, it seems a more sensible choice for those with no time to cook, while its powder format could have benefits for feeding people in areas hit by disasters such as flooding or famine. And faced with insects or bacteria as a replacement for that juicy steak, maybe powder doesn't seem such a big leap after all!

For the Robshaws it raises all kinds of questions. As Rochelle points out, it's just another meal that the family won't eat together, while in Brandon's view it may be nutritionally balanced but it's also completely processed. Is that where food is leading us – further away from a natural process that has sustained us as humans from the earliest stages of our existence?

The obesity crisis

As well as the world crisis of dwindling resources, there is another concern that calls for far-reaching changes to the food we eat. We've been tracking the steadily growing obesity crisis in the country since the Robshaws set out on their *Back in Time for Dinner* journey in 1950, a time when the state was in control of what we ate to an extent that had not existed before nor has done since. Research in 2012 revealed that since the start of the *Back in Time for Dinner* experiment in 1950

British people have gained an average three stone (19kg) in weight. Now it has been revealed that a report in 2007 that estimated that half the UK population will be obese by 2050 (which was itself a shocking figure) actually *under*estimated the problem. So do we once again need the government to step in and take control of our diets?

Obesity-related conditions, which are rocketing to new highs, are costing the NHS £5 billion a year. And by far its largest expenditure is on Type 2 diabetes, a disease that is almost always associated with obesity. The rising costs are bringing the health service to its knees, and if current trends continue could go on to cost the country £50 billion a year by 2050. With the challenges of an ageing population running parallel, we just can't afford these kinds of sums.

The director of health and well-being at Public Health England (PHE), Professor Kevin Fenton, has said that obesity is an international problem that requires action at 'national, local, family and individual level'. Another expert, Professor David Haslam, has called for government leadership and the need to ensure responsible food and drink manufacturing and retailing, alongside earlier intervention and support to enable the public to help themselves. He compares the crisis to that caused by smoking and thinks we need similar hard-hitting campaigns to tackle the issue. 'Brands that make sugary and fatty foods are in danger of becoming the new tobacco companies,' warns Richard Cope, senior trends consultant at market research company Mintel. 'Recommendations from scientists, nutritionists and governments are not going away,' he says. 'The smart brands realise that "fat taxes" are effectively coming.' For the Robshaws and the rest of us, a dinner out in future might well be one where unhealthy food is taxed by the government.

So what do we do? Health experts and academics from a campaign group called 'Action on Sugar' have a series of suggestions. They want levels of sugar in everyday products to be reduced dramatically; they also say that companies should be forced to stop advertising sugary drinks and snacks to children (they claim sugar has become 'the alcohol of childhood'); and they are calling on the government to impose fines on manufacturers who do not meet set reduction targets, and/or to impose a tax on sugar. The idea is that the money raised from fines and/or taxes will go towards the mounting obesity health bill. England's chief medical officer has also said such measures might be necessary. They are already being implemented in other parts of Europe: France, Finland, Denmark, Ireland and Romania have all either introduced food taxes or are talking about doing so. Hungary, which has one of the lowest life-expectancy rates in the EU, has introduced taxes on sugar, salt and fatty foods; the Hungarian prime minister has said that 'those who live unhealthily have to contribute more'. In 2011 Denmark too introduced a tax on saturated fats (sending the price of butter up by 30 per cent). But taxing food is a complicated strategy for changing eating habits – critics argue that it penalizes the poorest in society, who cannot afford healthier options, and may not affect the really overweight, who may well choose simply to increase what they spend on their food fix. It has also proved hard to implement: within a year, Denmark – under pressure from both the food industry and a population that simply crossed the border into Germany for its fat hit – had to backtrack and give up the tax. But health experts still believe that even a failed attempt like this is an important step on the road to altering unhealthy eating patterns.

Rochelle remembers that in the 1950s, cooking meals from strictly rationed ingredients, she hated serving the family with food no one liked or wanted to eat. She remembers looking in the larder and feeling anxious, worried that there was not enough food to sustain her active, growing children. But we know now that the period of rationing saw the British population at its fittest and most well-nourished. The government-controlled diet of the time was bland, boring and immensely unpopular, however. Most people who lived through the days of rationing are unlikely to recall them with any kind of fondness; food was most definitely there for fuel rather than pleasure. Would we want to go back to those kinds of restrictions now in order to be healthier? After experiencing the restrictions of the 1950s and comparing them with the freedom her family has to snack and graze outside her control half a century on, is Rochelle longing for a bit of back-up from the state to help keep them on the nutritional straight and narrow?

With its proven inventiveness, surely the food industry should be able to rise to the challenge facing us? A major problem is the fact that our ingenious and resourceful food producers have built their huge success – and huge profits – on 'added value' products. We pay for someone else to do the work for us: ready-made pots of hummus, quick pasta sauces, chilled meals that require just a little bit of prep from us to make us feel less guilty, stir-fry veg packs, etc., all cost more, use more packaging and keep us at a distance from the basic ingredients. Are we ready to step away from all this, to spend more time in the kitchen making things from scratch and so regain control of what we are eating? We wouldn't be happy to give up our washing machines, dishwashers, fridges or food processors, all of which offer time-saving and convenience, encourage a more sedentary life and stop us being as active as our grandparents – and nor does anyone seem to be suggesting that we should do so. So what makes benefiting from technological advances when it comes to food and cooking any different?

Smart kitchens and digital dining

Back in 1950, much of the technology that we now take for granted simply didn't exist. Modern mum Rochelle struggled with her back-to-basics kitchen, finding the domestic chores hard and monotonous. As sole 'cook and bottle-washer', she struggled with the tedium and repetitive nature of caring for her family and getting meals on to the table. As the decades whizzed by, technology transformed Rochelle's kitchen with a raft of labour-saving devices, beginning with the fridge that appeared in the 1960s to elevate food shopping to a different level and open up a new world of possibilities for both ingredients and meal styles. By 1981, with 55 per cent of women in work, for cash-rich and time-poor working mums the microwave was promoted as the ultimate time-saver; and finally in 1990, after four decades at the kitchen sink, the Robshaws got a dishwasher to help take the sting out of household chores. In the next twenty-five years they may be turning to a robot for help with the housework!

So what are the challenges that the next generation of appliances will be trying to solve? They are likely to deal with the foremost issues taxing the modern world – from use of precious resources (energy, water) to improving our health, and of course buying us that elusive commodity, time. The advances of the last fifty years would have been unthinkable for our predecessors, but we face a similar leap of belief over the next half-century. With companies such as Panasonic and Samsung vying to kit out our twenty-first-century kitchen, we will increasingly find smart technology migrating across from the rest of the home into our cooking and eating space. Everything will be controllable through our tablets and smartphones – you'll be able to chat to your smart fridge while you're in the supermarket to check if you've run out of eggs; then, if you are too busy, the fridge will talk to your oven to let it know you are on the way home so it can heat up all ready to cook when you walk in the door with your ready meal; and the cooker hob will allow you to read a recipe on its touchscreen as your stir-fry cooks alongside – and will let you tweet the developing recipe as you cook with a swipe of your finger. Precious water will be recycled around the house – reused from the dishwasher to water vegetables growing in a cultivator. And the new waterless washing machine that runs on dry ice, as envisaged by Electrolux, will leap into action in the same connected way, along with your lighting, door locks and CCTV.

Technology will also help us grow more of our own food, but to do so we won't need to head down to the allotment as Brandon and Fred did back in the 1950s. In the future we will be growing our own protein in the form of insects, such as grasshoppers, in a specially designed grower in the corner of the kitchen, while Philips have come up with a hive that fits into a glass window, allowing you to watch your bees as they come and go. Eating healthily should get easier too. 3D food printers are already able to print sweets and chocolate, but with help from NASA, currently researching the technology to provide food for its astronauts, it appears that at some time in the future we will be able to print an entire menu to our own specification. And kitchen scales will allow us to measure everything from nutritional content to level of toxins and even how fresh our food is.

Eating outside the home will also be transformed through the possibilities offered by new connectivity. Brandon might like to take Rochelle out for a specially designed menu to celebrate an anniversary, and might even invent a custom-made drink for the occasion. At Logbar in Tokyo's busy Shibuya district, customers are issued with iPad Minis as they arrive at the venue. The menu is all there on the tablet, and if you are a returning customer it will remind you of what you had last time; it also allows you to communicate with other drinkers and view, 'like' and order what they're drinking. You can invent your own cocktail and add it to the menu, earning a 50 yen (about 30p) commission when someone else orders one.

New technology has another trick up its sleeve for eating outside the home – one that will give us confidence about what we are eating and where it has come from. No matter how carefully we source the food we prepare in our own kitchens, it's much more difficult to check the provenance and origin of the food we choose when on the move. Sushi is a good example of a style of eating that relies on the finest, freshest ingredients, but seafood mislabelling is such a problem that a report from conservation group Oceana released in 2013 revealed a shocking 33 per cent of seafood fraud – one type of fish being passed off as another, potentially more harmful for the person eating it or the environment, such as farmed fish being passed off as wild – in restaurants and retail outlets in southern California, 48 per cent in Boston and 39 per cent in New York. They used DNA testing in twenty-one states and found that, with a third of all the fish they sampled mislabelled, it's a countrywide problem that is stopping customers from choosing fish that is both good for them and the environment. Harney Sushi, a restaurant in San Diego, has attempted to tackle the problem by devising edible rice paper QR codes (a type of barcode read by your smartphone). Using their phones, diners can scan the code which sits on top of slices of albacore tuna and call up detailed information about the provenance and global stocks of the fish they've ordered. A Spanish company has come up with another solution to checking up on the provenance of our foods – and one which will be welcome to those fed up with removing those little sticky labels from their fruit. Fruit tattoos etch a message or design on to the skin directly and will contain logos or information on place of origin, also saving on the cost and environmental impact of the current paper-and-glue system.

Little, often and local

In the early 1950s Rochelle's shopping trip to feed the family was a daily exercise in logistics and communication as, with no fridge, car or out-of-town superstore, she visited the range of small specialist shops on her local high street. In the period since then the supermarket has increasingly come to her rescue, offering ever more convenience, choice and quality all in one destination. Though we may demonize them for the control we see them exerting over our lives, the supermarkets have driven a level of consumer choice from which we've all benefited while at the same time hugely broadening our culinary horizons. But by 2014 the big four – Tesco, Sainsbury, Asda and Morrisons – are facing troubled times. Mark Price, MD of Waitrose, has accused them of living in the past, running supermarkets that are twenty years out of date. He sees the next few years as a 'once in a 50-to 60-year change' for the way we shop. Traditional supermarkets are likely to see food-shopping trends shift as more and more consumers buy their food on the move (continuing the pattern that saw sales of portable breakfast products rise by 10 per cent in 2013 alone) or drop into a convenience store on the way home from work to shop for the evening ahead. Middle-class foodies like to imagine a world where we will return to the high street, patronizing local fishmongers, bakers and greengrocers, but the reality is that we are more likely to continue our new habit of shopping in convenience stores owned and run by the big supermarkets – one in four people now visits a store such as Tesco Express or Sainsbury's Local at least once a day. As Mark Price points out, it is lifestyle changes resulting from the financial crisis paired with advances in technology that are driving development, rather than pressure from the discounters. Waitrose's annual *Food and Drink Report* in October 2014 reveals the impetus for change – the 'little and often' approach helps shoppers keep to budgets and manage the big issue of food waste. The desire to tackle the latter (for both environmental and financial reasons) has led to a decrease in food waste of 21 per cent over the last seven years, while another piece of research shows that three out of four people don't know what they will be eating for their evening meal at 4pm on the same day. Everything suggests that these trends will continue.

In many ways we seem to be coming full circle in the way we shop, back to where the Robshaws started out sixty years ago, but with all the benefits of more flexible shopping opportunities, technology, additional services, food-to-go, global cuisine and a far more sophisticated choice of food styles on offer. Choice and flexibility are what we will be looking for as the century rolls on. Online ordering is expected to double in volume by 2018 (but will still make up only around 5 per cent of the UK grocery market). And once again the ageing population will be a big factor in how our high streets not only look but also how we use them. Over the next ten years two thirds of all retail spending growth will come from those aged fifty-five and over; these older shoppers are less inclined, and may also be less able, to travel to do their shop. But at the same time the baby boomers have no intention of retiring quietly to a life of golf and knitting. While their needs may differ from those of younger consumers in some respects, they are just as likely to be using technology in similar ways, particularly as new technologies and mobile devices become more user-friendly and intuitive. Retailers will respond accordingly and we should see high streets evolve to reflect these changes, incorporating services and local amenities such as libraries and GP surgeries previously set on the edges of the main thoroughfare. Over the next ten years or so Rochelle may well find herself walking to her appointments and to do her shopping, just as she did back at the start of the *Back in Time for Dinner* experience in the 1950s.

Our food-to-go future

In post-war 1947 (just three years before the *Back in Time for Dinner* experiment's start date), when Gallup invited a cross-section of the British population to pick their 'perfect meal' (money no object), a glass of sherry, tomato soup and roast chicken were the conventional choices, with a trifle and cheese and biscuits to round off the meal. At that time, for most of the public eating out was confined mainly to canteens and school dining rooms. During our journey through the decades one of the biggest trends we have witnessed has been the constantly growing proliferation of food available outside the home, which has contributed enormously to the rise and rise of the snacking culture. By 2015 we are constantly grazing, and we eat everywhere – on the street, at our desks, on the bus. And inside the home we no longer sit down at the dinner table together for our three meals a day but, like the busy Robshaws, every member of the family might be eating at a different time and in a different place in or outside the house on every day of the week. The modern, informal nature of eating, with its diversity of time and place, plays straight to our wish for even more convenience products that are constantly on tap, and at the same time makes it even harder to keep track of how much we are eating. Apparently the worst offenders in the obesity epidemic are the foods that never get near a plate, the items such as sandwiches, burgers or snacks that we consume when we are eating on the go.

The frequency of eating out is only set to increase overall for every meal of the day, with corresponding challenges and opportunities to address the health of our nation. *The Taste of the Future* report by Allegra Strategies for the UK food and beverage industry in 2013 estimated that by 2020 consumers will be eating outside the home daily. It is Brandon and Rochelle who are the members of the family most likely to be leading this trend, as the country's ageing population changes the profile of diners. These high-spending consumers are recognized as a vital source of income for the industry, and as older consumers are likely to be educated and knowledgeable about food (after years of reading cookery books, watching food programmes on television and with a wealth of easily accessible information on the internet), they will expect and demand the highest standards of quality, service and also value for money. An appreciation of value, which took hold during the economic downturn, is now recognized as an established consumer trend. The 110 executives and consultants questioned for the report believe consumer expectation will lead to an overall rise in standards. And with a projected skills shortage in the food-service sector, maybe their children are the ones who will be cooking for, or serving, them!

What will our food-to-go be as the century evolves? Mintel sees the key areas of demand and growth as continuations of the trends we have seen already – healthy food that is both convenient and good value. Consumers will want to achieve a range of these perceived benefits in a single product, rather than having a single reason to buy something. For example, they will concentrate more on healthier versions of popular products, such as nutritionally balanced pizzas, rather than diet foods. New convenience foods – dubbed 'gourmet convenience' – will be required not only to taste good and deliver restaurant quality, but also to be nutritionally balanced. This desire for healthier eating is seen as the most important consumer trend in the long term, as people begin to take a more holistic approach to their health. This will feed into a demand for healthier global cuisines, and by 2020 we may well be looking to South East Asia and Latin America for new tastes and flavours. Fusion food, global and nordic trends are seen as the most likely to take over from Indian, Chinese and Italian dishes we enjoy now. Bold flavours and intense combinations will help bring dishes alive as manufacturers use less salt, sugar and saturated fats in their products. And we will be eating these dishes on the go – speed is the common denominator, and fast food ('healthy junk food') that takes inspiration from street food, along with pop-up restaurants, is expected to be the winning business model in the next three–five years in terms of growth, as retailers such as Leon, Chipotle and Pod offer healthier alternatives to the burger and pizza.

What about that other threat to public health that has also become part of our fast society – alcohol? The Robshaw children may well find a friend tapping them on the shoulder as they enjoy a post-work glass of wine in a bar. Alcohol-aware ice cubes in your drink will flash from green through amber and red as you drink more and go beyond the safe limit; and if you continue, a text will wing its way to a close friend via your smartphone to warn them that you have gone too far!

Changes and constants – the journey ends

So where have we ended up after this journey through half a century of family dining? Women have broken out of the drudgery of the 1950s kitchen, broadened their horizons and taken on the world of work and increasing equality with brio. The role of men in the family has changed as well. At the start of the exercise Brandon was excluded from the kitchen as effectively as Rochelle was tied to it. The strongly held belief that cooking and caring are essentially female occupations meant that social pressure kept men away from such roles, and that social pressure came mainly from other men. Change has come gradually, until now in many more families men and women are both responsible for feeding the family.

But freedom and equality has come at a cost. Even though we no longer buy into the 1980s dream of having it all, time-pressed families have been wooed by convenience, and the impact not only on the planet but also on our health, both mental and physical, seems to be part of the price we pay. With both partners under pressure of time, the food industry is keen to fill the gap and offer quick fixes. Outside and in the home, Rochelle and Brandon have less control over what their family is eating. They are not there, and the technology is now so easy that the kids can prepare food themselves. Brandon has pointed out that both he and Rochelle have full-time jobs – but she is the one who feels guilty about what the kids are eating. So it seems that mothers still worry about what their families eat and feel the pressure to create family life around the dining table.

But change is an ongoing affair and there are always two sides to every story. Would the Robshaws choose to go back to 1950s Britain and give up the world of the new millennium with all it has to offer – more freedom, technology, better health, longer lives? We take so much for granted in the twenty-first century. The *Back in Time for Dinner* experience has reminded us of that.

'Chips with everything' – the British way of eating has enabled us to absorb and assimilate all kinds of influences whilst just about managing to hold on to our own traditions.

Sources

Chapter 1

page 13 *Smell is extremely linked to our memories* . . .: Rachel Herz, http://www.npr.org/2010/11/26/131608865/remembering-the-scent-of-a-meal

page 18 *despite all the changes in lifestyle and increase in convenience* . . .: A. I. A. Costa, 'Conceptualization and Measurement of Personal Norms Regarding Meal Preparation', *International Consumer Studies*, 37, 2013, pp. 596–604

page 19 *to constitute one of the most important public health problems of our time* . . .: J. C. Waterlow, *Research on Obesity*, report of the DHSS/MRC Group, 1976

page 19 *the rapid rise in the prevalence of childhood obesity across the country* . . .: R. Foster and J. Lunn, 'Food Availability and Our Changing Diet', British Nutrition Foundation, *Nutrition Bulletin*, 32, 2007, pp. 187–249

page 21 *bread . . . was rationed for the first time* . . .: John Burnett, *Plenty and Want*, Scolar Press, 1979, p. 337

Chapter 2

page 25 *threadbare, bombed-out, financially and morally exhausted* . . .: Dominic Sandbrook, National Archives; http://www.nationalarchives.gov.uk/education/resources/fifties-britain/

page 26 *German air raids had damaged* . . .: Andrew Marr, *A History of Modern Britain*, Macmillan, 2007, p. 73

page 26 *From 1945 to 1951, 89 per cent of the 1.01 million houses built* . . .: Sophie Leighton, *The 1950s Home*, Shire Library, 2009, p. 9

page 26 *By 1999 owner occupation had increased . . .*: http://www.parliament. uk/documents/commons/lib/research/rp99/rp99-111.pdf

page 27 *These houses needed modernization . . .*: ibid., p. 16

page 28 *Many of the new builds also came with central heating . . .* : ibid., p. 26

page 28 *Notes from a 1950 parish meeting . . .*: http://www.greatbaddowparish council.co.uk/Parish%20Annual%20Assemblies%201950s.pdf

page 29 *At first only single women . . .*: http://www.bbc.co.uk/history/british/ britain_wwtwo/women_at_war_01.shtml

page 29 *However, most would be married . . .*: Geoffrey C. Warren, *The Foods We Eat*, Cassell, 1958, p. 64

page 29 *rather it was those who didn't embrace . . .*: Stephanie Spender, *Gender, Work and Education in Britain in the 1950s*, Palgrave Macmillan, 2005

page 29 *In the early 1950s many employers operated . . .*: Striking Women/ Women and Work, http://www.striking-women.org/module/women-and-work/post-world-war-ii-1946-1970

page 30 *figure had increased . . .*: Dora L. Costa, 'From Mill Town to Board Room: The Rise of Women's Paid Labor', *Journal of Economic Perspectives*, 2000, Vol. 14 (4 Fall), pp. 101–22

page 30 *Women of all classes joyfully . . .*: Nicola Humble, *Culinary Pleasures: Cookbooks and the Transformation of British Food*, Faber, 2005, p. 138

page 31 *Is it very much quicker than getting on with the job in the sink? . . .*: 'Domestic Diary', *Home & Country*, Women's Institute magazine, April 1954, p. 141

page 33 *Wars end tidily in history books . . .*: Susan Cooper, 'Snoek Piquante', in *Age of Austerity 1945–51* (ed. Michael Sissons and Philip French), Hodder & Stoughton, 1963, p. 44

page 33 Woman *magazine sold 2.25 million copies . . .*: Christina Hardyment, *Slice of Life: The British Way of Eating since 1945*, BBC Books, 1995, p. 53

page 34 *At the start of the decade, 70 per cent of men . . .*: Warren, *The Foods We Eat*, p. 63

page 34 *But the whole family would gather for tea . . .*: ibid., p. 116

page 35 *a look round the garden and a glass of sherry . . .*: ibid., p. 117

page 36 *But it was nutritionally better . . .*: http://hansard.millbanksystems. com/lords/1945/may/02/national-loaf

page 37 *the right kind of diet could even reduce juvenile delinquency . . .*: Doris Grant, *Dear Housewives*, Faber, 1955, p. 17

page 37 *Average consumption of fat and calories fell . . .*: Burnett, *Plenty and*

Want, p. 337

page 37 *Even when shortages had been at their most severe . . .*: Warren, *The Foods We Eat*, p. 2

page 37 *The average British family of the time . . .*: Andrew Alexander et al., 'The Co-creation of a Retail Innovation: Shoppers and the Early Supermarket in Britain', School of Management, University of Surrey, 2009, p. 11; http://epubs.surrey.ac.uk/7309/140/Alexander%20et%20al%20The%20Co-creation%20of%20a%20Retail%20Innovation.pdf

page 37 *each meal should provide at least 1,000 calories . . .*: Burnett, *Plenty and Want*, p. 353

page 38 *reaching 70 per cent of all children . . .*: John Burnett, *England Eats Out*, Longman, 2004, p. 260

page 40 *most stupendous event in British broadcasting . . .*: *Good Housekeeping: The Best of the 1950s*, Collins and Brown, 2008, p. 60

page 40 *eighty-two applications for people to roast oxen . . .*: www.royal.gov.uk

page 41 *Poulet Reine Elizabeth . . .*: full menu given in Constance Fry and Rosemary Hume, *The Constance Fry Cookery Book*, Dent, 1956, p. 1,030

page 42 *County Fare . . .*: Women's Institute booklet, 1954

page 42 *doubling the tonnage of potatoes grown . . .*: J. K. Bowers, 'British Agricultural Policy Since the Second World War', *Agricultural History Review*, xxxiii, 1985, pp. 71–2

page 42 *a stable and efficient agricultural industry . . .*: Agriculture Act 1947

page 43 *and the feeling of freedom . . .*: *History of the National Parks*, www.nationalparks.gov.uk

page 45 *exempted 2.5 million people . . .*: Pathé News, Budget Day, 1955

page 46 *It was for Gibbs SR toothpaste . . .*: http://news.bbc.co.uk/onthisday/hi/dates/stories/september/22/newsid_3131000/3131477.stm

page 46 *TV advertisements would become as famous . . .*: http://www.turnipnet.com/whirligig/tv/adverts/commercials.htm

page 48 *A History of the UK in 1000 Objects . . .*: History Association, www.history.org.uk/ resources/public_resource_4432_144

page 50 *By the 1950s the growing popularity of liquidizers ...*: Marguerite Patten, *Post-War Kitchen*, Hamlyn, 1998, p. 64

page 50 *In 1947 she took part in a new programme . . .*: Hazel Castell and Kathleen Griffin, *Out of the Frying Pan*, BBC Books, 1993, p. 12

page 52 *You know the contempt for garlic in this country . . .*: Peter Pirbright, *Off the Beeton Track*, Binnacle Books, 1946; quoted in Humble, *Culinary*

Pleasures, p. 118

page 54 *a symbol of security* . . .: Warren, *The Foods We Eat*, pp. 66–8

page 54 *Nearly two thirds of adults drank a cuppa* . . .: ibid., p. 75

page 56 *A feature from 1957 offers ideas* . . .: Rachel Ryan, 'Cooking with Offal', *Home & Country*, Women's Institute magazine, November 1957, p. 359

page 57 *by 1959 one in three married women was in employment* . . .: John Burnett, *England Eats Out*, p. 267

Chapter 3

page 63 *The Parker Morris report of 1961* . . .: Paul Evans, *The 1960s Home*, Shire Library, 2010, p. 8

page 66 *In 1956 Hotpoint had carried out market research* . . .: Huw Benyon et al., 'The Rise and Transformation of the UK Domestic Appliances Industry', University of Cardiff School of Social Sciences, 2003; www. cf.ac.uk/socsi/resources/wrkgpaper42.pdf

page 66 *By 1960 a quarter of British households had a fridge* . . .: www.retrowow. co.uk/social_history/britain_since_1948.php

page 66 *material goods now thought necessary* . . .: J. Goldthorpe et al., *The Affluent Worker in the Class Structure*, Cambridge University Press, 1969; cited in Benyon et al.

page 67 '*in 1958 most people drank six cups a day* . . .': Warren, *The Foods We Eat*, p. 9

page 68 *In 1959 only around a quarter of adults ate cereal* . . .: ibid., p. 20

page 70 *The Chorleywood process uses lower-protein wheats* . . .: www.talk healthpartnership.com/blog/2012/01/british-nutrition-foundation-confirms-there-is-no-evidence-that-sliced-bread-bloats-us/

page 70 *But even with this increase in ownership* . . .: Alexander et al., 'The Co-creation of a Retail Innovation', p. 11; http://epubs.surrey. ac.uk/7309/140/Alexander%20et%20al%20The%20Co-creation%20 of%20a%20Retail%20Innovation.pdf

page 71 'Jimi Hendrix heard the place mentioned so often . . .': 'M1 motorway and Watford Gap celebrate 50 years', *Daily Mail*, 2 November 2009

page 72 *Newport Pagnell service area began operations* . . .: Joe Moran, *On Roads*, Profile Books, 2009, p. 127

page 74 *Newport Pagnell had applied to the local council for a licence* . . .: ibid.; and motorwayservicesonline.co.uk/File:Postcard NP.jpg postcard of

Newport Pagnell in 1961

page 74 *more widespread provision of works canteens* . . .: Burnett, *Plenty and Want*, p. 352

page 75 *At the same time we started to visit the new 'supermarket' stores* . . .: Alexander et al., 'The Co-creation of a Retail Innovation', p. 12; http://epubs.surrey.ac.uk/7309/140/Alexander%20et%20al%20The%20Co-creation%20of%20a%20Retail%20Innovation.pdf

page 75 *Another nail in the coffin of the local store* . . .: Marr, *History of Modern Britain*, p. 320

page 76 *Vesta curries and chow mein* . . .: http://archive.museumoflondon.org.uk/SainsburyArchive/Themes/Products/Range/prodcon.htm

page 76 *Heinz tinned ravioli and spaghetti hoops* . . .: www.hatads.org.uk/catalogue/corporate-marketing/43/H-J-Heinz--Co-Ltd

page 77 *Pre-war, the average chicken flock was made up of only around 400 birds* . . .: www.henley.reading.ac.uk/web/FILES/management/050.pdf

page 81 *And before the final Geoff Hurst* . . .: Geoff Hurst, 'Set for a final fling', *Daily Telegraph*, 22 November 2003

page 81 *All except two national teams followed a controlled diet* . . .: http://www.fifa.com/mm/document/afdeveloping/technicaldevp/50/09/71/wc_66_tr_314.pdf

page 81 *New sweets such as Toffee Crisp* . . .: http://asenseofplaceblog.wordpress.com/2013/01/30/sweets-in-the-1960s-or-where-did-all-those-fillings-come-from/

page 81 *Smith's countered with Salt and Vinegar* . . .: http://joemoransblog.blogspot.co.uk/2011/01/crisp-at-crossroads.html

page 87 *A growing number of people were also starting* . . .: Burnett, *Plenty and Want*, p. 351

page 88 *A 1960s survey entitled* The British Eating Out . . . : Burnett, *England Eats Out*, p. 282

page 89 *whether it be the Mocambo in Knightsbridge* . . .: www.classiccafes.co.uk/Tour_central.html

page 89 *happy to while away an hour or two in a convivial place* . . . : Burnett, *England Eats Out*, p. 268

page 89 *La Terrazza in Romilly Street, Soho, opened in 1959* . . .: obituary, *Daily Telegraph*, 27 June 2011

page 90 *Another Italian, Alvaro Maccioni* . . .: obituary, *Daily Telegraph*, 29 November 2013 page 91 *a kind of 'internal tourism'* . . .: Pierre van den Berghe, *The Ethnic Phenomenon*, Greenwood Publishing, 1987

page 91 *there were 4,000 Chinese catering establishments in Britain* . . .: Burnett, *England Eats Out*, p. 283

page 92 *A survey in 1966 on 'The British Eating Out'* . . .: Burnett, *England Eats Out*, p. 290

page 95 *We moved from being a nation of beer drinkers* . . .: www.history andpolicy.org/opinion-articles/articles/the-highs-and-lows-of-drinking-in-britain

page 96 *There's proper food which is more French than anything else* . . .: Michael Bateman, *Cooking People*, p. 275

Chapter 4

page 102 *a survey by Birds Eye in 1976 did reveal* . . .: Burnett, *Plenty and Want*, p. 335

page 102 *At the time 90 per cent of beer was drunk in the pub, with only 10 per cent* . . .: http://www.publications.parliament.uk/pa/cm200809/cmselect/cmhealth/uc368-i/uc36802.htm

page 105 *In the 1960s an American scientist, nutritionist Ancel Keys* . . .: http://sevencountriesstudy.com/

page 106 *In 2012, with obesity levels ten times higher than when* . . .: 'John Yudkin: the man who tried to warn us about sugar', *Daily Telegraph*, 17 February 2014

page 108 *As the seventies progressed, the average diet became less heavy* . . .: Burnett, *Plenty and Want*, p. 243

page 108 *The average Briton's consumption of fats* . . .: National Food Survey statistical analysis, DEFRA Food Statistics Branch, September 2000

page 109 *But five years later in 1981* . . .: Chris Cowpe, *Chip Pan Fire Prevention*, Institute of Practitioners in Advertising report, 1984

page 109 *By 2012 chip/fat-pan fires had fallen* . . .: *Fire Statistics: Great Britain, 2011 to 2012*, Department for Communities and Local Government, 2012

page 110 *Feminism in the seventies was about all the things* . . .: Andy Beckett, *When the Lights Went Out*, Faber & Faber, 2010, p. 232

page 112 *By the middle of the decade, nearly half of us* . . .: 'Configuring Domestic Technologies: the Normalisation of Freezers in Finland, Norway and the UK', Consumption, Everyday Life and Sustainability Summer School, University of Lancaster, 1999; www.lancaster.ac.uk/fass/projects/esf/freezers.htm

page 113 *items such as fish fingers, boil-in-the bag fish, chips and frozen veg . . .*: Burnett, *Plenty and Want*, p. 345

page 114 *such a success that it outsold . . .*: Jill Churchill obituary, http://www.pressgazette.co.uk/node/36932

page 114 *It's not just what the freezer can do for you . . .*: http://www.retrowow.co.uk/retro_britain/70s/70s_high_tech_household.html

page 116 *Sainsbury stocked everyday basic products . . .*: http://archive.museumof london.org.uk/SainsburyArchive/Themes/Progress/Refrigeration/Frozenproduce.htm

page 117 *By the 1980s an estimated 6,000 flavours were being regularly added . . .*: http://www.eufic.org/article/en/expid/basics-food-additives/

page 117 *Flavourists had a wide palette to work from . . .*: Herta Ziegler (ed.), *Flavourings: Production, Composition, Applications, Regulations,* Wiley-VCH Verlag, 2008; and Bee Wilson, *Swindled: From Poison Sweets to Counterfeit Coffee – the Dark History of Food Cheats*, John Murray, 2008

page 118 *As early as 1972 artificial food dyes had been suspected . . .*: 'Hyperactivity and Artificial Food Colours', *Food Today*, European Food Information Council newsletter; http://www.eufic.org/article/en/artid/hyperactivity-artificial-food-colours/

page 118 *Artificial sweeteners such as aspartame . . .*: http://www.cspinet.org/reports/chemcuisine.htm

page 120 *There were over 25,000 ice-cream vans in the UK . . .*: http://www.vanquotedirect.co.uk/news/2012/10/chimes-of-the-ice-cream-seller-gradually-fading-away/

page 121 *by the 1970s accounted for half of all ice-cream sales . . .*: Lyons Maid in-house journal, http://www.kzwp.com/lyons/group2.htm

page 122 *when children as young as five, with mothers out doing essential war work . . .*: www.news.bbc.co.uk/1/hi/magazine/8704827.stm

page 124 *there will be no emancipation for women . . .*: Humble, *Culinary Pleasures*, p. 204

page 125 *M&S started selling alcohol in 1973 . . .*: 'Kipper ties, polyester flares and bad facial hair . . . dodgy dinner party style of the Seventies', *Daily Mail*, 23 October 2013

page 126 *By 1973 annual consumption per head stood at . . .*: http://www.
historyandpolicy.org/opinion-articles/articles/the-highs-and-lows-of-
drinking-in-britain

page 129 *In 1970 there were around 2,000 in high streets across Britain . . .*:
Burnett, *England Eats Out*, p. 283

page 132 *The first McDonald's opened . . .*: www.mcdonalds.co.uk/ukhome/
Aboutus/Newsroom/History.html

page 134 *Food prices were subject to massive inflation . . .*: http://econ.
economicshelp.org/2010/02/economy-of-1970s.html

page 134 *In the 1970s there were around 500,000 allotments in England . . .*:
http://ourlife.org.uk/silo/files/uk-allotments-briefing.pdf

page 135 *In an article in the* Daily Telegraph *their daughter Mary . . .*: 'Mary
McCartney: food from the heart', *Daily Telegraph*, 11 May 2012

page 136 *One commentator called the seventies the Brown Decade . . .*:
Hardyment, *Slice of Life*, p. 147

page 139 *industrial and social chaos . . .*: Marr, *History of Modern Britain*,
p. 375

Chapter 5

page 143 *pleasure without guilt . . .*: Jonathan Meades in 'Remembering the
80s', *Independent*, 12 May 2006

page 144 *Divorce rates rose, marriage rates decreased and more babies were born
outside marriage . . .*: http://www.ons.gov.uk/ons/dcp171778_291750.pdf

page 147 *However, it was the 1980s that saw sales really take off . . .*: http://www.
microwaveassociation.org.uk/factsheets/facts.php

page 149 *British supermarkets were set to become . . .*: Polly Russell, 'The history
cook: the Sainsbury's cookbook series', *Financial Times*, 15 February 2013

page 150 *In 1974, the average size of a supermarket was 2,800 square feet . . .*:
'Arrival of the Supermarkets', *The Ecology of Food Deserts*, School of
Geography, University of Leeds; http://www.geog.leeds.ac.uk/projects/h.
shaw/3.html

page 151 *A pack of two would have set you back . . .*: 'Chicken Kiev back in
fashion', *Daily Telegraph*, 12 June 2014

page 151 *It isn't kiev without the garlic . . .*: 'Cathy Chapman: the woman who
changed the way we eat', *Daily Telegraph*, 10 October 2010

page 152 *In November 2014 Aldi reported that sales of their version . . .*: 'Anne

Shooter the Savvy Shopper: Angel Delight is back . . .', *Daily Mail*, 4 November 2014

page 154 *since 1980 levels of obesity in the UK have trebled* . . .: *Obesity and Overweight*, World Health Organization Global Strategy on Diet, Physical Activity and Health, http://www.who.int/dietphysicalactivity/media/en/gsfs_obesity.pdf; and http://www.bbc.co.uk/news/health-25576400

page 155 *As a result, school-meal take-up* . . .: http://policybristol.blogs.bris.ac.uk/2013/08/15/school-meals-and-packed-lunches-how-important-is-government-policy/

page 157 *By 1987 they had twenty-five varieties* . . .:' Bee Wilson, *Sandwich: a Global History*, Reaktion Books, 2010, pp. 53–4

page 158 *The ciabatta – the term means 'slipper bread'* . . .: 'The secret life of ciabatta', *Guardian*, 30 April 1999

page 158 *Now, 60 per cent of us eat lunch at our desk* . . .: 'One in three eat lunch al desko, study finds', *Daily Telegraph*, 15 January 2013

page 159 *in the 1970s and 1980s children still played outside for more than two hours* . . .: 'Children today would rather read, do chores or even do HOMEWORK than play outside', *Daily Mail*, 11 April 2013

page 163 *Orange juice is one of the big success stories of the 1980s* . . .: C. Foster, A. McMeekin and J. Mylan, 'The entanglement of consumer expectations and (eco) innovation sequences: the case of orange juice', *Technology Analysis and Strategic Management*, Manchester Institute of Innovation Research, Sustainable Consumption Institute, Vol. 24, Issue 4, 2012, p. 15

page 163 *Changing diets and lifestyles had completely transformed body shape* . . .: 'The changing shape of women', *Daily Mail*, 14 November 2001

page 164 *people had turned with relief to Weight Watchers* . . .: Bob Batchelor and Scott Stoddart, *The 1980s*, Greenwood Publishing, 2007, p. 82

page 164 *The 1980s saw twenty-four diet books* . . .: ibid., p 81

page 165 *Jane Grigson dubbed her 'the Elizabeth David of India'* . . .: Castell and Griffin, *Out of the Frying Pan*, p. 133

page 168 *Across the country a large network of support for the miners* . . .: Andy McSmith, *No Such Thing as Society*, Constable, 2011, p. 160

page 172 *Sales of kiwi fruit went through the roof* . . .: R. Foster and J. Lunn, *Food Availability and Our Changing Diet*, British Nutrition Foundation, 40th Anniversary Briefing Paper, 2007, p. 215

page 174 Truffe en Brioche, *served by Raymond Blanc . . .*: Raymond Blanc, *A Taste of My Life*, Bantam Press, 2008, p. 177

page 176 *The number of wine drinkers in Britain rose . . .*: Pierre Spahni, *The International Wine Trade*, Woodhead Publishing, 2000, p. 69

page 177 *sales of 1970s favourite sweet tipple Blue Nun reached their peak . . .*: http://www.wine-searcher.com/m/2012/07/reviving-the-habit

Chapter 6

page 187 *75,000 in 1991 . . .*: Alwyn W. Turner, *A Classless Society: Britain in the 1990s*, Aurum Press, 2013, p. 32

page 189 *sales of raw ingredients for cooking fell . . .*: www.eatwellscotland.org/healthydiet/seasonsandcelebrations/howweusedtoeat/1990s/index.html

page 189 *By 2012 official data from the OECD . . .*: http://www.economist.com/blogs/freeexchange/2013/09/working-hours

page 189 *It is not so much that Britons do not have the time to cook . . .*: Joanna Blythman, *Bad Food Britain: How a Nation Ruined Its Appetite*, Fourth Estate, 2006, p. 77

page 190 *The number of people working from home doubled between 1981 and 1998 . . .*: Alan Felstead et al., *A Statistical Portrait of Working at Home in the UK: Evidence from the Labour Force Survey*, University of Leeds Working Paper, 2000; http://www.leeds.ac.uk/ESRCFutureofWork/downloads/workingpaperdownloads/fow_paper_04.pf

page 192 *by 2012 IKEA estimated it had sold . . .*: 'Ikea: 25 facts', *Daily Telegraph*, 31 October 21012

page 193 *in 1990 only 15 per cent of households owned one . . .*: http://www.statista.com/statistics/289151/household-dishwashing-in-the-uk/

page 193 *A 2003 report for the food industry looking back . . .*: Ruth Huxley, *A Review of the Food Market*, Cornwall Agricultural Council and Cornwall Taste of the West, June 2003

page 197 *In 2013 Tesco revealed that of all the bagged salads . . .*: www.tescoplc.com/index.asp?pageid=17&newsid=881

page 197 *the UK still produces more waste per head than any . . .*: www.cbenvironmental.co.uk/docs/Recycling%20Activity%20Pack%20v2%20.pdf

page 198 *Overall the number of supermarkets . . .*: John Dawson, 'Retail Change in Britain During 30 Years: The Strategic Use of Economies of Scale and

Scope', Research Papers in Retailing, No. 0402, Centre for the Study of Retailing in Scotland, 2004, p. 9

page 199 *In 2014 new data from Visa Europe showed that in the previous four years* . . .: 'Britain's biggest retailers split over Sunday hours', *Daily Telegraph*, 23 August 2014

page 200 *By 2000, the standard family food shop weighed* . . .: Select Committee on Environment, Transport and Regional Affairs, *Second Report on the Environmental Impact of Supermarket Competition*, 2000; quoted in Joanna Blythman, *Shopped: The Shocking Power of British Supermarkets*, Fourth Estate, 2004, p. 8

page 200 *equivalent to the weight of an average eleven-year-old child* . . .: Royal College of Paediatrics, http://www.rcpch.ac.uk/system/files/protected/page/NEW%20Girls%202-18yrs(4TH%20JAN%202012).pdf

page 201 *1,000 a week were destroyed at the peak of the cull* . . .: www.ukagriculture.com/livestock/bovine_spongiform_encephalopathy.cfm

page 203 *meat consumption dropped from 301g per head* . . .: www.gov.uk/government/statistical-data-sets/family-food-datasets

page 204 *By 1997, 14.3 per cent of the population polled in a RealEat survey* . . .: Joan Sabaté (ed.), *Vegetarian Nutrition*, CRC Press, 2001, p. 8

page 206 *in 2013 was voted one of the ten best* . . .: http://travel.cnn.com/explorations/shop/worlds-best-fresh-markets-316265

page 207 *2013 saw an increase in UK sales* . . .: Soil Association, Organic Market Report, 2014

page 208 *You should be able to eat produce without worrying* . . .: www.startupdonut.co.uk/startup/start-up-business-ideas/types-of-business/profile-the-organic-farmer

page 208 *I hate the way the term 'organic'* . . .: 'Riverford has the recipe for success', *Daily Telegraph*, 13 April 2014

page 210 *pasta was a small but rapidly growing market in the UK* . . .: Helen Peck et al., *Relationship Marketing: Strategy and Implementation*, Routledge, 1999

page 211 *this country has the largest Thai expatriate community* . . .: http://en.wikipedia.org/wiki/Thais_in_the_United_Kingdom#cite_note-RUN-5

page 214 *The survey also showed that a third of British women* . . .: 'Women buy wine – eight out of ten bottles, survey finds', *Guardian*, 2 April 2009

page 214 *The 1990s also witnessed the arrival of the soon-to-be-reviled* alcopops . . .: 'The quiet death of the alcopop', *BBC News Magazine*, 31 July 2013; http://www.bbc.co.uk/news/magazine-23502892

page 217 *Waitrose has seen sales of its takeaway sushi boxes . . .*: www.sushitrade.co.uk/why-sell-sushi/

page 217 *the proportion of the population eating in even the more relaxed pubs . . .*: Burnett, *England Eats Out*, p. 305

page 218 *Research in 2001 identified a new pattern . . .*: KeyNote, *UK Food Market Review*, 2001, 2003, 2.2.3 'Eating Habits'

page 219 *Today only one third of British families . . .*: 'Weekend Analyis – breakfast powerhouses save their bacon', *Financial Times*, 4 October 2014

page 219 *A coffee shops phenomenon has swept Britain's high streets . . .*: www.bbc.co.uk/programmes/articles/2QHz8CcHJV1wqxSjK77M4q7/women-and-the-coffee-shop-revolution

page 220 *By 2015 the number of coffee shops on the high street is expected . . .* : 'Which coffee shop chain? Snobbery in an age of austerity', *Guardian*, 15 July 2013

page 221 *one a day will provide nearly a quarter of the 2,000 calories . . .*: www.nhs.uk/chq/Pages/how-many-calories-do-children-need.aspx?CategoryID=62&SubCategoryID=65

page 221 *In a survey for market research company Nielsen . . .*: 'Weekend Analysis – breakfast powerhouses save their bacon', *Financial Times*, 4 October 2014

page 222 *Almost a third of a Tracker Roasted Nut bar . . .*: 'Cereal bars healthy image a myth', *Which?*, 18 August 2012; http://press.which.co.uk/whichpressreleases/cereal-bars-healthy-image-a-myth/

page 228 *four in ten British schoolgirls had never cooked . . .* : 'Why students can't cook, won't cook', *Daily Telegraph*, 24 July 2004

page 228 *distinctive brand of enthusiasm and desire . . .*: 'The Jamie Oliver effect', *Daily Telegraph*, 5 February 2011

page 230 *In 1994 a COMA Report issued specific guidelines . . .*: Verner Wheelock, *Implementing Dietary Guidelines for Healthy Eating*, Jones & Bartlett Inc., 1997, p. 435

page 230 *in 1996 fat and saturated fat became the focus of government policy . . .*: www.gda.cl/medios/profesores/Origen_GDA.pdf

Chapter 7

page 238 *The sandwich is now the most frequently eaten meal . . .*: 'It'll be sandwiches for supper again', *The Times*, 27 March 2014

page 239 *A study in 2012 found that for both chefs . . .*: 'Jamie and Nigella's meals unhealthy', *Daily Telegraph*, 17 December 2012

page 240 *a take on the traditional Bloody Mary . . .*: http://www.thedrinksbusiness.com/2014/01/top-10-food-and-drink-trends-for-2014/2/

page 240 *Another trend I welcome is the one favoured by . . .*: ibid.

page 240 *women with families will struggle to be top chefs . . .*: 'Prue Leith: Women cannot be top chefs, mostly', *Daily Telegraph*, 14 March 2014

page 241 *Sugar is our number one eating problem . . .*: 'Why cupcakes are the new cocaine', *Daily Telegraph*, 18 May 2012

page 242 *since 2007 sales of Thai meals . . .*: http://www.foodmanufacture.co.uk/Ingredients/Ethnic-foods-shaping-UK-market

page 242 *the UK accounted for 42 per cent . . .*: http://www.open.edu/openlearn/body-mind/health/health-studies/the-lure-the-ready-meal

page 242 *A 2013 Mintel report entitled* Kids Snacking . . . : http://www.mintel.com/blog/food-market-news/snack-market-trends-in-uk

page 243 *Since 2007 food prices have risen by 12 per cent . . .*: *Food Statistics Pocketbook*, National Archives, 2013, update, p. 9

page 244 *median household incomes have fallen across the board . . .*: *Middle Income Households, 1977–2011/12*, Office for National Statistics, 2013

page 244 *78 per cent of shoppers were buying British food . . .*: http://www.j-sainsbury.co.uk/media/latest-stories/2014/0101-sainsburys-gathered-over-100-british-farmers-and-growers-to-share-views-on-food-supply-trends-for-the-year-ahead/

page 245 *in the first ten years of the decade we increased our recycling . . .*: 'UK increased recycling rates fastest in Europe', *Guardian*, 19 March 2013

page 246 *by the end of the century men would still earn . . .*: http://www.bbc.co.uk/history/british/modern/jmurray_01.shtml

page 246 *just one in ten married men took on . . .*: 'Forty years of feminism – but women still do most of the housework', *Guardian*, 10 March 2012

page 246 *feminism – known in some quarters as the f-word . . .*: http://www.bbc.co.uk/history/british/modern/jmurray_01.shtml

page 246 *How (Not) to React to Anti-Feminist Women* . . .: http://news.nationalpost.com/2014/07/25/not-all-feminists-how-modern-feminism-has-become-complicated-messy-personal-and-sometimes-alienating/

page 247 *it is estimated that by 2050 we will have to find* . . .: http://www.worldometers.info/world-population/

page 248 *five key food and drink trends* . . .: http://www.foodnavigator.com/Market-Trends/What-key-trends-will-be-driving-the-food-and-drink-industry-in-2014

page 249 *In the 1950s meat was also scarce* . . .: 'What will we be eating in 20 years' time', *BBC News Magazine*, 30 July 2012; http://www.bbc.co.uk/news/magazine-18813075

page 250 *Professor Mark Post, who led the team* . . .: 'Lab-grown meat is first step to artificial hamburger', *BBC News Magazine*, http://www.bbc.co.uk/news/science-environment-16972761

page 251 *Molecular biologist Dr David Steele* . . .: ibid.

page 252 *In comparison to diets rich in animal products* . . .: http://www.ncbi.nlm.nih.gov/pubmed/24898222

page 253 *The United Nations, meanwhile, is committed* . . .: *Edible Insects: Future prospects for food and feed security*, Food and Agriculture Organization of the United Nations, 2013

page 253 *One man at the forefront of this new world* . . .: http://robrhinehart.com/?p=298

page 253 *Soylent is a food replacement* . . .: http://www.soylent.me/#/

page 256 *Obesity-related conditions, which are rocketing* . . .: 'Junk food: we need to tackle Britain's obesity crisis', *Daily Telegraph*, 4 February 2014

page 256 *if current trends continue could go on* . . .: 'Sugar is as dangerous as alcohol and tobacco, warn health experts', *Daily Telegraph*, 9 January 2014

page 256 *obesity is an international problem* . . .: http://www.bbc.co.uk/news/health-25708278

page 259 *and will let you tweet the developing recipe* . . .: http://www.foodtechconnect.com/2014/01/14/8-smart-kitchen-innovations-from-ces-2014/

page 260 *At Logbar in Tokyo's busy Shibuya district* . . .: 'Food trends in 2014: from digital dining to healthy junk food', *Guardian*, 6 January 2014

page 260 *a report from conservation group Oceana* . . .: 'New Oceana study finds 33% of seafood mislabeled', *National Geographic*, 21 February 2013

page 261 *But by 2014 the big four* . . .: 'Supermarkets are 20 years out of date, says Waitrose boss', *Daily Telegraph*, 22 October 2014

page 262 *with all the benefits of more flexible* . . .: http://www.igd.com/our-expertise/Retail/Convenience/17433/Three-trends-driving-growth-in-convenience-/

page 263 *Over the next ten years two thirds of all retail spending growth* . . .: http://www.kpmg.com/uk/en/issuesandinsights/articlespublications/newsreleases/pages/how-will-demographic-trends-in-the-uk-affect-the-retail-sector.aspx

page 264 *The frequency of eating out is only set to increase* . . .: Allegra Food Strategy Forum, *A Taste of the Future*, Allegra Strategies Ltd, 2013

page 264 *Mintel sees the key areas of demand and growth* . . .: http://www.rts-resource.com/Blog/Latest-Trends/Future-trends-in-food-and-drink-2013-and-beyond/2012/7/26.aspx

page 265 *fast food ('healthy junk food')* . . .: 'Food trends in 2014: from digital dining to healthy junk food', *Guardian*, 6 January 2014

Select Bibliography

Andrews, Maggie, *Domesticating the Airwaves: Broadcasting, Domesticity and Femininity*, Bloomsbury, 2012

Avila, Kay, *Take Twelve Cooks,* Thames Macdonald, 1986

Barr, Ann, and Levy, Paul, *The Official Foodie Handbook*, Olympic Marketing Corp, 1984

Bateman, Michael, *Cooking People*, Cookery Book Club, 1966

Beckett, Andy, *When the Lights Went Out*, Faber & Faber, 2010

Berghe, Pierre van den, *The Ethnic Phenomenon*, Greenwood Publishing, 1987

Berry, Mary, *Popular Freezer Cookery*, Octopus, 1972

Blanc, Raymond, *A Taste of My Life*, Bantam Press, 2008

Blythman, Joanna, *Bad Food Britain: How a Nation Ruined Its Appetite*, Fourth Estate, 2006

Blythman, Joanna, *Shopped: The Shocking Power of British Supermarkets*, Fourth Estate, 2004

Burnett, John, *England Eats Out*, Longman, 2004

Burnett, John, *Plenty and Want*, Scolar Press, 1979

Castell, Hazel, and Griffin, Kathleen, *Out of the Frying Pan*, BBC Books, 1993

David, Elizabeth, *An Omelette and a Glass of Wine*, Penguin Books, 1984

David, Elizabeth, *English Bread and Yeast Cookery,* Penguin Books, 1977

Deighton, Len, *Len Deighton's Action Cook Book,* Jonathan Cape, 1965

Evans, Paul, *The 1960s Home*, Shire Library, 2010

Fry, Constance, and Hume, Rosemary, *The Constance Fry Cookery Book*, Dent, 1956

Goldthorpe, J., et al., *The Affluent Worker in the Class Structure*, Cambridge University Press, 1969

The Good Housekeeping Cookbook, Ebury Press, 1985

Grant, Doris, *Dear Housewives*, Faber, 1955

Hardyment, Christina, *Slice of Life: The British Way of Eating since 1945*, BBC Books, 1995

Humble, Nicola, *Culinary Pleasures: Cookbooks and the Transformation of British Food*, Faber, 2005

Leighton, Sophie, *The 1950s Home*, Shire Library, 2009

Lewis, C. S., *The Lion, the Witch and the Wardrobe*, Geoffrey Bles, 1950

Marr, Andrew, *A History of Modern Britain*, Macmillan, 2007

McSmith, Andy, *No Such Thing as Society*, Constable, 2011

Moran, Joe, *On Roads*, Profile Books, 2009

Patten, Marguerite, *Post-War Kitchen: Nostalgic Foods and Facts from 1945–54*, Hamlyn, 1998

Patten, Marguerite, *Cookery in Colour*, Hamlyn, 1960

Pollan, Michael, *The Omnivore's Dilemma: The Search for a Perfect Meal in a Fast-Food World*, Bloomsbury, 2006

Reader's Digest Cookery Year, Reader's Digest, 1976

Robinson, Jane, *A Force to be Reckoned With: A History of the Women's Institute*, Virago, 2011

Sandbrook, Dominic, *Seasons in the Sun: The Battle for Britain, 1974–1979*, Penguin Books, 2012

Sandbrook, Dominic, *State of Emergency: The Way We Were, Britain 1970–1974*, Allen Lane, 2010

Sissons, Michael, and French, Philip (eds), *Age of Austerity 1945–51*, Hodder & Stoughton, 1963

Slater, Nigel, *Toast: The Story of a Boy's Hunger*, Fourth Estate, 2003

Smith, Delia, *How to Cheat at Cooking*, Ebury Press, 1971

Spencer, Stephanie, *Gender, Work and Education in Britain in the 1950s*, Palgrave Macmillan, 2005

Turner, Alwyn W., *A Classless Society: Britain in the 1990s*, Aurum Press, 2013

Turner, Alwyn W., *Rejoice! Rejoice!: Britain in the 1980s*, Aurum Press, 2010

Warren, Geoffrey C., *The Foods We Eat*, Cassell, 1958

White, Florence, *Good Things in England*, Jonathan Cape, 1932; reissued Persephone Books, 2010

Whitehorn, Katharine, *Cooking in a Bedsitter*, Penguin Books, 1963 (first published as *Kitchen in the Corner*, MacGibbon & Kee, 1961); reissued Virago, 2008

Wilkinson, Philip, *The High Street*, Quercus, 2010

Woman & Home Cordon Bleu Cookery, Fleetway Publications, 1962

Yudkin, John, *Pure, White and Deadly*, Viking, 1972

Acknowledgements

This book has been written to support the series *Back in Time for Dinner*, made by Wall to Wall for the BBC, so has had input from a wide range of people. I would like to thank Alison Kirkham at the BBC and Emily Shields and all her team at Wall to Wall for providing me with information, research and support, whilst they were working hard to produce the series. Thanks also to Polly Russell for her programme notes, Giles Coren for his entertaining and perceptive foreword, and of course the Robshaw family for their patience with my questions and their commitment to the whole project.

The publishing team at Transworld has been fundamental in ensuring that this book has been a pleasure to write from start to finish. It's a very rare privilege to work with a team in such harmony with one another, and every single person involved has smoothed the path for me as the author and been instrumental in the look and feel of the final product. My huge thanks to Susanna Wadeson, Brenda Updegraff, Sheila Lee, Kate Samano, Phil Lord, Mic Alcaino, Alison Martin and Lizzy Goudsmit. Thanks are also due to my agent, Heather Holden Brown, and her team at HHB.

Finally, thanks to my family, who have been unfailingly patient and understanding throughout. I couldn't have done this without them!

Picture Credits

Images in the text

Colour illustrations

Credits run from top left clockwise.

First section

John Bull, cover, 1957: © Pictorial Press Ltd/Alamy.
Kitchen interior, Ontario Buildings, Preston's Road Estate, London, 1959: London Metropolitan Archives, City of London (SC/PHL/02/59/2897); detail of an MFI advertisement, 1989: © Jeff Margan 14/Alamy; kitchen interior, Skipton, Yorkshire, 2009: © Paula Solloway/Alamy; kitchen interior, 1968: Popperfoto/Getty Images.
1950s magazine illustration: image courtesy of The Advertising Archives; Jamie Oliver, title shot, 2001: Rex/Moviestore Collection; Sainsbury's TV advertisement, 2011: image courtesy of The Advertising Archives; Kenwood Chef advertisement, 1960s: image courtesy of The Advertising Archives.
Vesta curry advertisement, 1970s: image courtesy of The Advertising Archives; still from *Abigail's Party*, TV production, 1977: © Moviestore Collection Ltd/ Alamy; still from *Come Dine With Me*, September 2013: Rex/Lifetime/Everett. Supermarket interior, 1964: Evening Standard/Getty Images; Lidl store interior, Tottenham, London: Jason Alden/Bloomberg via Getty Images.

Second section

Oxo advertisement, 1950s; stills from Oxo TV advertisements, 1984 and 2009: all images courtesy of The Advertising Archives.
Lyons Corner House, Piccadilly, 1966: Les Lee/Express Getty Images; Wimpy menu, 1972: image courtesy of The Advertising Archives; tower of octopus and radish: © Bon Appetite/Alamy; Trevor Gulliver (left) and Fergus Henderson, co-founders of St John restaurant, London, October 2013: © Andrew Testa/ Panos/for The Washington Post via Getty Images; kitchen at Cranks, 1960s: photo courtesy Cranks.
Marguerite Patten on the BBC television show *Designed For Women*, April 1948: Kurt Hutton/Picture Post/Hulton/Archive/Gettty Images; Nigella Lawson, October 2000: Rex/Brooke Webb; Graham Kerr and Cilla Black, 1970s: Rex/Dezo Hoffmann; Rick Stein with Bombil Fish in Mumbai, during shooting of *Rick Stein's India* broadcast in 2013: Denhams; Keith Floyd, 1989: Rex/Ian Bradshaw; Delia Smith, 1973: © David Reed/Alamy.
Butter advertisement, 1970s British Heart foundation advertisement, 2006; Kellogg's advertisement, 1961; Mars TV advertisement, 2008; Health Education Authority advertisement, 2000s; Flora advertisement, 1980: all images courtesy of The Advertising Archives.
Food Revolution Day, May 2014: Anthony Devlin/PA Archive/Press Association Images; grasshopper tempura: photo Charlotte Tolhurst

Index

Mary Gwynn was deputy food editor of *Woman and Home* magazine, founding editor of *BBC Vegetarian Good Food* and subsequently editor of the M&S magazine. She worked as a consultant editor and trainer for Waitrose for fourteen years and now writes for their publications. She is the author of many cookery books, including *The Busy Mum's Cookbook* (2011), *The Busy Mum's Vegetarian Cookbook* (2013) and *The WI Cookbook: the First 100 Years*. Mary lives in East Sussex.

@busymumcooks
www. trufflehound.wordpress.com